VARIETIES OF SOUTHERN HISTORY

Recent Titles in
Contributions in American History

Northern Labor and Antislavery: A Documentary History
Philip S. Foner and Herbert Shapiro, editors

Loyalists and Community in North America
Robert M. Calhoon, Timothy M. Barnes, and George A. Rawlyk, editors

Abraham Lincoln: Sources and Style of Leadership
Frank J. Williams, William D. Pederson, and Vincent J. Marsala, editors

Zebulon Butler: Hero of the Revolutionary Frontier
James R. Williamson and Linda A. Fossler

Clio Confused: Troubling Aspects of Historical Study from the Perspective of U.S. History
David J. Russo

Federal Antitrust Policy During the Kennedy-Johnson Years
James R. Williamson

The Home-Front War: World War II and American Society
Kenneth Paul O'Brien and Lynn Hudson Parsons, editors

Portrait of an Abolitionist: A Biography of George Luther Stearns
Charles E. Heller

No King, No Popery: Anti-Catholicism in Revolutionary New England
Francis D. Cogliano

James Glen: From Scottish Provost to Royal Governor of South Carolina
W. Stitt Robinson

The Journalist as Reformer: Henry Demarest Lloyd and *Wealth Against Commonwealth*
Richard Digby-Junger

Reconciliation and Revival: James R. Mann and the House Republicans in the Wilson Era
Herbert F. Margulies

VARIETIES OF SOUTHERN HISTORY

New Essays on a Region and Its People

Edited by
BRUCE CLAYTON
and JOHN SALMOND

Contributions in American History, Number 169
Jon L. Wakelyn, Series Editor

GREENWOOD PRESS
Westport, Connecticut • London

Library of Congress Cataloging-in-Publication Data

Varieties of southern history : new essays on a region and its people / edited by Bruce Clayton and John Salmond.
p. cm.—(Contributions in American history, ISSN 0084–9219 ; no. 169)
Includes bibliographical references and index.
ISBN 0–313–29860–2 (alk. paper)
1. Southern States—History. I. Clayton, Bruce. II. Salmond, John. III. Series.
F209.V35 1996
975—dc20 95–53106

British Library Cataloguing in Publication Data is available.

Library of Congress Catalog Card Number: 95–53106
ISBN: 0–313–29860–2
ISSN: 0084–9219

First published in 1996

Greenwood Press, 88 Post Road West, Westport, CT 06881
An imprint of Greenwood Publishing Group, Inc.

Printed in the United States of America

The paper used in this book complies with the Permanent Paper Standard issued by the National Information Standards Organization (Z39.48–1984).

10 9 8 7 6 5 4 3 2 1

Copyright Acknowledgments

The editors and publisher gratefully acknowledge permission to use selected excerpts from the following sources:

Jack P. Greene, ed., *The Diary of Colonel Landon Carter of Sabine Hall, 1752–1778* (Charlottesville, Va., 1965). Courtesy of the Virginia Historical Society.

Weevils in the Wheat, edited by Charles L. Perdue, Thomas E. Barden, and Robert K. Phillips (Charlottesville: University Press of Virginia, 1992). Used by permission of the University Press of Virginia.

The letter from Reverend John Venn to Bishop Sherlock, June 15, 1751, General Correspondence, Jamaica, Volume 18, pp. 45–52, 46 (quote), The Fulham Papers in the Lambeth Palace Library, American Colonial Section.

Ames Family Papers at the Sophia Smith Archives. Courtesy of Oakes Ames Plimpton.

Adelbert Ames Papers, the Percy Lee Rainwater Papers, and the James W. Garner Papers. Courtesy of the Mississippi Department of Archives and History.

Lillian Smith Papers, Hargrett Rare Book and Manuscript Library, University of Georgia Libraries; reprinted in *How Am I to Be Heard? Letters of Lillian Smith*, edited with an introduction by Margaret Rose Gladney (Chapel Hill, 1993).

Lillian Smith Papers. Courtesy of Esther Smith, Literary Executor of the Lillian E. Smith.

The song, *Mill Mother's Lament* in Jo Lynn Haessley, "Mill Mother's Lament, Ella May, Working Women's Militancy and the Gaston County Strikes of 1929" (M.A. thesis in history, University of North Carolina at Chapel Hill, 1987).

An interview with Solomin Barkin, conducted by Jim Cavanaugh, January 1994.

Operation Dixie Archives, Perkins Special Collections Library, Duke University, Durham, North Carolina.

Textile Workers Union of America Collection and Textile Workers Union of America Oral History Project. Courtesy of the State Historical Society of Wisconsin.

Contents

II. Southern History through Life History

III. Labor in the New South

Acknowledgments

Many people and institutions have given a helping hand to the preparation of this book. We would like to say an appreciative word to the contributors whose work enlarged our own understanding of southern history; their enthusiasm and creativity are inspiring. Special thanks to Samantha Stephens of Allegheny College and Laraine Dumsday of La Trobe University who unstintingly used their superb secretarial skills to bring order out of chaos on many occasions. Don Vrabel and Jane Westenfeld, reference librarians at Allegheny College, were, as always, particularly helpful. We are also indebted in a variety of obvious and subtle ways to the counsel and encouragement of our friends and colleagues, Orville Vernon Burton, W. J. Breen, Richard L. Watson, Jr., Paula Treckel, Judith Bassett, Fred Frank, Lucy Frost, Barry Shapiro, Michael Bassett, Alan Frost, Jack Roper, and Robert Hohner. And once again we would like to express our appreciation to our home institutions La Trobe University and Allegheny College for constant encouragement and support.

Introduction

In the late 1980s the editors solicited, assembled, and published *The South Is Another Land* (1987), a book of essays on carefully chosen topics in the history of the twentieth-century South. We were deeply impressed by the quality of scholarship pursued by our colleagues in southern history, whether in America or elsewhere in the Western world, and we asked them for samples of their ongoing work. To our delight, we attracted informed, lively contributions. Essays came from above and below the Mason Dixon line, from neighboring Canada, and from as far away as Australia and New Zealand. Southern history was alive and robust—and as the twenty-first century looms, it shows no signs of any hardening of its intellectual arteries.

Just the opposite. We knew this. But this we now know even more convincingly after reading and editing the eleven essays selected for this volume. The historians appearing here approach the South armed with an infectious enthusiasm for the region, for all of its people, and for innovative research as well as a passion (palpable on every page) for bringing the best of current, sophisticated ways of historical thinking to doing southern history. Although they share broad and fundamental areas of agreement as to what constitutes the basic themes of the South's past, each historian has a distinct point of view and approach. Hence our title, *Varieties of Southern History: New Essays on a Region and Its People*. Our opening section illustrates the fruitful link between "The Social Sciences and Southern History." We begin with a welcomed installment of Rhys Isaac's ethnographic analysis of Landon Carter's diary. Isaac, the Pulitzer Prize-winning author of *The Transformation of Virginia, 1740–1790* (1982), shows how a prominent and haughty slaveholder's diary can be used to tease out poignant insights into the life not only of a master but, in this instance, of a slave as well. This "person-centered ethnography," says Isaac, allows us "quite properly to turn to the very particular locus of experience, that smallest place of all within the scope of social-cultural studies, the individual person."

Charles Joyner heartily agrees. In "Texts, Texture, and Context," Joyner builds upon Isaac to explore "an ethnographic history of slave resistance." In Joyner's hands, as he indicated in his acclaimed book, *Down by the Riverside* (1984), the folk life of the slaves must be central to anyone who would pretend to talk about the South. Joyner boldly announces that since the "slaves did the work and the slave holders enjoyed the profits," the old question, "How did the masters provide for the slaves?" must be replaced with "How did the slaves provide for their masters?" Both Isaac and Joyner, by looking at "what happened, not what happens," probe slavery imaginatively and, in the process, forcefully rebut the charge that ethnographic history calmly ignores human cruelty and the suffering of society's "others."

Shane White and Graham White are related not only by their Australian heritage—but also by their perceptive methodology and angle of vision on history. Their essay, "Reading the Slave Body: Demeanor, Gesture, and African-American Culture," looks at what can be recovered as to how slaves maintained, in spite of oppression, a vital culture with distinct "signs" and a group identity, partly through facial expressions, modes of dance, clothing, and quilts. Here is "new" history indeed, history that helps to pry open the iron gates of the everyday past.

Like the Whites, indeed, like every author in this book, Grace Elizabeth Hale and Terence Finnegan, two younger scholars, understand the haunting importance of race in the history of the region. Both concentrate on lynchings. But neither shirks from facing and documenting the almost unbelievable bestiality of racism's ugliest manifestation in the decades before and immediately after 1914. Hale's title—"Deadly Amusements: Spectacle Lynchings and Southern Whiteness, 1890–1940"—announces her argument. Mob lynchings, far from being the work of the inflamed lower orders or the temporarily deranged masses, "were rituals increasingly bound up with the way southern whites shaped the practices of modern consumption to their own ends . . . and helped ease white fears of a race-less consumer society, even as they helped structure segregation."

Hale probes the "what" and the "why" surrounding the barbaric violence of Judge Lynch; Finnegan asks "Who Were the Victims of Lynchings?" His contentions, based on exhaustive statistical analysis of lynchings in Mississippi and South Carolina, demand attention. Finnegan underlines the value of the techniques of social science. And his conclusions pointedly challenge some of the traditional and most recent assessments of who got lynched and why.

None of the scholars mentioned—and certainly not Finnegan or Hale—is ever in danger of forgetting that history must always have a human face. The artistry of biography must occupy the chair next to the science of history. Such is demonstrated in part 2: "Southern History through Life History." Here two younger scholars (Trevor Burnard and Sam Elworthy) join with two senior biographers (Warren A. Ellem and Bruce Clayton) to search for the defining moments or values in someone whose life touched or was shaped by the South.

Writing from his native New Zealand, a nation with a long history of attachment to England, Burnard concentrates on how an Englishman adapted to his new home in Jamaica in the mid-eighteenth century. In "Thomas Thistlewood Becomes a Creole," Burnard explores an expatriate's fulsome diary in an attempt to discover how and why an otherwise humane newcomer to the island, where entrenched black slavery dominated the culture, adapted himself so seemingly effortlessly to its "racially oppressive psychology." Race, racism, white hegemony—all were central to Thistlewood's acculturation, as they were to that of every southerner, and in the eighteenth century, Jamaica was clearly part of the colonial South.

But not every newcomer or visitor (or native white or African American) succumbed to the racism in the age of slavery and racial segregation. Some abhorred racism; some battled it with all their might. Such is true of the Yankee Republican Adelbert Ames, the embattled carpetbag governor of Mississippi during Reconstruction. Warren Ellem, whose earlier work on carpetbaggers and scalawags helped clear away old myths, details the way Ames, a former general in the victorious Union army, saw himself "Doing God's Service" by staying true to his commitment not only to national unity but to equality for the freed slave, what C. Vann Woodward has called "The Deferred Commitment."

Has race been "the central theme of southern history?" Of late, it has been fashionable to discredit U. B. Phillips's admittedly overblown claim. But make a counterfactual argument, that is, subtract race, and the lives of Thistlewood and Ames, to say nothing of the South's great black population, would have been changed in incalculable ways. So, too, would the lives of Frank Cushing and W. E. B. Du Bois. Both were Yankee social scientists—one a white anthropologist, the other America's most influential African-American intellectual—who journeyed south, confronted race, and were never the same again. Such is Sam Elworthy's view as he links "Religion, Social Science, and Traveling South in the Late Nineteenth Century." Cushing went to the Southwest and was transformed by his experiences with the "other," the Zuñi; Du Bois's sojourns in Nashville and rural Tennessee and Atlanta, Georgia, made him see that "the problem of the twentieth century is the problem of the color line."

Race dominated the thinking of Lillian Smith, arguably the first white southerner in the age of Jim Crow to embark on a radical intellectual journey of emancipation from racism. As Bruce Clayton shows in "Race, Gender, and Modernism: The Case of Lillian Smith," she fathomed in her own life history the intricate ways racism poisoned the well, especially for women, white and black. What accounts for her emancipation? Clayton, biographer of her contemporary W. J. Cash, points to her immersion in modernist thought, mainly Sigmund Freud, and suggests that her Freudianism led both to intellectual emancipation and personal complications.

The last section of this book shifts attention from race to economics, particularly in the changing lives of textile workers in the first half of the twentieth century. Part 3, "Labor in the New South," begins with an analysis of the great strike at Gastonia, North Carolina, in 1929. John Salmond, in "Aspects of Modernization in the Loray Mill Strike of 1929," concentrates concisely on class and the crucial heroism and significance of women in the struggling union movement—as he did in his 1988 biography of Lucy Randolph Mason. Standing tall on the picket line, fending off abuse, going to jail—usually in very un-Victorian, "unladylike" modern garb—the young and old women of Loray Mill reflected the rapidly changing modern mind inching into the South. This essay revises our knowledge of what happened at Gastonia—spelled out more fully in John Salmond's recent book *Gastonia 1929*.

It would take at least another twenty years after the failure at Gastonia for anyone to say that textile workers were even slowly "Coming into the Real World," as Timothy J. Minchin says in this volume's concluding essay. Minchin, a young scholar writing from England, examines the immediate post-1945 era to see what accounts for the failure of unions to organize southern textile workers. While mindful of traditional answers—lack of community support, the workers' deep-grained individualism, the political climate—Minchin looks for clues in the rising wages, generated at first by World War II, and the workers' modern consumer-minded attitudes.

To the editors it is strikingly revealing that twelve historians—separated by gender, nationality, age, and oceans—concentrate not on traditional political, economic, social, or racial values or assumptions of what used to be called the South's master race or master class. Rather, the emphasis, by and large, is on what might be called the South's have-nots or various "others," those frequently seen only as "problems" or lumps of humanity. In *Varieties of Southern History*, attention focuses on the individual slave, slaves expressing their individuality, the charred victims of lynchings, an idealistic carpetbagger, courageous intellectuals, and on women and men on the picket lines—on workers hoping to enjoy the fruits of their labor in the modern age. In this, we believe, lies the volume's significance.

I

THE SOCIAL SCIENCES AND SOUTHERN HISTORY

1

Stories of Enslavement: A Person-Centered Ethnography from an Eighteenth-Century Virginia Plantation

Rhys Isaac

Nowhere have the achievements of the new social history been greater than in the analysis of colonial and antebellum slavery in the American South. Yet we still search anxiously for ways to encompass what we think of with more and more insistence as "the experience" of slavery. We have therefore to ask what are the ways in which experience can be apprehended and rendered in historical writing? Intensely personal studies seem to offer great possibilities as we engage in such an elusive quest. Experience is, after all, ultimately personal. The particular cultural-anthropological approach adopted in this study, I have designated as "person-centered ethnography."

The careful study of a well-documented individual can illuminate much more than just that individual. It can become a powerful way to intensify understanding of past social-cultural systems and a way to discover larger processes of historical change at the level of experience. Colonel Landon Carter (1710–1778) of Sabine Hall, Virginia, is the person through whose rich self-documentation I have been for some time working to open windows at once on individual experience and on the wide world of which he was a part.[1]

In the documentation surrounding the colonel—above all, in the writings he styled variously as "Farming Observations," "diary" or "journal," and, in its last form, "my monthly books"—I have made first attempts to trace some of the great changes in family values and of household orientation that we associate with the ideology of domesticity and the emergence of the home as a sacred center in our world. The same set of documents will also support a particularizing study of cultural aspects of early stages of the great reorganization of labor—its calculated rationalization by the subjection of its operations to the interested gaze of science (or "natural philosophy") in the very important agricultural component of what we, fixated on later manifestations, style "the industrial revolution." Both these developments, domestication and rationalization, can be traced as strongly present transforming historical processes in Landon Carter's diary; certainly they had profound implications for his slaves and for the whole system of slavery.[2]

If the richly documented individual was also a storyteller of note and left a fund of stories, so much the better; if the fund of stories is replete with direct representations of actual experiences, then the opportunity (and the challenge) for person-centered ethnography is great. At least a prima facie case exists for regarding the story as one of the most powerful, if not *the* most powerful means for socializing or acculturating—and so communicating—raw and often recalcitrant experience.

Here I need to enter at least in a small way into the welter of discourses and polemics concerning narrative. By the time Roland Barthes's influential conceptualizing synthesis appeared, a consensus had emerged that there scarcely *is* a relationship between story and reality. This view was arrived at from the argument that the inclusion of occurrences and events in stories, and their relationship there, is governed by a logic that belongs to narrative and not to the world outside of the story. In a very telling critique, David Carr made the objection to this received wisdom that it is based on an intense scrutiny of the structure of stories and a scandalous inattention to the structures of the world in which stories are sustained—structures that, in a spirit of "scientism," had been taken to be the vast concatenation of causal sequences or interacting systems that *physicists* imagine! Carr finds that view of the human world to be not so much wrong as quite inadequate, because it is amazingly innocent of the insights arrived at in the social phenomenology of Gerhardt Husserl and Alfred Schutz—best known perhaps in Peter Berger and Thomas Luckmann's great synthesis, *The Social Construction of Reality*. There it is urged that reality for humankind is produced and sustained out of the meaningful actions of participants and the communicated understandings that inform them. Human participants, then, are not randomly moving particles of physical reality; they are to a marked degree participants in stories that they are forever busy constructing for themselves. Humans proceed, as Carr points out, from beginnings (initiatives of which they are conscious), through intermediate steps (developments from the initiating actions), toward anticipated outcomes (endings). People have, then, powerful "story-structures" in life as they live it, reality as they know it. Developments and outcomes in life, as opposed to those plotted in stories, are, of course, quite commonly different from what had been intended. To note this, however, is only to come upon the difference between anticipation and retrospection. This contrast gives a very different aspect, to be sure, to stories in the living and stories in the telling. Nevertheless, Carr must certainly be right to assert that there is not a total dissimilarity of structure but rather a large measure of correspondence between stories and "real" life.[3]

It was not part of David Carr's particular concern to address the cultural relativity of stories and so to challenge the bland assertions of Roland Barthes (and, subsequently of Hayden White and others) about the universality of narrative. Historians and anthropologists, however, must have this concern. If the viability of narrative derives in part from its correspondence with the social construction of everyday life, then we need a systematic study of the highly variant realities that different cultures manifestly sustain and the interrelationship between the stories people tell and those that they enact in such worlds. Or more properly—since such culturally relative studies have long been conducted—we need for those who are accepted as the source of wisdom upon the nature and functioning of narrative in our own cultural tradition to be attentive to culturally relative aspects of the life-story-life relationship. Most particularly, for present purposes, we historians of the South need such a systematic study of the relationship of masters' stories to slaves' stories. This chapter is offered as a small contribution toward that great project.[4]

Stories from life have, of course, played a conspicuous part in discourses of slavery in different ways at different times. In a consideration of the colonial era they stand out for their matter-of-fact acceptance of slavery, its situations, and its relationships. I think here of the incomplete narrations of William Byrd's diary—Jenny being whipped for throwing water on the sofa, Eugene being made to drink a pint of urine as a "cure" for his habit of bed-wetting. I think also, knowing it only in a single striking instance, of the stoic framing of slavery in a little report in a *Virginia Gazette* of the 1750s, telling of the newly landed African slave who, upon observing the punishment of a fellow slave in the yard where he was working, went to a grindstone, sharpened a knife to razor keenness, and, cutting his own throat, poured out his lifeblood rather than submit to slavery.[5]

As the changes in worldview associated with the American Revolution began to render slavery problematic for an ever-increasing number of people in the North Atlantic world, so slavery stories began to have a wider and wider circulation, dramatizing situations, relationships, and agonies in the sentimental mode in which experiences within the culture were being reorganized. The activists of the Abolitionist movement both collected real-life narratives from escaped slaves and constructed fictional stories of their own to sustain and intensify their condemnatory representations of the institution of slavery. The Civil War produced a flow of rather different stories from life; Reconstruction and the rise of the New South produced yet other sets. By the later nineteenth century, Western "high" culture's great project to discover and recover "the culture of the folk" had been activated in North America, and was adding collections of Negro tales and other expressive forms to the stock of stories from life. This stock of stories was simultaneously being expanded also among the literary white folk by nostalgic stories of the plantation remembered. Moving forward in time, I must also note the great fund of stories gathered in the WPA projects of the New Deal era under the rubric of Slave Narratives—a fund used to great effect, along with earlier accumulations, by Charles Joyner in his rich ethnographic reconstruction of the antebellum Waccamaw Neck.[6]

Understandably, the new social history of more recent times has mistrusted stories as it embarked on its great project to establish with cliometrics the social facts of slavery times. Even if we accept that these most valuable demographic forms of systematic analyses of data have by no means exhausted their potential to enhance our understanding of plantation slavery as a troubling phase of our world's past, we may yet feel that the time is right for a return to stories—and an equally systematic review of what they can contribute in the way of a commentary on slavery as an experience rather than just as a condition of life. By treating a small sample of stories from the writings of the diarist who is the focus of my person-centered ethnography, I hope to open for discussion some of the possibilities of a systematic attention to slavery stories from life.

Colonel Landon Carter, as revealed in his diary, was a prolific and accomplished storyteller. His writings are full of mundane stories of everyday life. There are incessant stories of slaves and overseers under the diarist's lordship; there are equally numerous stories of disloyal sons and of outrageous neighbors, and stories of contriving merchants and corrupt officials beyond his immediate world. The actions of these people are almost as predictable as the cast of characters—the slaves idle, steal, drink, and conspire; the overseers lie, subvert instructions, and embezzle; the sons seek constantly to humiliate—perhaps symbolically to kill—the father; the neighbors trespass across Carter's boundaries and fabricate countercharges of trespass, for which they exact reprisals, and always they circulate rumors and slanders; the merchants systematically cheat through arranging to buy produce cheap and sell goods dear; and the officials arrange to divert public charges to their own private accounts. Besides this, at all levels, there are those yet more devious and uncontrollable Others, the female creatures that make up womankind. There are the willful "Jades" among the slaves; and there is "madam," Carter's daughter-in-law, who must surely have Louis XV's Madame de Maintenon for her pattern in pride and intrigue.

More would have been made of all these stories before now had they not come from a male of Landon Carter's social rank—a category concerning whom we are often told we know too much already. What we most crave, of course, is the experiential perspective that such stories would give us if they came from the ladies' withdrawing room, the back stairs, or the slave quarter. And that, of course, is what we so seldom get—and so we have to keep working indirectly by way of transformations of the lordly male's inscribed versions. Meanwhile, his lordship's stories are what we have, and they must be used for the experiential insights they afford into "being there" in the master's place on a great plantation. Though the possible approaches to a collection of personal stories are certainly various, I shall briefly review two only, and then introduce and attempt to develop a third—with an extended illustration.

Following the example of cultural anthropologists, one must go to fundamentals, and seek the grounding of the stories, asking, In what kind of world does the doing take place? This is where the relation of story to myth becomes important—if myth is taken to mean not so much a certain kind of story, as that aspect of storying through which it is made known what cosmos contains the action. "Myth" thus understood is the storytelling's evocations of kinds of agency—beings, forces—that are at work in the world imagined and what kinds of actions those beings perform.[7]

Myth is always both fragmentary and partisan—that is a way in which it is more elusive, pervasive, and dynamic than cosmology. Where cosmology attempts to expound or extrapolate a system whole, myths and the narratives that carry them tell only a part—a selected part. The invocation of this or that portion of myth in story at once highlights an aspect of the whole and the claims of the speaker or writer. That is one of the advantages of approaching myth through storying in the context of person-centered ethnography. We can discern these claims because we are taking up located fragments.[8]

The principal myths latent in Landon Carter's telling of the world, as I read it, are twofold. There is the version—great, overarching, and containing—of the world created perfect in seven days by the Almighty, only to be plunged into confusion and misery by the transgression of the first Man at the prompting of the first Woman. God had told Adam, "Cursed is the ground for thy sake; in sorrow shalt thou eat of it all the days of thy life" (Gen. 3.17). Landon Carter glossed this explicitly when he wrote: "The first judgement denounced against man was that he should surely die. The second that he should get his bread by the sweat of his brow. Every day's experience demonstrates the truth of the first and every year's labor proves the latter." He glossed it implicitly in nearly every line that he inscribed about agriculture—the great bulk of what he wrote. Husbandry was the working out of God's curse: incessant toil for the laborers in the field; incessant care for the master as he watched their waywardness and the uncertainties conditioned by wet, dry, cold, pests, and plagues.[9]

But—a great theme already sounding insistent notes in this Enlightenment diary—there is an emergent countermyth. Within the dominant myth of God's curse and the sorrow of the life of labor, there developed an opposing myth of improvement. There had been ancient counterparts for the idea of material advancement; Prometheus is only the most famous of a host of mythic men who, unlike Pandora, gave improving gifts of technological know-how to humankind. There is, however, a great difference between the technology myths of the ancients and the emergent myth of progress in which Landon Carter so revealingly participated: the one was epic or opportunistic, involving bold or cunning access to the powers of the gods; the other (with dire consequences for slaves) was bourgeois, and involved the systematic application of calculating reason, which—as this myth came into the ascendant—began to replace nobility as the dominant attribute of triumphant man.

In the first portion of Landon Carter's plantation diary, the myth of improvement is distinctly dominant. This is the record of the active engagements of a man in the prime of life, the project book for the methodization of the plantation. He actually gave it the heading "Farming Observations," using a vocabulary in which the word "farming" was a term chosen with deliberation to stand for English, rational "improving agriculture," as opposed to merely "planting" according to the century-and-a-half old wasteful vernacular ways of the Chesapeake. Stories in this early part of the diary are few and mostly incidental or accessory to strong non-narrative modes. There is the chilling, proto-Tayloristic story of the application of systematic performance tests to the gang of oat threshers in order to discover the "lazy" ones and raise the productivity of the group, but more developed in the diary at this time, looming larger, were non-narrative modes of representation that better expressed the concerns of the agricultural improver. For example, there was the engineering construction project for tide gates to drain a marsh, and the design for the systematic planting of a field of indigo—both of these accompanied by diagrams—and there were elaborate specifications for a wheat kiln to kill the fly-weevil in the egg stage.[10]

Another very fruitful approach to the stories scattered in the documents that form the sources for this person-centered ethnographic history would be to follow the example of folklorists. One might analyze the tale types to which the stories are assignable. In this again one could be both drawing on a powerful body of generalized scholarship and usefully particularizing it, since these tale tellings, like the myth fragments, are socially located in ways that most of the tales, as folklorists view them, are not. In that field the analysis is usually, perforce, of tales severed from their contexts or tales that have been generated by contexts created by the collectors rather than by the tellers of the tales and their communities. The folkloric approach to Colonel Carter's diary, attending to strong and persistent forms in the culture, is in itself appealing, especially because it offers the chance to analyze an out-of-the-usual instance—not the peasants' cycle of tales, but the repertoire attached to the equally ancient role of the master of the estate house. Here we have stories, then, of the lazy or faithless servant and of the perplexities as to whether the servant is most knave or fool.

It is neither of these merely sketched approaches but a third, and somewhat contrary, approach that I want to take up and attempt to develop for the remainder of this essay. I want to look at the story from life as a means to explore not just what can too neatly be expressed as "the limits of culture" but rather to register the presence of the dark and unspeakable in the world. I do not mean by this the unknown with its undoubted terrors; I mean the all-too-well-known; I mean the gut-wrenching pain and the agony of what others do to us that we most would have them not do—experiences, then, for which there are words, but no ways for those words or other conventionalizing forms to even begin to encompass the brutal reality of the experience for the person suffering.[11]

The ethnography of slavery, whether it is mainly directed to the institutional systems and the meanings of the masters or to the resiliences, defensive and counteroffensive strategies of the slaves, is certain to be inadequate, even seriously distorted, as long as it is fixed in too fascinated a fashion on the ordered play of cultural forms. There must be ways to stare into the pit—even if we know we cannot truly see. There must be ways to look into the dark places where we know are lurking the experienced agonies that are part of life in all places—especially slave places—but that we also know defy telling or indeed any representation. Generalized or statistical studies—of punishment records, incidences of injury and mortality, and other forms of quantifiable suffering—may be very suggestive in this regard, but such knowledge is all experience-far. Stories, of course, are themselves conventionalizing assimilations of experience into social reality, and in that sense they belong in the domain of culture and not that of the unacculturatable experiences that remain unspeakable for the sufferer. Nevertheless, it may be an important part of the operation of stories in life—whether tales or recollections from life—to speak the unspeakable, to contemplate the inscrutables of experience. An approach to the ethnography of slavery by way of stories that seem to have undertaken that assignment or that seem to give us a chance to undertake it experientially will now be assayed, using a cluster of stories told in Colonel Landon Carter's diary.

In the welter of socially located plantation stories, there are many that point to misery—including Carter's own—and point to ways in which the demoralizing anguish could be at least partially objectified. Death might be the occasion. Landon lost, when she was at a tender age, his "dear little daughter Susannah," his last-born child, to whom his heart had clearly gone out and to whom he had looked for "the support of Grey hairs."[12] Recurrent anguish was, however, mainly centered on sorrowful, destructive contests—with his eldest son, Robert Wormeley Carter, who he feared wished him dead, and with his daughter-in-law, Winifred Travers Beale Carter, who he believed was ever beguiling his son into conspiracies to destroy his authority. It would be instructive to review these stories, so universal in one sense, so particular in historic setting and ethos, in another. But I shall rather take a different striking series of confrontations with pain and death; I shall follow the stories involving Landon Carter's slave, Nassau.

An extensive web of reports surround Nassau. Some are stories in the sense of being fully structured narratives, others—in some ways even more revealing—are only implicit narratives or undeveloped items of information. The narratives often exemplify David Carr's contention that persons engage to a considerable extent in conducting their lives along story lines, since many of them are told before the sequence that they narrate is concluded. The ending is supplied not in retrospect but in anticipation, as in the ominous conclusion: "There will come a warm day for the punishment of those things."[13]

Nassau, who emerges from the reports in a close, intimate relationship to Landon Carter, is a slave who was his constant attendant at home and abroad, "waiting" on him, as the master termed it, his body servant, in other words. But Nassau was deemed an extension of the person of this indefatigably medical diarist in another deeply significant respect: Nassau was a skilled surgeon, pharmacist, and, indeed, assistant physician, and as a member of Landon Carter's household, was also in his turn a body to be physicked. Sadly, he was also a drinker whose indulgences either increased in frequency or came to attract increased attention. The Nassau we meet in the record was also a family man; his wife, his children—some grown up, some infants yet—his still-living father, and at least one sister are all part of the person that emerges from the stories.

The records form a spectrum that can be divided more or less into those that are stories and those that are not. The records that are not stories (or are only implicit ones) are among the most instructive, since they highlight the taken-for-granted role of the personal slave in stressed situations and relationships and forms of engagement of which no account is taken by the master/narrator. Even when there is little stress, the nonstories can be revealing. The slave is the gentleman planter's eyes and, where need be, hands, sent into the fields to assess crop prospects or cope with ailing livestock, but no notice is taken of the play of the slave's own expertise in this situation unless there is detected and permitted a note of challenge, as in this note: "I believe both my colt and John Carter's . . . will dye; though Nassau differs; mine he says will live but Jack's must go." Rarer still—generated, it seems, by a moment of shared laughter sufficiently relished to be recorded—there might be a fleeting recognition of expertise, albeit in mocking parody. On Sunday June 23, 1771, the colonel noted: "I walked about in these home fields . . . and sent Nassau all over them. I thought it [the tobacco] stood . . . very well indeed, and Dr. Nassau says he has seen much tobacco, and never saw any stand better."[14]

As one who was expected to be the immediate extension of the master's eyes, ears, and arms, Nassau was, inevitably, involved in the conflicts and aggressions that the master knew to be part of the exercise of his authority on the plantation—at a cost to Nassau that would never be reckoned. So, Nassau must check tallies to expose livestock losses that a fellow slave's shepherding daughter had tried to conceal; he must even go down into the home field to verify his master's suspicion that his own sister, Maryan, was engaged in deception about the rate of progress of the gang she led. In what was probably a very stressful confrontation, he must "strip" a fellow home-quarter slave's "cloaths off" to show that the master's blow upon the man's arm, since there was "not the least swelling upon it," had not *really* disabled the slave as he claimed it had.[15]

The stressful was usually at least implicit in the half-tellings of Nassau's work in caring for the sick. In this work Nassau carried great responsibility—to heal or to ease the way to death—but the master's reports, except in particular circumstances to be noted shortly, are unconcernedly matter of fact. This could be so whether Nassau's role has been to watch all night with Landon's fevered daughter Judy and to report in the morning; or, as it might be, to go, though quite ill himself, to minister to a neighbor's sick boy whose death he cannot avert; or it might be to watch continually over the dying slave carpenter, McGinnes, and the decline and death of the extremely aged old slave retainer, Jack Lubbar. Nassau's reports were noticed—so we know he was there—but his cares were not. He must even be assumed as an unreported attendant carer at the death of his own very young but pregnant daughter, Sukey, when, "being Near her time," she was believed sent into decline by the sight, at "her mother's Cabbin . . . door," of a snake—"her father's aversion to an amazing degree."

Nassau once, however, virtually compelled the telling of a story in which the master must allow him a part. On one occasion he "waked" the colonel "in the night" to see to his own little son, Meridith, "concluding him dying" from the way "the child's pulse [had] sunk." But, of course, the slave father's alarm is, in the diary story, only incidental to the master's working of a cure "by [a] very bold Practice, but yet a rational one." There is—but only once—an explicit recognition of the slave surgeon's skill, care, and commitment. The master, lamenting his own anxious situation, sick himself and with a household full of sick persons, recorded that Nassau, two days before, had "sent in a list of 19 very ill." Now he did for once notice that his assistant was desperately overworked, "running from one to the other who are sick."[16]

Some more fully developed stories do involve Nassau but scarcely feature him, so that the disregard is a revealing statement of the situation, as well as of the partial nature of stories. A story recorded for July 13, 1777, is directly concerned with the dismissal of an overseer—but the occasion of it was that the master had "yesterday ordered [the overseer] to whip Nassau naked," whereas the overseer "it seems only gave . . . a stroke or two over his cloaths." And a month later, the drama narrated is over a man from another plantation who came to visit his "whore," bringing liquor for her father, Nassau. There is at least the suggestion in the narration that Nassau was prostituting his own daughter in return for the indulgence of his own great vice—yet the point of the story, as it is told, is that Landon "was obliged to threaten to shoot the [visiting] fellow before he would go." We simply do not know Nassau's story here, nor yet his daughter's; all we have are the colonel's judgmental phrases.[17]

There is nothing surprising in the unquestioned hierarchical assumptions that ensure that the cares of the man will not be much, if at all, a part of the stories of the master. Nor, perhaps, would Nassau have expected them to be; in that relationship, more of his master's concern with his feelings might have been experienced as an unwelcome increase of oppression. There was far too much of that sort of concern anyway. Nevertheless, the story frames that marginalize Nassau, even when the record notes his presence and participation in dramatic situations and forms of action, are a sort of striking commentary, not only on the place of the body servant in the world in which he often moves, but on the power and privilege of the narrator, who assigned roles in stories even more imperiously than in life. We have to assume that Nassau constructed and experienced, and would have told, his role quite differently. And yet these sets of roles—self-assigned and master-assigned—so separated in the stories the one tells us and the ones the other cannot tell us belonged to persons continuously and intimately linked. This perception of deadly intimacy is sharpened when it is recalled that it was on a Sunday that "Dr. Nassau" went to report on how the tobacco stood—and there had been reports from him on the previous two Sundays. There was no structured "off time" for Nassau; he was, in principle, always on call.

The full stories in which Nassau was assigned a pronounced role give further insight into the painful intimacy of the relationship. Through some of those stories we are able to look—though we cannot see—into blacknesses of desolation and longings for an end to the burden of life itself.

These fully told stories are, as told, mostly mundane enough. They divide into a few distinct but related types. There is, for instance, the "story type" of the servant as knave, conspiring with other knavish servants to make matters in the household appear other than they are, in order to shield yet another servant, the runaway Simon the Oxcarter, and to deny his just reward to a further more "honest" servant, Mangorike Will, who lived, indeed, at a different quarter.[18] There is also the story type of the faithless servant, who, together with the son he led into villainy, has been heedless of duty and the master's safety. The son is reported to have "mired my horse up to his saddle in crossing a marsh that none but a blind drunkard could ever venture upon," so that the colonel had "to plung[e] home 5 or 6 miles upon this mired horse without one person to assist." He resolved, as he inscribed the story, to have both the delinquents flogged; "though [the father, Nassau, is] my old Servant[,] I am too old a Master to be thus inhumanely treated."[19]

More insistent, and in their nature more caught up in a tangle of inescapable miseries quite other than those merely of a master, chilled and unassisted on the road, is the abundantly narrated story type of the drunken surgeon. Related also to the mired-horse episode is the account of the occasion when—after an elaborate contrivance to secure a horse to go riding out in search of liquor—the servant is too intoxicated to bleed the master. Stories mount up in the record, however, of failures more unpardonable than that, because they were life threatening. Nassau, on Saturday, November 24, 1770, was, according to his master, "most inhumanly drunk and what is worse blooded a two year old child and his [own] father in that fit." For that, together with the lies he was said to have told about the treatments he had administered, he was "clapped in irons to lye all night and feel his drunkenness." Or he was so drunk that he could not even "give an account" of his physicking. Even when Nassau was too sick to minister, his sickness was blamed on his drinking; his having, at an earlier stage, "by drink . . . grown stupid" was held against him.[20]

When Nassau was on the job, it was perhaps worse, because the master, intent on the healing work, felt he had been constantly thwarted in it: "I have nobody but him to bring me account of them [the sick], nor to give what medicine I order; and when he gets drunk he lies, and only remembers to do so, by telling me he has done what he has not done." On the occasion of this complaint, the master felt "obliged to give the slave physician a severe whipping"—although only after he had himself been vomited and blooded. So Nassau's body was the object of the master's practice in multiple ways—purging, flaying, and then more physicking. The case seemed hopeless: "and yet" the diary's scolding went on, "he will drink; he can't say he can't help it, because he could help sending for liquor." Violent attacks upon Nassau's body were not enough, however; a different kind of cure had to be sought—one that was even more invasive than the physicking and flogging. Evidently disturbed at the flogging of the surgeon on whom he relied, the colonel inscribed his justification for what he was doing, in a mode that commences a transcendance of the mundane story type concerning the undutiful servant and begins to show a more inward menace to Nassau: "I have threatened him, begged him, Prayed him, and told him the consequences if he neglected the care to one of the sick people; that their deaths . . . must be an evidence against him at the great and terrible day, [I have] talked a great deal to him in [a] most religious and affectionate way." The story type has become something else, invoking explicitly now the ultimate truths of salvation and damnation. The master tells that he had kept up this pressure "day by day," so that we might think that he was himself thus aggravating the problem by exacerbating the psychic insupportability for Nassau of being given the task of the surgeon without being allowed the identity. This appeared at least dimly to Landon himself: "And yet all will not do; he seems resolved to drink in spight of me, and I beleive in order to spight me." A stern patriarchal idea, however, of "justice," had still to prevail over any search for understanding: "He knows he never gets a stroke but for his drinkings, and then he is very sharply whipped; but as soon as the cuts heal he gets drunk directly. I am now resolved not to pass one instance over[,] and think myself justified both to God and man." Having thus put his resolve firmly in a religious frame, the colonel went on: "I confess I have faults myself to be forgiven, but to be every day and hour committing them, and to seek the modes of committing them[,] admits of no Plea of frailty." He concluded, nevertheless, relentlessly: "I hope then I may still save his soul."[21]

The pressure, and perhaps the guilt it was intended to induce, took its toll. A week after the whipping and the intensified daily sermonizing, while in the middle of being interrogated about the symptoms of his patients, Nassau was "accused . . . of being drunk." That may have been for the moment too much: "at dark he went off," leaving his master to fulminate on what "a cursed Villain he must be," since "he knows his own Father, his sister Maryan, a child of his, [and] another of Nelly's [together with members of the Carter kindred itself], are all sick[,] and yet he gets drunk and goes off." But not without conscience, or perhaps a heartrending plea for acceptance as a caring healer. "Having the key of the [dispensing] Shop[,] he came back in the night and laid that down on the steps of the Narrow Passage." He was gone some time—"harbored" by "Somebody," the narrator surmised, "as it has rained ever since he has been out." Meanwhile, the results of his drunken doctoring were angrily noted.[22]

In the summer of 1775, it seems—plotting the story, between the separate stories in the diary—the nexus of enslavement to drink and to a master who kept at him about it seemed to draw more excruciatingly tightly about Nassau than ever. First—or as a first indicator in the story as we pick it up—is a story that almost seems not to be a story, though it carries powerful action beneath its almost casual surface:

Talbot, Nassau's son[,] proved more of a drinker than he was of a fool; therefore I made a plowboy of him, having catched him asleep with a Piece of a bottle of Grog in the Closet window, and *for his father's sake* I will have no more of such creatures, as he [Nassau, the boy's father] is *as unhappy a drunkard as can live.*[23]

The master's moralizing story has sententiously redirected lives—"I made a plowboy of him." And from this high-handed determination of the slave son's destiny according to an inscribed judgment of what was known to be for the slave father's good, the strains in the relationship appear, not surprisingly, to have intensified. Six weeks later, Landon Carter, himself troubled in his own fatherhood by bitter quarrels over the elopement of one of his remaining unmarried daughters, tells the story of a dramatic renewal of his divine father-judge role vis-à-vis Nassau. He tells of taking the parts, in sequence, first of the punishing and then of the forgiving "Father," and, throughout, of the redeeming "Father." Nassau had once again conspired to acquire liquor, and then had engaged in potentially murderous surgery on an overseer whose sickness and fear for his life had particularly enlisted the master's "endeavors after humanity." When the comatose drunk was finally found and dragged home, his master "offered to give him a box on the ear." We know suddenly at this point, from the narration itself, that Nassau had a different construction of the situation—which, in the diarist's view, clearly called for penitent submission. Nassau "fairly forced himself against" his menacing master, for which the master "tumbled him into the Sellar and there had him tied Neck and heels all night."[24]

The next day the master's enactment of the story he was also determined to tell was intensified. And with that escalation we must suppose Nassau's misery also intensified, almost beyond what we can bear, as we follow the narrative:

I . . . had him stripped and tied up to a limb and, with a Number of switches Presented to his eyes and a fellow with an uplifted arm, He encreased his crying Petitions to be forgiven but this once, and desired the man to bear witness that he called on God to record his solemn Vow that he never more would touch liquor. I expostulated with him on his and his father's blasphemy of denying the wholy [holy] word of God in boldly asserting that there was neither a hell nor a devil, and asked him if he did not dread to hear how he had set the word of God at nought [, God] who promised everlasting happiness to those who loved him and obeyed his words and eternal torments [to those] who set his goodness at nought and dispised his holy word. After all I forgave this creature out of humanity, religion, and every virtuous duty[,] with hopes[,] though I hardly dare mention it[,] that I shall by it save one soul more Alive.[25]

The menacing, yet still mundane, stories of the drunken surgeon have now given way to an intense dramatization of Landon Carter's primal myth of cosmic Fatherhood and Redemption. Nassau's rebellion against oppression—the story he seems to be telling—has also entered this plane, with his denial of the reality of damnation of the soul. The agony of this confrontation cannot have been less, even if Nassau—as he may well have—had at some stage in his promises sincerely entered into the action, longing for the release from the bondages of drinking bouts, repeated failures, and the hell of the stand-over preachings of his master.

The way for Nassau was yet deeper into the pit, his master still looking down on him there. Perhaps Nassau's other life—his own, apart from what his master could or would "script" and "story" in his compulsions to continue this destructive intimacy—was becoming unsustainable under all this pressure. Two weeks and three days later, after some intervening cures in which he was trusted again, Nassau was overcome once more with drink. He was called upon—in a situation stressful for everyone—to physick Reuben Beale, "the monster" who had eloped with the master's beloved daughter, Judy, and who had only recently, in the aftermath of that previous round of threatening and forgiving, found his banishment from Sabine Hall lifted. Nassau "was so very drunk he could not Assist. . . . At night he crawled about the room and did not know a chamber pot from a bottle of water." In consequence, his master, renewing resolutions to be sternly punitive, "ordered him to be [tyed?] and imprisoned." By the next day, however, "he will not eat" and said "he desires to die." Landon does not convince when he declares, "I don't care." Perhaps he would have done something to release the slave if he had not cared, for his obvious care was such an added affliction: "I say he may [die] but he is [so?] far [damned?] . . . he certainly has forfeited his solemn promise before heaven. . . . If he goes, I shall be rid of a Villain, though a most capable servant." There follow some largely illegible words about "ingratitude."[26]

If life were indeed a story instead of being something of infinitely more strands into which threads of stories are constantly woven, this narrative would perhaps have to end there, or be resolved into the redeeming or damning death that the master's storying conjures. But life is not a story; it drags on. Drinking and punishment, protestation and return to duty continued for Nassau. His daughter died after childbirth in the sequel to the snake alarm already noticed—in itself so peculiarly terrifying to Nassau. We read that "for the last time he was excused on a most [so]lemn Promise never more to drink." Then there was the story—"last" in a different sense—of the ailing Landon Carter preparing some mulled wine with cinnamon to ease a bowel condition; it did, but the next day he found, when he needed more of it, that Nassau had "drank up most of the rest" and that he had "run off on the discovery of it." The comment—"This fellow is proof against his oaths never to drink and gets so drunk every morn as to contradict every time I speak"—merely shows that this painful, destructive relationship will indeed only be ended by the separation of death. So it was, some four months later—when the master died.[27]

Stories we hear, stories we tell; stories historians read, stories historians write. . . . In the cultured forms of the stories Landon Carter told of Nassau—as well as in the stories he did not tell, because Nassau was only a slave—and in the stories we make out of those stories and nonstories, we see something of the situation, and the culture-formed definitions of the situation, with which Nassau's master and constant associate confronted him. The master—with the power he commanded, including the power of book and pen—could readily gloss his own so-much-smaller part of all this anguish in the storying of it; he could refer the most painful parts to his own certainties of a Fall and a Redemption, which give a cosmic aspect to the patriarchal role he assigned himself. We can scarcely even hear a whisper of the stories Nassau might tell. Some of them could be transformations of the now justly celebrated trickster tales, as Landon Carter's are of the knave-or-fool, faithless servant tales. But we surely see enough to perceive where ethnography cannot guide us. We see the limits of the capacity of cultural forms to give shape and meaning to recurrent experiences of threatened annihilation—experiences of oppression, denial, the stand-over from without, and experiences of the sense of failure and despair welling from within.

Thus slavery? That formulation gives too much to the particular, and certainly allows too little to ethnography and the study of those cultural forms whose most profound role may be to curb, contain, and give recognizable, manageable shapes to the experiences of suffering in the passage from birth to death that is human life. Forms like the African-American folktale have been convincingly interpreted as lessons in coming to terms with the harshness of the world; the spirituals have been presented as forms for building on communal warmths to create richly recurrent experiences of transcending that harshness. Yet our accounts of the cultures of the world—certainly of the worlds that slaves and masters made together—must also address the limits of culture; and stories from life, even if they seem mostly to give the master the last word, can be used to explore experiences of slavery with its forms of domination and resistance.

Landon Carter did, and did not, have the last word. His last will and testament bequeathed "my man Nassau" to his son Robert—along with Mulatto Betty (almost certainly Nassau's wife) and Nat, their coachman son. A codicil, written two months before the master's death, decreed that Nat and Mulattoe Betty should be paid "an annuity of Ten pounds per Annum" and, "on every Christmas day," should have "liberty to make choice which one so ever of my . . . sons and daughters they shall desire to live with."[28] Evidently still enraged with Nassau, the master did not include him in this largesse.

The actual last written word I can find is a bland entry in the son's account book: "1786, May 22 Nassau cut 18 Lambs." Or was that really the last word? Not long before his death, Colonel Carter took note of Nassau's habits of self-assertion. This African-American surgeon physician was proud of his healing powers: such outspokenness surely did not cease with the master's death, which ended both his stand-over and his diary recording of their conflicts. The master had made his usual dismissal of "drunken Nassau" whom "I am obliged to make do everything," but then he added a protest that points to a professional pride that Nassau surely continued, even augmented—after the diarist was dead. The Colonel noted crossly that in every case–despite all his own care and supervision, Nassau claimed the credit: "On any recovery it is all"–the surgeon would boast "his doing".[29]

"On any recovery," the master complained, Nassau would say: "It is all *my* doing."[30]

NOTES

First I must express my gratitude to Mary Aitken and Rowan Ireland for sharing and helping to develop my interest in stories, and similarly to Alton Becker and Bernard Newsome.

This chapter owes a great deal to Colleen Isaac, who demands more people and less academic guff in her history. It was also read, and timely help was given, by Inga Clendinnen, Greg Dening, and Gwynedd Hunter. Special thanks to Charles Joyner—now a great friend to historians of the Great South Land as well as of the South—for inviting me to his wonderful 1989 Myrtle Beach conference, for which the first version was prepared.

1. References to Jack P. Greene, ed., *The Diary of Colonel Landon Carter of Sabine Hall, 1752-1778* (Charlottesville, Va., 1965) will be by date *and* page number. I have found when reading diary-based histories that I want to have the date of the entry in that most time-marked of genres.

2. See Rhys Isaac, "Communication and Control: Authority Metaphors and Power Contests on Colonel Landon Carter's Virginia Plantation, 1752–1778," in Sean Wilentz, ed., *Rites of Power: Symbolism, Ritual, and Politics since the Middle Ages* (Philadelphia, 1985), pp. 275–303, esp. pp. 295–300; and Rhys Isaac, "Imagination and Material Culture: The Enlightenment on a Mid-Eighteenth-Century Virginia Plantation," in Anne Yentsch and Mary Beaudry, eds., *The Art and Mystery of Historical Archaeology: Essays in Honor of James Deetz* (Boca Raton, Fla., 1992), pp. 401–26.

3. David Carr, "Life and the Narrator's Art," in Hugh J. Silverman and Don Ihde, eds., *Hermeneutics and Deconstruction*, (Albany, 1985), pp. 108–121; Roland Barthes, "Introduction to the Structural Analysis of Narratives," in his *Image, Music, Text*, ed. and trans. Stephen Heath (New York, 1977), pp. 79–124. Peter Berger and Thomas Luckmann, *The Social Construction of Reality: A Treatise in the Sociology of Knowledge* (Garden City, N.Y., 1966). The technicalities of "story" and "narrative" need not be entered into here; "story" for me entails a degree of shaping, development, and implied comment well above what is found in the "narrative" fragments that are more usual in diaries. For recent overviews of this burgeoning topic—which, along with "story" has now become an almost modish concern—see Jerome Bruner, "The Narrative Construction of Reality," *Critical Inquiry* 18 (1991), pp. 1–21, and Charlotte Linde, *Life Stories: The Creation of Coherence* (New York, 1993).

4. Hayden White, "The Value of Narrativity in the Representation of Reality," in W. T. J. Mitchell, ed., *On Narrative*, (Chicago, 1981), pp. 1–23. See, for an example of a distant culture's narrative principles, Alton L. Becker, "Text-Building, Epistemology, and Aesthetics in Javanese Shadow Theatre," in A. L. Becker and A. A. Yengoyan, eds., *The Imagination of Reality: Essays in South-East Asian Coherence Systems* (Norwood, N.J., 1979) pp. 211–43.

5. Louis B. Wright and Marion Tinling, eds., *The Secret Diary of William Byrd of Westover, 1709–1712* (Richmond, Va., 1941), pp. 79, 117; *Virginia Gazette*, July 10, 1752, p. 3.

6. Charles Joyner, *Down by the Riverside: A South Carolina Slave Community* (Urbana, Ill., 1984). The classic landmark work on the slaves' repertoire of stories as historical document is Lawrence W. Levine, *Black Culture and Black Consciousness: Afro-American Folk Thought from Slavery to Freedom* (New York, 1977). See also Roger D. Abrahams, *Afro-American Folktales: Stories from Black Traditions in the New World* (New York, 1985).

7. My thinking toward this conception of myth has been assisted a great deal by attention to the dialogue, as it were, set up between Marshall Sahlins and Greg Dening. See Sahlins, *Historical Metaphors and Mythical Realities: Structure in the Early History of the Sandwich Islands Kingdom* (Ann Arbor, 1981), and Greg Dening's very powerful historian-anthropologist's response, *History's Anthropology: The Death of William Gooch* (Washington, D.C., 1988), now revised as *The Death of William Gooch: A History's Anthropology* (Melbourne, 1995).

8. Here I am indebted to an illuminating discussion at the Shelby Cullom Davis Seminar, Princeton University, in December 1981. The paper was Elizabeth Traube's "Order and Events: Responses to Colonial Rule in Two Eastern Indonesian Societies." The discussants who underscored the fragmentary and contestable aspects of the myths treated in the paper were Hildred Geertz and Jerry Sider.

9. Greene, *Diary of Carter*, 8/14/1770, p. 465. See also Isaac, "Imagination and Material Culture," in Beaudry and Yentch, eds., *Art and Mystery*, pp. 403-6.

10. Greene, *Diary of Carter*, 3/7/1757, pp. 151–54; 10/20/1757, pp. 180–85; 10/25/1757, pp. 185–87. (From comfortable positions in an affluent society—though in anything but an affluent world—readers may have to remind themselves of the harsh aspect of these optimistic devices that embodied the myth of "improvement." The application of measured and calculated method promised increased yields, but there is really no suggestion in them that either increased benefits or shorter hours would flow on

from this to the laborer, whose task had now become more exacting, if sometimes slightly less physically effortful.

11. I have been impelled to wrestle more intensely with the problems specially addressed in this paper by a critique of my assemblage of ethnographic studies in *The Transformation of Virginia, 1740–1790* (Chapel Hill, N.C., 1982) that was developed by Jean-Christophe Agnew in a paper to the Shelby Cullom Davis Center, Princeton University (October 24, 1986), subsequently revised and published as "History and Anthropology: Scenes from a Marriage," *Yale Journal of Criticism* 3 (Spring 1990), pp. 29–50. My thoughts in response have appeared as Rhys Isaac, "Power and Meaning: Event and Text: History and Anthropology," in Donna Merwick, ed., *Dangerous Liaisons: Essays in Honour of Greg Dening* (Melbourne, 1994) pp. 297–316, and "Explanation and Terrifying Power in Ethnographic History," *Yale Journal of Criticism* 6 (Spring 1993), pp. 217–36.

12. Greene, *Diary of Carter*, 4/25/1758, pp. 221–22.

13. Carr, "Life and the Narrator's Art," in Silverman and Ihde, *Hermeneutics and Deconstruction*, pp. 108–21; Greene, *Diary of Carter*, 3/25/1767, p. 347.

14. Greene, *Diary of Carter*, 9/12/1771, p. 628; 6/23/1771, p. 583.

15. Ibid., 2/6/1764, p. 254; 4/12/1770, p. 385; 6/2/1771, p. 568; 3/31/1770, p. 378.

16. Ibid., 9/12/1772, pp. 652–53; 7/27 & 28, 8/24/1774, pp. 840–42, 853; 5/9/1776, p. 1036; 3/12/1772, p. 658; and 9/3/1773, p. 765.

17. Ibid., 7/13/77, p. 1110; 8/11/1777, p. 1124.

18. Ibid., 4/24–27/1766, pp. 289–92. This episode has already been treated by me at some length—though with somewhat different intent. See Isaac, *Transformation of Virginia*, pp. 332–36.

19. Greene, *Diary of Carter*, 3/23/1770, p. 373; 2/26/1770, p. 363.

20. Ibid., 9/15/1770, p. 412; 11/25/1770, p. 527; 10/31/1770, p. 520; 4/1/1772, pp. 665–67. See also 9/22/1773, p. 776.

21. Ibid., 9/22/1773., p. 776; 9/23/1773, p. 778.

22. Ibid., 9/30/1773, p. 782; 10/1–2/1773, pp. 783, 785.

23. Ibid., 7/25/1775, p. 927 (emphasis added).

24. Ibid., 9/11/1775. p. 941.

25. Ibid., 9/11/1775., p. 941. Colonel Carter's emulation of divine justice and mercy in these episodes is given fuller treatment in Isaac, *Transformation of Virginia*, pp. 344–46, and in Isaac, "Communication and Control," in Willentz, *Rites of Power*, pp. 295–97.

26. Greene, *Diary of Carter*, 9/28/1775., p. 953.

27. For drinking and punishments, see ibid., 3/4–9/1776, pp. 993–97; 4/21/77, p. 1096; 7/13/1777, p. 1110; 8/11/1777, p. 1124; the snake episode: 5/2–9/1776, pp. 1034, 1036; and for late episodes: 4/4/1777, p. 1088, and 8/16/1778, p. 1145.

28. The Will of Landon Carter, Esq. (proved Feb. 1, 1779), Will Book 7, Richmond County, Va., microfilm in Virginia State Library, Richmond.

29. Diary of Robert Wormeley Carter, May 22, 1786, typescript in Research Library, Colonial Williamsburg Foundation, Williamsburg, Va.; Greene, *Diary of Carter*, 7/14/1777, p. 1111.

30. Ibid.

2

Texts, Texture, and Context: Toward an Ethnographic History of Slave Resistance

Charles Joyner

> With regard to my factual reporting of . . . events . . . I have made it a principle not to write down the first story that came my way, and not even to be guided by my own general impressions; either I was present myself at the events which I have described or else heard of them from eye-witnesses whose reports I have checked with as much thoroughness as possible. Not that even so the truth was easy to discover: different eye-witnesses give different accounts of the same events, speaking out of partiality for one side or the other or else from imperfect memories. And it may well be that my history will seem less easy to read because of the absence in it of a romantic element. It will be enough for me, however, if these words of mine are judged useful by those who want to understand clearly the events which happened in the past and which (human nature being what it is) will, at some time or other and in much the same ways, be repeated in the future. My work is not a piece of writing designed to meet the taste of the immediate public, but was done to last forever.
>
> —Thucydides, *The Peloponnesian War*, Book 1, Chapter 22

The day dawned bleak and chill that Friday in the Virginia Tidewater, and a gray light out of the northeast seemed to envelop everything. The dry leaves whispered a little in the windless November. Around noon the jailor unlocked the condemned hole of the Southampton County Jail. It was cold and musty in the hole, and the rank smell fouled the air.

For nearly two weeks, Nat Turner had been there in darkness, secured with manacles and chains. For nearly two weeks he had been lying there, on a pine board, neither asleep nor awake, as though his very being were itself a part of darkness and silence. All he had done, all he had felt and suffered, had passed before his mind as he had tried to explain his actions to an uncomprehending white man named Thomas Gray. It was strange to him that whites could apprehend neither motivation nor explanation for his actions. To them he seemed to have erupted out of nowhere with a shadowy band of avenging angels to cut a red swath through Southampton County in the summer of 1831. But as Nat Turner lay upon his hard pine board in his ragged garments, he saw again how the actual and urgent need to accomplish his purpose had been revealed to him in the heavens. There had been no choice, just one right thing, without alternatives. It had been as though the opposed forces of his destiny and his will had drawn swiftly together toward a foreordained mission.

Now armed guards took Nat Turner from his cell and struggled through a morass of hostile white faces. Eventually the party approached a field northeast of the town. A large crowd, sullenly inert and immobile, had gathered around a gnarled old live oak. The sheriff asked the prisoner if he had anything to say. Turning slowly, quietly, holding his body erect, Nat Turner answered in an unexpectedly pleasant voice. "I'm ready," was all he said. Then, waiting under the tree without impatience or even emotion, he stared out beyond the mob of angry white faces into the distant skies. They threw one end of the rope over a limb of the tree and pulled him up with a jerk. Eyewitnesses said Nat Turner did not move a muscle; he hung there as still as a rock.

So they hanged Nat Turner from a live oak tree in 1831. They skinned his body and rendered his flesh into grease. They sliced a souvenir purse from his skin and divided his bones into trophies, to be handed down as family heirlooms.[1] If all this was supposed to have killed Nat Turner, it would seem to have failed miserably. Nat Turner still lives in history, for he led the greatest slave revolt ever to take place in the greatest slave republic in the New World. No one has yet been able to explain satisfactorily the tragic enigma of Nat Turner, the spiritual and charismatic young carpenter with visions of apocalypse who at the age of thirty-one was taken to Jerusalem to hang upon a tree.[2]

The rapprochement between history and anthropology is relatively recent, and it takes many forms. Ethnographic history tries to negotiate between the Scylla of a theoretical empiricism that characterized the field of anthropology in the first half of the twentieth century and the Charybdis of neo-evolutionary determinism that has dominated the second half. Ethnographic historians (and historical ethnographers) seek not merely to delineate the surface of events but also to comprehend the skeletal substructure beneath the tough hide of behavior and expression—the attitudes and emotions of the historical actors expressed in events. Not readily apparent in everyday life, this skeletal substructure can only be glimpsed through the interaction of people within the boundaries they place around their own cultural categories. These boundaries and categories are constantly shifting, as Greg Dening notes, like sand on a beach, now piled up around the bulkheads of social structure now eroded by the riptides of historical events. The effort to comprehend these underlying attitudes and emotions is what makes ethnographic history ethnographic. The effort to comprehend this constant negotiation is what makes ethnographic history historical.[3]

Jean-Christophe Agnew defines ethnographic history as an example of something he calls "textualism," and he finds it exemplified in Rhys Isaac's *The Transformation of Virginia*. In its search for finely spun meanings, Agnew complains, "textualism" ignores the cruel actuality of pain, and terror, and death upon which the powers of domination over human life rest. He considers ethnographic history inimical to what he regards as the historian's responsibility to explain events, to account for what happened in the past, not merely to give an account of what happened.[4] Agnew's simplistic equation of ethnography with textualism is problematical. He does not employ the word with precision; in his hands it is more epithet than specifier. But I would not deny that episodes of slave resistance may be read like a collection of "texts" in which the slaves as cultural actors reveal how they perceive their world. If that makes me a "textualist," whatever that is, I shall wear the label proudly.[5]

A more serious problem is Agnew's demand for "explanation." He is by no means clear about just what he might consider a satisfactory "explanation," except that accounting *for* what happened must go beyond giving an account *of* what happened. Accounting *for* an occurrence would seem to require demonstrating that what happened *had* to happen, that it *necessarily* happened. After all, if accounting *for* any given historical event or process does not rule out the possibility of it having failed to happen, how can one claim to have accounted for why it *did* happen in that case, and why it happened in the manner it did? Similarly, since ethnographic history seeks to penetrate beneath the surface of events, accounting *for* the underlying attitudes and emotions would seem to require establishing a necessary connection between historical actors having certain thoughts and acting certain ways. And a necessary connection between the various independent variables considered "causes" and the dependent variable considered "effect" would seem to be clearly implied in the idea that the "causes" in a given historical event make the "effect" inevitable. But in the world of historical "explanation," could a "cause" fail to produce an "effect"? Could a cause be "necessary" only in the sense that there would otherwise be no reason for the "effect," without the "effect" necessarily following the occurrence of the "cause"? Perhaps subsuming events under general covering laws, and thus making them predictable, constitutes a satisfactory historical "explanation" for Agnew. But is every historical event merely an instance of a general law? Or is each historical occurrence unique in itself? Does not each example of human behavior represent a particular constellation of forces in a particular situation? Is not each human personality a unique (and therefore unpredictable) wellspring of unique (and therefore unpredictable) actions? Instead of demonstrating that certain conditions lead to certain inevitable consequences, has history not revealed over and over again how unpredictable events actually are? If each individual historical occurrence is unique, yet "explanation" requires making generalizations that render it nonunique, is "explanation" not inherently deterministic and inherently false? Does it not impose a nonexistent order and coherence upon a chaotic and contested historical terrain? Does it not reduce the indescribably intricate experience of real men and women to the inevitably simplified pages of what Stuart Marks calls "the monologue of knowledge"?[6]

In a particularly cogent response to Agnew entitled "Power and Meaning: Event and Text: History and Anthropology," Rhys Isaac rejects Agnew's artificial dichotomy of meaning and explanation as radical opposites and ponders "the dilemmas of being 'ethnographic'—[that is,] descriptive and interpretive of meanings—in the face of [the] death and maiming that ultimately sustain power in the cruel world in which we live." Is ethnography really so preoccupied with the pursuit of meaning as to be dangerously unconcerned with death and death threats, unconcerned with the brutal realities of power? In particular, Isaac affirms ethnographic *narrative* as a significant mode of explanation, as the distinctive contribution of historians to humane discourse in a "harsh world of dominators and dominated." Historical actions must be seen as forming a whole. Not only do later actions realize purposes anticipated by earlier ones, but earlier actions were also affected by the anticipation of later ones. Thus the relationship is in some sense reciprocal. And thus the attempt to explore intrinsic relationships among actions *in time* through ethnographic narrative would seem to be a more promising—and distinctively historical—contribution to explanation than some that have already been tried.[7]

As Isaac has been haunted for more than two decades by a slave suicide in 1752, I have been haunted by the insurrection and execution of Nat Turner, haunted by what it may yet teach us about the meaning of human bondage and about the meaning of the human struggle for freedom. And thus I offer the narratives that follow to the ongoing discourse on ethnographic history. By converging many narratives, by blending metaphors and models, and by letting the historical actors speak for themselves, I hope to allow meanings to become more visible, to generate not proofs but possibilities. By converging *texts* with the *context* of power and resistance on the slave plantations, I hope to be able to reveal something about the emotional *texture* of life within an institution that—however humanized it may have been by occasional human kindnesses—rested ultimately upon violence and the threat of violence. To come to grips with the events and texts of slave resistance in the Old South is thus to contend also with the broader dynamics of power and resistance in other human relationships.[8]

"Good masters had good slaves 'cause they treated 'em good," a Virginia slave told an interviewer in the 1930s, "an' bad masters had lyin' thievin' slaves 'cause they made 'em that way."[9] Bad masters punished often and cruelly, and they made their slaves work hard. When Victoria Perry's master got mad at any slave, he whipped them all—and he got mad often. He would tie slaves to posts or trees, strip their clothes to the waist, and whip them until he exhausted himself. Perry had seen her own mother whipped in such a manner until she bled. Solomon Bradley described a beating he had seen on his South Carolina plantation. A woman was stretched out face down with her hands and feet fastened to stakes. Her master struck her repeatedly with his carriage harness, the force of his blows raising welts on the flesh of her back and legs. When she cried out with pain he would kick her in the mouth. After he grew tired from whipping her he sent to his house for sealing wax and a lighted candle and, melting the wax, dropped it upon the woman's lacerated back. Her offense was having burned the edges of the waffles that she had cooked for his breakfast.[10]

If masters and overseers were inhumane, slaves might go to the plantation mistress for help, for protection, for justice. Fanny Kemble, an English actress married to Georgia slaveholder Pierce Butler, was particularly incensed at the driver's harsh punishments of women. In her journal, she described how on one occasion several slave women were "fastened by their wrists to a beam or a branch of a tree, their feet barely touching the ground, so as to allow them no purchase for resistance or evasion of the lash, their clothes turned over their heads, and their backs scored with a leather thong." She complained to her husband, but to no avail. Such punishments continued on the Butler plantations. Her marriage to Pierce Butler did not.[11]

The mistress was not always aware of beatings that took place on the plantation.[12] And the plantation mistress could be as cruel as the master. In fact, in some cases it was the master who restrained his wife.[13] Cruel plantation mistresses often turned special ire upon female slaves, inflicting punishments prompted by a slave's failure to perform some task to the mistress's satisfaction. George King described seeing his mother abused when the mistress "pull his mammy's clothes over her head so's the lash would reach the skin." While his mother writhed in pain, "the mistress walk haway laughing." When Ida Henry was "passing around the potatoes, Old Mistress felt one as if it wasn't soft done. She exclaimed to de cook, 'What you bring these raw potatoes out here for?' and grab a fork and stuck it in her eye and put hit out.'" Delia Garlic remembered vividly the temper of her Arkansas mistress: "One day I was playin' wid de baby. It hurts its li'l han' an' commenced to cry, an' she whirl on me, pick up a hot iron an' run it all down my arm an' han'. It took off de flesh when she done it."[14]

The worst punishments were reserved for slaves who attempted to emancipate themselves by flight. Jack Frowers was captured during an escape attempt near Aiken, South Carolina: "Just as soon as Master Holley got me home, he set the dogs to . . . bit me. . . . After he got tired of that fun, he took me to a blacksmith, who put a ring around my ankle, bending the ends in when it was red hot." Jacob Stroyer recalled that after a fugitive from his plantation was caught, "they killed him, cut him up, and gave his remains to the living dogs."[15]

The most dramatic threat to the well-being of the slave family was the auction block. Settlement of the Old Southwest was accompanied by widespread disruption of slave families back in the East. Parvenu cotton planters in the Deep South cotton lands opened up in the 1820s and 1830s acquired their labor forces on the auction blocks of the older slave states. Whenever slaveholders broke up slave families to satisfy creditors or heirs, whenever they deemed it necessary or desirable to convert slaves into cash, the mask of paternalism was ripped away. A traveling slave trader separated a despairing slave woman from her husband much against her will. "The woman will complain," he wrote callously to his manager. "I think she will need correcting. I could not buy her husband," he added. He urged his manager to "try to get $1300 for the woman and daughter."[16]

Henry Laurens shared half-interest in a South Carolina plantation with his brother-in-law, John Coming Ball. When Ball died in 1764, the plantation and its force of nearly eighty slaves faced division among Laurens' and Ball's heirs. Laurens wrote to the executor of the estate lamenting what he called the "inhumanity of separating and tearing assunder my Negroes' several families," which he said he would never "cause to be done but in case of irresistable necessity." Laurens offered either to sell his own share of the estate's slaves or to buy the other half "in preference to an act which has always shocked me too much to submit to it." Nevertheless, after nearly a year's wrangling, the estate was divided, and with it several slave families. One family that was split was that of a woman named Isabel, who was taken from her husband, Mathias, and sent to another plantation. When she learned that Mathias was living with another wife, Isabel returned to the plantation and murdered her.[17]

Viney Baker vividly recalled losing her mother in North Carolina. "One night I lay down on de straw mattress wid my mammy," she said, "an' de nex mo'nin I woked up an' she wuz gone. A speculator comed dar de night before an' wanted ter buy a 'oman. Dey had come an' got my mammy widout wakin' me up. I has always been glad somehow dat I wuz asleep." Jacob Stroyer recalled that the slaves on his South Carolina plantation sang a spiritual to console the unfortunates who were being sold away.

> When we all meet in Heaven,
> There is no parting there;
> When we all meet in Heaven,
> There is no parting more.

Shipping slaves to the market became so common in Virginia that the slaves made up a different kind of song about it—"Massa's Gwine Sell Us Tomorrow."[18]

Henry Walker remembered his Arkansas mistress saying, "'If you don't be good and mind we'll send yare off and sell you wid 'em.'" That threat, he recalled, frightened him more than any beating he ever received. Some slaveholders seemed to take sadistic delight in parting families. For instance, "Old Man Rogan" in South Carolina

> always love to take er baby away from he me and sell it, and take he ma somewhere else and sell her, and ain't luh 'em see one another again. He love to part a man and he ooman, sell de man one place and sell de ooman another, and dat look like all Ole Man Rogan live for, and when he ain't 'casion 'stress dat er way, he been on restless. He love to see a man wid he head bowed down in 'stress, and he love to see chillun holdin' out dey arms cryin' for dey mother, and he always looked satisfied when he see tear runn' down de face of er ooman when she weepin' for her chile.[19]

The auction block was one of the strongest forms of psychological control any slaveholder possessed.

Another major threat to the stability of the slave family was the sexual liberty taken by some white men with female slaves. If a slave family had an attractive daughter, she might be taken from her home and moved to the Big House where the "young masters could have the run of her," as a former Virginia slave described it. Henry Clay Bruce wrote in his memoirs, "We would have been pure black, were it not that immoral white men, by force, injected their blood into our veins." Another writer complained, "One of the reasons why wicked men in the South uphold slavery, is the facility which it affords for a licentious life. Negroes tell no tales in courts of law of the violation by white men of colored females." Such violations were even upheld by the South's leading men of letters. In his *Morals of Slavery* (1838), William Gilmore Simms characterized slavery as a beneficial institution because it protected the purity of white women by allowing slaveholders to vent their lust "harmlessly" upon slave women.[20]

House servants were more often at risk of sexual exploitation by their masters or his guests than were field hands. But women in the slave quarters were also at risk of sexual exploitation. The twenty-four-year-old overseer on Argyle Island in the Savannah River fathered a mulatto son. The groom on Jacob Stroyer's South Carolina plantation shared his cabin with a slave mistress and their two daughters. After emancipation, one of their daughters married a white man. Both the father and son who managed Pierce Butler's Georgia plantations sexually abused female slaves and fathered mulatto children by them. Butler's ex-wife Fanny Kemble wrote of the younger manager, "It would be hard to find a more cruel and unscrupulous [man,] even among the cruel and unscrupulous class to which he belonged."[21]

"Any man with money can buy a beautiful and virtuous girl, and force her to live with him in a criminal connection," wrote self-emancipated slave William Craft. In Edgefield District, South Carolina, a lecherous master tried to entice a slave named Charlotte into a sexual relationship. When she resisted, he stripped her and forced her to sit naked upon a pile of manure until she eventually submitted. After she had borne him a child, he passed her along to his cousin, to whom she bore another child.[22] Mulatto children fathered by slaveholders were rarely acknowledged on the slave plantations. According to Mary Boykin Chesnut, mistress of Mulberry Plantation in South Carolina, a slaveholder's "wife and daughters in the might of their purity and innocence are supposed never to dream of what is plain before their eyes as the sunlight, and they play their parts of unsuspecting angels to the letter." The large numbers of plantation mulattoes contributed to the hostility felt by some mistresses toward their slaves. They considered black women promiscuous and directed their anger toward the slaves instead of toward their husbands. Under the slavery system, Mary Chesnut lamented,

> we live surrounded by prostitutes. . . . Like the patriarchs of old our men live all in one house with their wives and their concubines, and the mulattoes one sees in every family exactly resemble the white children—every lady tells you who is the father of all the mulatto children in every body's household, but those in her own she seems to think drop from the clouds.[23]

Mothers resented the young slaves who attracted their sons, and wives feared the female slaves who attracted their husbands. Such slaves threatened the position of the plantation mistress.

Their fears were not entirely misplaced. Some plantation sons and husbands engaged in sexual relationships with slave women that were more than fleeting. Some slaveholders even flaunted their relations with slave women, risking condemnation by the public and by their own families. James Henry Hammond, governor of South Carolina, took an eighteen-year-old slave to be his mistress. When her daughter reached the age of twelve, Hammond made her his mistress too. When he brought his slave mistress into the Big House, his wife moved out and refused to return until he sent the mistress away. The slave mistress moved out, and the wife returned. But soon the slave mistress returned as well.[24]

A classic example of the tensions inherent in such situations is the story told by Mary Reynolds, a former slave in Louisiana:

> Once Massa goes to Baton Rouge and brung back a yaller gal dressed in fine style. She was a seamster nigger. He builds her a house 'way from the quarters. This yaller gal breeds fast and gits a mess of white young-uns. She larnt them fine manners and combs out they hair. Oncet two of them goes down the hill to the dollhouse where the Missy's children am playing. They wants to go in the dollhouse and one of the Missy's boys say, "That's for white children." They say, "We ain't no niggers, 'cause we got the same daddy as you has, and he comes to see near every day."

As the children quarrel, the plantation mistress hears their conversation from her bedroom window. Mary Reynolds recalled vividly what happened later that day.

When Massa come home his wife hardly say nothin' to him, and he asks her what the matter, and she tells him, "Since you asks me, I'm studying in my mind 'bout them white young-uns of that yaller nigger wench from Baton Rouge." He say, "Now, honey, I fotches that gal just for you, 'cause she a fine seamster." She say, "It look kind of funny they got the same kind of hair and eyes as my children, and they got a nose look like yours." He say, "Honey, you just paying 'tention to talk of little children that ain't got no mind to what they say." She say, "Over in Mississippi I got a home and plenty with my daddy and I got that in mind." Well, she didn't never leave, and Massa bought her a new span of surrey hosses. But she don't never have no more children, and she ain't so cordial with the Massa. That yaller gal has more white young-uns, but they don't never go down the hill no more."[25]

Sometimes, then, a master's infidelity prompted a mistress's cruel and unfair behavior toward the slaves.[26]

Occasionally the slave families fought back. But few efforts to deter white sexual aggression were successful. In one case, a cruel master lusted after a woman in the slave quarters. He would come to her cabin, wake her family, and tell her husband to leave while he vented his lust upon the wife. One night the husband waited outside. As the master was leaving the cabin, the husband strangled him. For that act the husband was swiftly executed. In Missouri a slave woman named Celia was sexually abused by her master. She resisted by killing him and burning his body. For that act she was tried, convicted, and hanged.[27]

White slave owners were sometimes inclined to sell their slave offspring in order to protect them from the abuse of their stepmothers, half-brothers, and half-sisters. Frederick Douglass noted, "As cruel as the deed may strike anyone to be, for a man to sell his own children to human flesh-mongers, it is often the dictate of humanity for him to do so: for unless he does this, he must not only whip them himself, but must stand by and see the white son tie up his brother, of but a few shades darker complexion than himself, and ply the gory lash to his naked back." The master's mulatto children, if they were not sold, were quite often made personal slaves in the Big House. In many cases the body servants of the young people were their half-brothers or half-sisters.[28]

Slaves might pretend to be satisfied with their lot around whites, but it is not true that they simply accepted their condition because they had no conception of freedom. To see the advantages whites had that slaves lacked was to perceive all too clearly the difference between freedom and slavery. Slave responses took many forms: slaves not only pretended to be sick, they also slowed work, fought back, committed suicide or homicide, and emancipated themselves by flight. Slave resistance, whatever its form, created a problem of discipline for slaveholders. Acts of resistance, whether they were mild and sporadic or bold and persistent, threatened property or threatened safety, weakening the institution that held human beings in bondage.[29]

Malingering—pretending to be sick in order to get out of work—was one way that slaves engaged in day-to-day resistance to slavery. A former slave testified to the Freedman's Inquiry Commission that he knew at least twenty former slaves "who were considered worn out and too old to work under the slave system who are now working cotton . . . and their crops look very well." A Georgia slave reported that his father had "beat ol' marster out 'o 'bout fifteen years work. When he didn't feel like workin' he would play like he wus sick an' ol' marster would git de doctor for him."[30] A more subtle method of resistance was for slaves to perform assigned work poorly, sabotaging the system through intentional failure. One slaveholder complained to Frederic Law Olmsted that his slaves "never do more than just enough to save themselves from being punished, and no amount of punishment prevent their working careless and indifferently."[31]

Slave dogs disrupted white society to such an extent that in 1859, after a decade and a half of controversy, the South Carolina General Assembly passed a law to prevent slaves from having dogs. There were complaints that slave dogs were too hostile, or that slave dogs were too friendly, or that slave dogs were too ugly or too mean, or that they barked all night, or that they attacked innocent plantation visitors. "One can scarcely step out at night," one planter averred, "without being liable to be dog bit." One of the most irritating activities of slave dogs was their propensity to trot into church and try to sing along with the hymns or eat the communion wafers. In 1846 Salem Presbyterian Church, near Mayesville in Sumter District, resolved that "no negro shall fetch a Dog to the Church." Slaveholders maintained that slaves also used their dogs to warn of approaching slave patrols when they went out to steal at night. *The Farmer and Planter*, a publication for slaveholders, warned that slaves should not be allowed to keep dogs because it "often leads to mischief" and illicit activities subversive of the institution.[32]

One of the most common methods by which slaves resisted was stealing. By theft a slave could simultaneously take revenge upon oppressors and supplement a family's meager food supply. Few acts of slave resistance irritated the masters more. Food was the primary object of slave theft. Children began at an early age to take food from pantries and hen houses. Sometimes older slaves punished the children for such deeds, but they rarely informed on them to the masters.[33]

Literacy was used as a form of resistance by the slaves. Learning how to read and write was of great advantage for sabotage and day-to-day resistance. Frederick Douglass overheard his master forbid his wife to teach the young slave to read and write on the grounds that it would make him "unfit to be a slave." Douglass concluded that "the pathway from slavery to freedom" was literacy. An Alabama slave came to the conclusion, "Ol' Miss taught de niggers how to read an' write an' some of 'em got to be too good at it, 'case dey learned how to write too many passes so's de pattyrollers wouldn't cotch 'em."[34]

The "pattyrollers," or slave patrols, were considered the most virulent elements of white society by the slaves. Slaves moving about after dark, whether visiting wives or sweethearts on other plantations or making an escape attempt, were subject to capture and punishment by patrols with dogs, horses, and whips. Sometimes slaves fought back. One effective method of fighting back was arson, which was a more obviously rebellious act than stealing. A patroller who had been engaged in harassing slaves might suddenly awake at night to find his barn aflame. Edmund Ruffin, puzzled for years at how many buildings on his plantation mysteriously burned to the ground, eventually came to realize that his slaves were torching the structures as retaliation against a hated overseer.[35]

Some slaves took their own lives rather than continue to submit. Former slave Adeline Marshall told of a Texas slave who "done hang himself to 'scape he mis'ry." But others turned violence upon their oppressors rather than upon themselves. The overseer on a Mississippi plantation attempted to beat a slave named Mose. Pulling up the stakes intended to hold him down, Mose attacked the overseer with one of the stakes before being clubbed unconscious. Mose's master, however, abandoned his effort to break the slave and auctioned him off.[36]

Women resisted as fervently as men. "Ole Miss," according to John Rudd, "had a long whip hid under her apron and began whippin' Mama across the shoulders 'thout tellin' her why. Mama wheeled around from whar she was slicin' ham and started runnin' after Old Missus Jane. Ole Missus run so fas' Mama couldn't catch up wif her so she throwed the butcher knife and struck it in the wall!" Mama's punishment was the auction block. Mary Armstrong, a former slave in Texas, recalled her master and mistress as "the meanest two white folks what ever live, cause they was always beatin' on their slaves. . . . Old Polly, she was a Polly devil if there ever was one, and she whipped my little sister what was only nine months old, and just a baby, to death. She come and took the diaper offen my little sister and shipped till the blood just ran—just 'cause she cry like all babies do, and it kilt my sister." Mary Armstrong never forgave her mistress for killing her baby sister. Eventually she had an opportunity to take revenge on her. "You see, I'se 'bout ten year old and I belongs to Miss Olivia, what was that old Polly's daughter, and one day Old Polly devil comes to where Miss Olivia lives after she marries, and tries to give me a lick out in the yard, and I picks up a rock about as big as half your fist and hits her right in the eye and busted the eyeball, and tells her that's for whippin' my baby sister to death." Seven decades after emancipation, Mary Armstrong had still not forgiven her mistress: "But that Old Polly was mean like her husband, Old Cleveland, till she die, and I hopes they is burnin' in torment now." Age did not always prevent slaves from fighting back. After her young master whipped her, an elderly Mississippi mammy took a pole from her loom and beat him "nearly to death," shouting with each stroke, "'I'm goin' to kill you. These black titties sucked you, and you come out here to beat me!'"[37]

Sometimes the slaves' revenge was even more forceful. "Accidents" were a means of taking revenge without necessarily having to take blame. An

Alabama ex-slave told of

> a mean man who shupped a cullid woman near 'bout to death. She got so mad at him dat she tuk his baby chile what was playin' roun' de yard and grab him up an' th'owed it in a pot of lye dat she was usin' to wash wid. His wife come a'hollerin' an' run her arms down in de boilin' lye to git de chile out, an' she near 'bout burnt her arms off, but it didn't do no good 'case when she jerked de chile out he was daid.

An Oklahoma slave, unwilling to endure the indignities of slavery any longer, suddenly turned upon his tormenters and "just killed all of 'em he could."[38]

Self-emancipation—the slaveholders called it "running away"—was perhaps the most important form of protest against human bondage. Those who sought permanent freedom naturally tried to get out of the slave states altogether. A former slave in South Carolina recalled a big black man who "stole away one night" and made his way as far as Charleston before he was apprehended. Questioned by the overseer upon his return to the plantation, he said: "Sho', I try to get away from this sort of thing. I was goin' to Massachusetts, and hire out 'till I git 'nough to carry me to my home in Africa." To attempt self-emancipation was to undertake a perilous flight for freedom in the dead of night along dangerous and unfamiliar paths. "Every once in a while slaves would run away to de North," recalled an Alabama slave. "Most times dey was caught an' brought back. Sometimes dey would git desp'rit an' would kill demse'ves 'fore dey woud stand to be brought back."[39]

Those who pondered escape from slavery had to consider that their chances of success were poor and the penalty for failure was dire. Most of the time, a flight for freedom ended in failure. Punishment was certain and execution was common. Self-emancipation seemed impractical except for slaves in border states. For the great majority of slaves, the free states were all but unreachable. Instead of striking out in quest of freedom against all odds, many chose the less rewarding but more practical approach of taking a sabbatical from slavery, of stealing away from the plantation and hiding out in the woods for a time. An escapee from a South Carolina plantation dug a hillside cave and took up residence in the woods, slipping out at night to obtain food. When the slave catchers apprehended him five months later, he had in his possession a hog, two geese, some chickens, and some dressed meat—apparently "liberated" from a plantation smokehouse.[40]

Perhaps most slaves fled for reasons other than the pursuit of permanent freedom. Often slave resistance was prompted by clear personal grievances. Cruelty was certainly one reason, but slaves of masters with kindly reputations sought freedom as eagerly as those of masters with cruel reputations. Slaves did not necessarily have to be prodded by any specific punishment or incident to take flight. Two slaves in the Abbeville District of South Carolina slipped away from their plantation in 1862. Their bemused overseer informed the slaveholder that "I was uncertain whether they had run away or were only absenting themselves from work and particularly as they had not reason for leaving no fault being found with them or punishment inflicted."[41]

Slave women were less likely than men to escape, not because they loved freedom less, but because most slave women between fifteen and thirty-five years of age were either pregnant, nursing an infant, or caring for a small child. When slave women did resort to flight, it was more often response to immediate personal grievances than an effort to emancipate themselves. Martha Bradley, an Alabama slave, was "workin' in de field and de overseer he come 'round and say sumpin' to me he had no bizness say. I took my hoe and knocked him plum down. I knowed I'se done sumpin bad so I run to de bushes." Her escape did not last long, however. "Marster Lucas come and got me and started whippin me. I say to Marster Lucas whut dat overseer sez to me and Marster Lucas didn' hit me no more."[42]

But slave women were often intimately involved in planning and aiding the escape attempts of others. Even trusted house servants were coconspirators in runaway efforts. Mary, a "highly favored servant . . . in charge of the house with the keys" on a South Carolina rice plantation, helped many of her family to escape in 1864. Not only did her sons run off, but also her daughter and her daughter's family and her brother and all of his family. Ultimately, her mistress became suspicious. There were, she wrote a friend, "too many instances in her family for me to suppose she is ignorant of their plans and designs." Aiding and abetting fugitive slaves could be as dangerous as an escape attempt itself. Harriet Miller's grandfather ran away from his master's Mississippi plantation to escape an overseer's brutality. He hid out nearby, and his family secretly supplied him with food and information. But the overseer came to the man's cabin and questioned his family about his whereabouts. When the man's daughter refused to answer, the overseer beat her to death.[43]

When slave catchers attempted to apprehend them, runaways rarely surrendered peacefully. Facing punishment and perhaps death if returned to slavery, fugitives often elected to stand and fight. Occasionally the slaves had the better of the battle. "Lots of times," an Alabama slave recalled, "de patterollers would git killed." A slave catcher in South Carolina sued for damages caused by the slave he had attempted to apprehend.

> A runaway slave named George, the property of a Gentleman of Chester District, stole two horses, broke open several houses and committed other offences in Richland District for which a warrant was issued against him but it was found impossible to arrest him. He was at length taken in Columbia on the 4 July last but broke from custody. A hue and cry was immediately raised and your petitioner joined in the pursuit and first overtook the fellone where a contest ensued between them in which the slave cut out your petitioner's eye with a razor blade. . . . The fellone has since been tried, convicted, and executed.

More often than not freedom seekers fell to overwhelming odds.[44]

Some runaways formed armed maroon bands, hid out in the woods or swamps and raided storehouses for arms and food. Maroon bands were especially prevalent in South Carolina during the Civil War. "On Monday I commenced hunting down Cosawhatchie Swamp," Thomas Allen reported, and

> during the afternoon the dogs struck a warm trail which we followed about one mile into the swamp through water and bog[,] sometimes swimming and sometimes bog down[,] when the dogs trailed a negro boy . . . who has been out since August last. The said boy stated that there was two others with him that day and four at the camp seven or eight miles below—all armed with guns and pistols.[45]

The most dramatic form of slave resistance was insurrection. At least five major insurrectionary plots and numerous smaller revolts or conspiracies disturbed the consciousness of the Old South. Since most of them were aborted, their full dimensions remain unknown. The major insurrections included the Stono rebellion in South Carolina in 1739, Samba's conspiracy in Louisiana in 1763, Gabriel Prosser's rebellion in Virginia in 1800, Denmark Vesey's in South Carolina in 1822, and Nat Turner's in Virginia in 1831. And there was a significant slave conspiracy in Adams County, Mississippi, in 1861, for which at least twenty-seven slaves were executed.[46]

The most important of the rebellions was the one led by Nat Turner. Stories of "Ole Nat" lived in oral tradition among Virginia slaves. One of them, Allen Crawford, described the rebellion vividly.

> It started out on a Sunday night. Fust place he got to was his mistress' house. Said God 'dained him to start the fust war with forty men. When he got to his mistress' house he commence to grab him missus baby and he took hit up, slung hit back and fo'h three times. Said hit had bin so playful setting on his knee and dat chile sho did love him. So third sling he went quick 'bout hit—killing baby at dis rap.

The insurrectionists then went to another house, Crawford said, and "went through orchard, going to the house—met a school mistress—killed her."[47]

Fannie Berry, another Virginia slave, remembered well the fear of the white folks. "I can remember my mistress, Miss Sara Ann, coming to de window an' hollering, 'De niggers is arisin', De niggers is arisin', De niggers is killin' all de white folks—killin' all de babies in de cradle!'" Harriet Jacobs wrote in her memoirs, *Incidents in the Life of a Slave Girl*, that she thought it strange that the whites should be so frightened "when their slaves were so 'contented and happy'!"[48]

The following day, the militia was mustered to search the quarters of all slaves and free blacks. Jacobs said the militia planted false evidence to implicate some slaves in the rebellion: "The searchers scattered powder and shot among their clothes, and then sent other parties to find them, and bring them forward as proof that they were plotting insurrection." Allen Crawford recalled that "Blues and Reds—name of soldiers—met at a place called Cross Keys, right down here at Newsome's Depot. Dat's whar they had log fires made and every one dat was Nat's man was taken bodily by two men who catch you and hold yer bare feet to dis blazing fire 'til you tole all you know'd 'bout dis killing." In the wake of the Turner insurrection, Henry Box Brown wrote in his memoirs that many slaves were "half-hung, as it was termed—that is, they were suspended from some tree with a rope about their necks, so adjusted as not quite to strangle them—and then they were pelted by men and boys with rotten eggs." The air was filled with shrieks and shouts. Harriet Jacobs said she "saw a mob dragging along a number of colored people, each white man, with his musket upraised, threatening instant death if they did not stop their shrieks." Jacobs could not contain her indignation. "What a spectacle was that for a civilized country!" she exclaimed. "A rabble, staggering under intoxication, assuming to be the administrators of justice!"[49]

According to Allen Crawford, "Ole Nat was captured at Black Head Sign Post, near Cortland, Virginia—Indian town. He got away. So after a little Nat found dem on his trail so he went back near to the Travis place whar he fust started killing and he built a cave and made shoes in this cave. He came out night fur food dat slaves would give him from his own missus plantation." After about a month, Nat Turner's hiding place was discovered, and he was taken into custody. Turner's captors, Crawford said, "brought him to Peter Edward's farm. 'Twas at this farm whar I was born. Grandma ran out and struck Nat in the mouth, knocking the blood out[,] and asked him, 'Why did you take my son away?' In reply Nat said, 'Your son was as willing to go as I was.' It was my Uncle Henry dat they was talking about." Then, Crawford said, Virginia "passed a law to give the rest of the niggers a fair trial and Nat, my Uncle Henry, and others dat was caught was hanged."[50]

The shock of Nat Turner's revolt was followed by the appearance of a new and militant abolitionist newspaper, William Lloyd Garrison's *The Liberator*. Slaves took heart. Slaveholders concentrated their energies on trying to defend slavery against the criticism of an aroused and critical world. The institution that many white southerners had once considered an evil destined for eventual elimination they now praised as a positive good, the secret of their region's putative perfection. The slaveholders staked everything—their fortunes, their honor, the lives of their sons—on its defense. Unlike slaveholders anywhere else, they went to war to preserve their "Peculiar Institution." South Carolina's Edward Bryan bellowed, "Give us slavery or give us death!" In the gubernatorial election of 1860, his friend Francis W. Pickens proclaimed his support for slavery today, slavery tomorrow, slavery forever, committing his state and region to a disastrous course. "I would be willing to appeal to the god of battles," Pickens defiantly declared, "if need be, cover the state with ruin, conflagration and blood rather than submit." He won the governorship, and his state was indeed covered with ruin, conflagration, and blood. In the end South Carolina submitted anyway.[51]

So what can we conclude from the foregoing narratives? We have seen that slaveholders subjected their slaves to "horrors unbefitting even to wild animals," including forced separation from family and friends, "piercing with forks, burning with tar, skinning with knives, and killing outright with whips and pistols." And we have seen that the slaves resisted through theft, arson, self-emancipation, and a "collective assault on the will of the masters."[52]

And I have not even mentioned the ways that slaves used their cultural creativity as a form of resistance.[53] It has become stylish in some quarters to see almost any form of independent behavior on the part of the slaves as a form of resistance. Historical anthropologist Sidney Mintz questions the value of dividing slave actions into categories of "accommodation" and "resistance" as though the lines between such categories were always clear. "Some acts with consequences that can be read as resistance did not originate with resistance," he notes. "Some acts with consequences that can be read as accommodation did not originate with accommodation." And some forms of slave behavior, in his opinion, may be read as both accommodation and resistance simultaneously. "We must try," he says, "to understand how the slaves coped as whole persons with their condition."[54]

Still, the basic dynamics of power and resistance in the master-slave relationship seem to have varied surprisingly little from place to place and from time to time in human history. In all places and in all times, from the ancient world to the modern, slaveholders were parasites who lived off the labor of the people they claimed to own. Everywhere the slaves did the work and the slaveholders enjoyed the profits. Everywhere the slaveholders reaped what they did not themselves sow. Everywhere the slaveholders received greater returns than they earned by the sweat of their own brows. The question "How did the masters provide for their slaves?" should be replaced by the question "How did the slaves provide for their masters?" The related question "How were slaves treated?" should be replaced by the question "What portion of the wealth the slaves produced was taken from them and what portion was left to them?" Everywhere slaves resented the expropriation of their labor, and everywhere slaves resisted their enslavement.

But regardless of how much slaves resisted, they remained slaves. Their enslavement itself forced them to struggle, for slavery forced upon them a need that no other human beings have ever felt so acutely—the need to have their inherent human dignity recognized, the need for the condition we now call freedom. The idea we call freedom, according to historical sociologist Orlando Patterson, was inconceivable before slavery. How could people in nonslaveholding premodern societies conceive of the removal of restraint as a positive value? What they yearned for was membership. What they yearned for was belonging. What they yearned for was the security of being anchored in a network of power and authority. But membership was not freedom. Belonging was not freedom. Security was not freedom. Slaves were the first men and women able to conceive of freedom as it is defined in modern terms, and slaves were the first men and women to struggle for that freedom. To most Western thinkers, the deep links between the love of freedom and the denial of freedom to others are unsettling and deeply embarrassing. But the ironic fact is that the ideal of freedom, the ideal that we cherish above all others, emerged from the resistance of slaves to oppression.[55]

NOTES

1. Petersburg, Virginia, *Intelligencer* quoted in *Richmond Enquirer*, November 22, 1831. Thomas Gray's interviews with Nat Turner, the key source for practically everyone who has written on the subject, are published as Thomas T. Gray, *The Confessions of Nat Turner, the Leader of the Late Insurrection in Southampton County, Va., as Fully and Voluntarily Made to Thomas T. Gray, in the Prison Where He Was Confined, and Acknowledged by Him to Be Such when Read before the Court of Southampton* (Baltimore, 1831). Gray's *Confessions* have been widely reprinted.

2. C. Vann Woodward was the first, I believe, to call attention to Nat Turner, as "a kind of Christ-figure. Consider his age, his trade as a carpenter, his march on Jerusalem, his martyrdom." See C. Vann Woodward and R.W.B. Lewis, "The Confessions of William Styron," an interview with William Styron on November 5, 1967, in James L. W. West, III, ed., *Conversations with William Styron* (Jackson, Miss., 1985), p. 88 (hereinafter cited as *Conversations*) and C. Vann Woodward, "Confessions of a Rebel: 1831," *New Republic*, October 7, 1967 p. 26.

3. Greg Dening, *Islands and Beaches: Discourse on a Silent Land, Marquesas 1774–1880* (Honolulu, 1980). Ideologically, such interactions derive from shared and contested definition. Stuart Marks contrasts models and metaphors as modes of cultural understanding. "Models are constructed from the truncated experiences and visions of observers and scholars," he writes, while "metaphors belong to and are understood by those who express their meaning within their daily lives." He considers metaphors to be "the graphics through which people control and expand their universe," while models represent the ways that outsiders simplify a culture so that they can understand it. See his *Southern Hunting in Black and White: Nature, History, and Ritual in a Carolina Community* (Princeton, 1991), p. 5.

4. Jean-Christophe Agnew, "History and Anthropology: Scenes from a Marriage," *Yale Journal of Criticism* 3 (1990), pp. 29–50, esp. pp. 38–42, 45–47; Rhys Isaac, *The Transformation of Virginia, 1740–1790* (Chapel Hill, 1982).

5. Rhys Isaac, "Power and Meaning: Event and Text: History and Anthropology," unpublished manuscript, pp. 8–9. This paper has been published as "On Explanation, Text, and Terrifying Power in Ethnographic History," *Yale Journal of Criticism* 6 (1993), pp. 217–36. All quotations are from the unpublished manuscript.

6. Questions of historical epistomology are explored in more detail in Charles Joyner, "A Model for the Analysis of Folklore Performance in Historical Context," *Journal of American Folklore* 88 (1975), pp. 263–64. See also Dominick LaCapra, *Rethinking Intellectual History: Texts, Contexts, Language* (Ithaca, 1983); Hayden White, *The Content of the Form: Narrative Discourse and Historical Representation* (Baltimore, 1987); and Marks, *Southern Hunting in Black and White*, p. 5.

7. Isaac, "Power and Meaning," pp. 1–3, 5, 8.

8. Joyner, "Model for the Analysis of Folklore Performance," p. 264; Marks, *Southern Hunting in Black and White*, p. 8. Cf. J. David Sapir and J. Christopher Crocker, eds., *The Social Use of Metaphor: Essays on the Anthropology of Rhetoric* (Philadelphia, 1977), and James W. Fernandez, *Persuasions and Performances: The Play of Tropes in Culture* (Bloomington, 1986).

9. Beverly Jones, interviewed by William T. Lee, Gloucester Court House, Va., n.d., in Charles L. Perdue, Jr., Thomas E. Barden, and Robert K. Phillips, *Weevils in the Wheat: Interviews with Virginia Ex-Slaves* (Charlottesville, 1976), pp. 11, 181.

10. George P. Rawick, *The American Slave: A Composite Autobiography* (Westport, Conn., 1972), Supplement Series 1, Vol. IX, 1501. In all future references to Rawick, the volume number will be given in uppercase Roman numerals and all sections within each volume will be indicated by lowercase Roman numerals. "Testimony of Solomon Bradley," *American Freedman's Inquiry Commission: Testimony* (Microfilm), Reel 200, File III, pp. 95–96, National Archives.

11. Frances Ann Kemble, *Journal of a Residence on a Georgian Plantation in 1838–1839* (New York, 1863; Brown Thrasher ed., Athens, 1984), pp. 160–61, 215, 274, 283.

12. Alabamian Henry Cheatam recalled, "A heap of times old Miss didn't know nothin' 'bout it, an' de slaves better not tell her, 'case dat oberseerer whup 'em iffen he finds out dat dey done gone an' tol." See Rawick, *The American Slave*, VI, p. 120; VII, p. 89; VI, p. 311; VI, p. 67.

13. Charles Ball, *Slavery in the United States: A Narrative of the Life and Adventures of Charles Ball, a Black Man* (New York, 1937), pp. 348–51; Rawick, *The American Slave*, VII, p. 347; VII, p. 301; VI, p. 62; Jacob Branch, "Double Bayou Settlement, near Houston, Texas," in Norman R. Yetman, ed., *Life under the Peculiar Institution: Selections from the Slave Narrative Collection* (New York, 1970), p. 40.

14. Rawick, *The American Slave*, VII, pp. 166–67; VII, p. 135; VI, p. 130. Cf. Jacob Branch, in Yetman, *Life under the Peculiar Institution*, p. 40.

15. Langdon Cheves to Langdon Cheves, Jr., May 2, 1864, Cheves Family Papers, South Carolina Historical Society, Charleston; Jacob Stroyer, *My Life in the South* (Salem, Mass., 1890).

16. A. J. McElveen, Sumterville, S. C., to Z. B. Oakes, Charleston, February 7, 1854, in Edmund L. Drago, ed., *Broke by the War: Letters of a Slave Trader* (Columbia, S. C., 1991), pp. 70–71.

17. Failure "to keep the families together," Laurens feared, might "cause great disruption amongst the whole" of the slaves. Nothing could be more distressing, he said, "than this unnecessary division of Fathers, Mothers, Husbands, Wives, & Children who[,] tho[ugh] slaves[,] are still human creatures." Henry Laurens to Elias Ball, April 1, 1765, George C. Rogers, Jr., et al., eds., *The Papers of Henry Laurens* (Columbia, 1968–),vol. 4, p. 595; Henry Laurens to David Graeme, January 23, 1764, The Papers of Henry Laurens 4, p.141; Will of John Coming Ball, Ball Family Papers, South Carolina Historical Society, Charleston, S. C. Cf. Joyce Chaplin, "Slavery and the Principle of Humanity: A Modern Idea in the Lower South," *Journal of Social History* 24 (1990), p. 306.

18. Rawick, *The American Slave*, XIV, p. 97; Stroyer, *My Life in the South*, p. 41; Elizabeth Sparks, interviewed by Claude Anderson, Matthews Court House, Virginia, in Yetman, *Life under the Peculiar Institution*, p. 299.

19. Rawick, *The American Slave*, XI, vii, p. 29; E. C. L. Adams, *Congaree Sketches: Scenes from Negro Life in the Swamps of Congaree and Tales by Tad and Scip of Heaven and Hell with Other Miscellany* (Chapel Hill, 1927), pp. 50–51.

20. Robert Ellett, interviewed by Claude W. Anderson, Hampton, Virginia, December 25, 1937, in Perdue, Barden, and Phillips, *Weevils in the Wheat*, p. 84; Henry Clay Bruce, *The New Man: Twenty-Nine Years a Slave, Twenty-Nine Years a Free Man: Recollections of H. C. Bruce* (York, Pa., 1895), pp. 130–31; Rev. J. D. Long, quoted in Catherine Clinton, *The Plantation Mistress: Woman's World in the Old South* (New York, 1982), pp. 208–11; William Gilmore Simms, *Morals of Slavery* (Charleston, 1838).

21. James Clifton, ed., *Life and Labor on Argyle Island* (Savannah, 1978); Stroyer, *My Life in the South*, pp. 30–37; Kemble, *Journal*, p. 207.

22. William Craft, *Running a Thousand Miles for Freedom; or, The Escape of William and Ellen Craft from Slavery* (London, 1860), pp. 16–17, in Arna Bontemps, ed., *Great Slave Narratives* (Boston 1969), p. 279; Orville Vernon Burton, *In My Father's House Are Many Mansions: Family and Community in Edgefield, South Carolina* (Chapel Hill, 1985), pp. 185–86.

23. C. Vann Woodward, ed., *Mary Chesnut's Civil War* (New Haven, 1981), pp. 29, 168–69.

24. Drew Gilpin Faust, *James Henry Hammond and the Old South: A Design for Mastery* (Baton Rouge, 1982), pp. 314–17.

25. Rawick, *The American Slave*, Supplement 2, IX, vii, pp. 92–94.

26. Ibid., VII, p. 347; Henry Ferry, n.p., n.d., in Perdue, Barden, and Phillips, *Weevils in the Wheat*, p. 91.

27. Author(s) unknown; cited as Fisk University, *Unwritten History of Slavery*, in Rawick, *The American Slave* 18, I, p. 2; Melton A. McLaurin, *Celia: A Slave* (Athens, 1991).

28. Frederick Douglass, *Narrative of the Life of Frederick Douglass, an American Slave, Written by Himself* (Boston, 1845), pp. 3–4; Rawick, *The American Slave*, Supplement 2, VI, p. 219.

29. Philip J. Schwarz, *Twice Condemned: Slaves and the Criminal Laws of Virginia, 1705–1865* (Baton Rouge, 1988), p. 3.

30. *American Freedman's Inquiry Commission: Testimony*, June 30, 1863 (Microfilm), Reel 200, File III, National Archives; Rawick, *The American Slave*, XII, ii, p.59.

31. Harriett Robinson, Oklahoma City, Oklahoma, in Benjamin A. Botkin, *Lay My Burden Down: A Folk History of Slavery* (Chicago, 1945; Brown Thrasher ed., Athens, 1989), p. 3; Olmsted, *Journey in the Seaboard Slave States*, I, p. 86.

32. *Farmer and Planter* 5 (1854), pp. 177, 259–60, 300; 7 (1856), p. 274; 8 (1858), p. 198; 9 (1859), p. 338; John Campbell, "Slaves, Their Dogs, and the State in Nineteenth-Century South Carolina" (Paper presented at African American Work and Culture conference, University of Rochester, April 23–25, 1993), pp. 1–5, 8–9.

33. See passim.

34. Douglass, *Narrative*, p. 40; Rawick, *The American Slave*, VI, p. 190.

35. Schwarz, *Twice Condemned*, p. 299. See also Rawick, *The American Slave*, Supplement series 1, VI, p. 47.

36. Rawick, *The American Slave*, V, iii, p. 46; Supplement series 1, XI, i, p. 6.

37. Ibid., VI, p. 171; Mary Armstrong, Houston, Texas, n.d., in Yetman, *Life under the Peculiar Institution*, p. 19; Rawick, *The American Slave*, VIII, ii, p. 42.

38. Rawick, *The American Slave,* VI, p. 60; VII, p. 17.

39. Ibid., III, p. 130; VI, p. 390.

40. Ibid., III, iv, p. 113.

41. Ibid., II, i, pp. 26–28; Charles T. Haskell to Langdon Cheves, Abbeville, S. C., June 16, 1862, Cheves Family Papers, South Carolina Historical Society, Charleston, S.C.

42. Rawick, *The American Slave,* VI, p. 46.

43. Adele Petigru Allston to Col. Francis W. Heriot, May 31, 1864, in J. Harold Easterby, ed., *The South Carolina Rice Plantation as Revealed in the Papers of Robert F. W. Allston* (Chicago, 1945), p. 199; Rawick, *The American Slave,* Supplement series 1, IX, pp. 1500–1501.

44. Ibid., VI, p. 418; Petition of John Rose, Richland District, 1831, Slavery Files, South Carolina Archives, Columbia, S. C.; Rawick, *The American Slave,* XV, p. 132.

45. Thomas G. Allen to General Walker, February 3, 1863, in Francis W. Pickens and Milledge L. Bonham Papers, Library of Congress.

46. Winthrop D. Jordan, *Tumult and Shouting at Second Creek: An Inquiry into a Civil War Slave Conspiracy* (Baton Rouge, 1993).

47. Bruce, *The New Man,* pp. 25–26; Allen Crawford, interviewed by Susie R. C. Byrd, North Emporia, Va., June 25, 1937, in Perdue, Barden, and Phillips, *Weevils in the Wheat,* pp. 75–76.

48. Perdue, Barden, and Phillips, *Weevils in the Wheat,* p. 35; Jacobs, *Incidents in the Life of a Slave Girl,* p. 97.

49. Jacobs, *Incidents in the Life of a Slave Girl,* pp. 98–99, 102; Crawford, in Perdue, Barden, and Phillips, *Weevils in the Wheat,* pp. 75–76; Henry Box Brown, *Narrative of the Life of Henry Box Brown, Written by Himself* (Boston, 1852), p. 19.

50. Crawford is quoted in Perdue, Barden, and Phillips, *Weevils in the Wheat,* pp. 75–76.

51. Quoted in John B. Edmunds, Jr., *Francis Pickens* (Chapel Hill, 1986), p. 152.

52. Norrece T. Jones, Jr., *Born a Child of Freedom, Yet a Slave: Mechanisms of Control and Strategies of Resistance in Antebellum South Carolina* (Hanover, N.H., 1990), pp. 87-88, 168.

53. I have explored slave culture as a form of resistance in "History as Ritual: Rites of Power and Resistance on the Slave Plantation," *Australasian Journal of American Studies* 5 (1986), pp. 1–9, and *Remember Me: Slave Life in Coastal Georgia* (Atlanta, 1989).

54. Sidney W. Mintz, "Tasting Food, Tasting Freedom," in Wolfgang Binder, ed., *Sonderdruck aus: Slavery in the Americas* (Wurzburg, 1993), pp. 257–75, quotations on pp. 269, 271.

55. Orlando Patterson, *Slavery and Social Death* (Cambridge, 1982), and *Freedom: Freedom in the Making of Western Culture* (New York, 1991).

3

Reading the Slave Body: Demeanor, Gesture, and African-American Culture

Shane White and Graham White

On May 24, 1854, the runaway Virginia slave Anthony Burns was recaptured in Boston. Within hours, Richard Henry Dana, best known to us as the author of *Two Years before the Mast* (1869) but also a prominent lawyer, had volunteered to defend him. The fugitive was a solidly built man, about six feet in height, and possessing a considerable presence, but he did not make a favorable impression on his putative advocate: Dana thought him "a piteous object, rather weak in mind & body," who "seemed completely cowed & dispirited," and who, when questioned by the presiding judge, had "looked round bewildered, like a child." The lawyer left the courthouse convinced that his services were not wanted, that the slave runaway, fearing retribution from his master and having no wish to delay proceedings, was willing to return meekly to a life of bondage. That night, however, Burns was visited by friends who convinced him that Dana was trustworthy and would prove a powerful ally, and when the two men met the following day the prisoner's demeanor had entirely altered. Burns now seemed, as Dana expressed it, "a very different man"—"self possessed, intelligent" and imbued with "considerable force both of mind & body."[1]

Though of little importance in the larger scheme of things, this incident serves to show the way in which kinesics or communicative bodily movement formed a crucial, if generally neglected, element in the social interactions of the past. Undoubtedly Burns had been intimidated by his predicament, and when brought face-to-face with Dana, who must have been marked as a gentleman by everything from his clothing and demeanor to the deference accorded him by court officials, had drawn on the gestural vocabulary of slavery to guide him in his dealings with the lawyer, creating an impression of resignation and abject docility. Once Dana's antislavery credentials had been established, however, not only the words Burns used but his body language—his bearing, gestures, facial expressions—combined to create in the lawyer a radically different impression. Much the same kind of reclamation of the body, a shucking off of the vestiges of a hated institution, would often occur as slavery ended. Elizabeth Barker, a black hairdresser born in 1900 and interviewed in the 1970s, recalled hearing of the determined efforts former slaves had made to stamp out all reminders of their bondage. To that end they had "insisted their children stand ramrod straight so they could look any man in the eye, as contrasting to the way slaves had to look at masters, with heads bowed and eyes cast down."[2]

It is at the point of transition between slavery and freedom—either in individual cases, such as that of Anthony Burns, or more generally—that the crucial role of gestures and bodily movements takes on a particular clarity, but it is also the case that such nonverbal language formed an indispensable part of the myriad transactions that occurred on plantations every day. What follows, then, is an exploratory and necessarily speculative chapter, an attempt to recover something of black kinesics and to show what the repertoire of black gesture and bodily movement can reveal about the cultural codes that existed within the African-American slave community. We begin with the gestures used in the most constrained of situations—face-to-face interactions between blacks and whites—and then move on to a consideration of black dance, an expressive realm in which slaves enjoyed considerable liberty in the use of their bodies and in which cultural differences were often dramatically displayed.

There was always a tension in the slave South between the "ideal" master-slave relationship imagined by planters and the often recalcitrant behavior of their "troublesome property," but generally the realities of power and control on the plantation were such that there was little scope for direct verbal resistance. Examples of such open defiance do occasionally appear in contemporary sources. Quamina, a seventeen-year-old runaway and skilled carver and chair maker, "well known in and about Charlestown by his impudent behaviour," told his master to his face that he intended to go where he pleased and that his master could "do nothing to him, nor shall I ever get a copper for him." The aggrieved owner of Limus, a slave "well known in Charles-Town from his saucy and impudent Tongue," invited anyone who discovered Limus "out of my Habitation without a Ticket" to administer a severe thrashing, "for though he is my Property, he has the audacity to tell me, he will be free, that he will serve no Man, and that he will be conquered or governed by no Man."[3] These stark verbal challenges to their authority had clearly made a considerable impression on the owners who placed these advertisements, but incidents of this kind must have been rare.

In her superb explication of Aztec culture, Inga Clendinnen has suggested that when speech is "curbed there might well be an equivalent expansion of a vocabulary of demeanor and gesture, where understanding must be sought through an analysis of observed action." We cannot, of course, directly observe the repertoire of demeanor and gesture of African-American slaves, but we can examine contemporary descriptions of such nonverbal communication, in order to determine whether it was culturally distinctive in any sense. Frederick Law Olmsted thought that it was. As he watched the day-to-day activities of African Americans in the Washington marketplace, he concluded that not only "in their dress," but in their "language, *manner, [and] motions*—all were distinguishable almost as much by their color, from the white people who were distributed among them, and engaged in the same occupations—chiefly selling poultry, vegetables and small country produce."[4] But Olmsted did not elaborate upon this typically acute observation.

Though travelers' accounts contain occasional comments on blacks' gestures, facial expressions, eye movements, and so on, by far the richest source of such descriptions is the thousands of notices slave owners placed in the contemporary press appealing for the return of slaves who had run away. Such advertisements described not merely the runaway's clothing, hairstyle, visible signs of mutilation, and so on, but also, very frequently, any physical mannerisms that could aid identification. Thus we can learn from the Maryland slaveholder William Colyer's description of his slave Warwick that "the balls of [Warwick's] eyes are uncommonly white, and, when talked to, he rolls them unusually." We discover that Clem, another runaway, had "a swaggering Air with him in his Walk" and that "when spoken to," the Virginia runaway Samuel "often turns his head on one side, and shuts one of his eyes."[5] Were the eye movements, mode of walking, and manner of inclining the head as described different from those of whites, and if they were, what did those differences signify?

The distinctive nature of black kinesics begins to emerge when we compare contemporary descriptions of African Americans with the informal codes that operated to regulate social interaction. Elsewhere we have shown that the codes relating to dress were often reasonably precise, even, on occasion, written into law.[6] But ideas of how slaves ought to look embraced not merely notions as to how they should be clothed but expectations relating to demeanor and posture, to the way slaves held their heads, directed their gaze, moved their bodies, and so on. Just as there was opposition to slaves who dressed too grandly, so, too, was there resistance to slaves (and free blacks) who stood too proudly, approached too nearly, gazed too directly, walked too confidently. If slaves were not supposed to appropriate the garb of the elite, neither were they expected to adopt their manners or bearing. Slaves, in short, were expected to look the part.

The so-called courtesy manuals, English publications to which, as Richard Bushman has shown, the higher social orders in the eighteenth-century colonies and later America paid close attention, attempted to impose social standards governing interaction between various groups in society. Those aspiring to gentility were advised to "remain erect, . . . keep[ing] the line from the base of the spine through the neck to the back of the head as straight as possible." But if a proud, upright carriage was appropriate in the elite, signifying, as Jonathan Prude has pointed out, not merely gentility but power, it was hardly so for those further down the social scale, and most emphatically not for slaves, whose bearing was expected to be deferential, not to say servile. In much the same way, members of the lower orders were instructed, for instance, that "in Speaking to men of Quality," they ought neither to "lean nor Look them full in the Face, nor approach too near them."[7] The personal space of the elite was to be respected.

Unwritten rules governing African Americans' lives emerge, too, in the testimony of former slaves. One man recalled being whipped for his "sullen, dogged countenance." Another told how, though in agony from a flogging, he had had to temper his response to a sympathetic inquiry as to his condition: "A slave must not manifest feelings of resentment," Charles Ball explained, "and I answered with humility."[8] "We have been taught a cringing servility," the former slave Edward Wilmot Blyden declared. "We have been drilled into contentment with the most undignified circumstances." Ex-slaves' recollections of their first experience of freedom also reveal the rules that had formerly bound them but that no longer applied. One black soldier remembered how, having gained his freedom, he had "walked fearlessly and boldly through the streets of a southern city" without being "required to take off his cap at every step" or move off the sidewalks for planters' sons. "Now we sogers are men—men de first time in our lives," an exultant Sergeant Prince Rivers of the First South Carolina Volunteers, United States Colored Troops, told an interviewer during the Civil War. "Now we can look our old masters in de face."[9]

Slaves' eyes may or may not have been windows to their souls, but they did provide a number of clues to what we now call African-American culture. Some contemporaries certainly thought that this was so. When Frederick Law Olmsted discussed with a number of Mississippi overseers the problem of identifying a very light-skinned person as a slave, one of them "thought there would be no difficulty; you could always see a slave girl quail when you looked in her eyes." For other white southerners—and without prejudging the issue too much we would suggest that they were the more perceptive ones—the eyes of slaves were rather more opaque; these observers were certainly less sure of their ability to read facial features than the chillingly confident overseer Olmsted had memorialized. Prompted by the Civil War, the murder of a nearby slave owner by her slaves, and her own considerable doubts about the morality of the slave system, Mary Boykin Chesnut started to look at the surrounding sea of black faces in a fresh way, trying to decipher their meaning in what seemed an almost surreal semiotics of survival, but quickly realized that they "are as unreadable as the sphinx." Although Chesnut was "always studying these creatures," the slaves were "inscrutable," indeed, "past finding out," and that recognition of unknowability, in spite of all her years of close contact with slaves, became an anxious refrain in her justly famed diary. Decades later, W. J. Cash echoed Chesnut, and distanced himself from the easy conclusion of the white South that it "knew the black man through and through," suggesting that "even the most unreflecting" must feel, when dealing with a black, "that they were looking at a blank wall," and that "a veil was drawn which no white man might certainly know he had penetrated."[10] Cash's metaphor of the veil, alluding to Du Bois before him, with its suggestion of the partly concealed, conveys well the difficulties of discerning meaning from the descriptions and words of slave owners. But for all that, the slave owners' often scrupulous and fascinated attention to detail, their search for precision as they attempted to represent slave gestures and eye movements that were at once everyday and familiar yet still disconcertingly strange, indicates that they recognized that slaves' actions were different. That the slave owners were also frequently unable to understand what they saw was partly caused by the misunderstandings and clumsy translations that inevitably ensue whenever cultures come in contact, but mostly it was the result of the reasonable and sensible desire of slaves to conceal their feelings from whites. Nowhere are the resulting ambiguities and ambivalences more clearly seen than in the eye movements of slaves.

Consider the so-called down look, the practice among blacks when in the presence of whites of inclining their heads and directing their gaze toward the ground. As Jonathan Prude has pointed out, this gesture "fit the polite conviction that plebeian types should neither stand erect nor stare back," and this may be part of the reason why so many references to it appear in the runaway advertisements.[11] There is little doubt, however, that the phrase "down look" did accurately describe one aspect of the appearance of many slaves. Advertising for the return of a young slave, his Georgia owner noted that Isaac "has a down look when any white person speaks to him." Likewise Quash, a young Virginia slave who ran away in 1776, had "a down Look when spoken to," and Kate, aged about twenty, also of Virginia, was said by her master to have "a down look when she talks." Expressing the matter rather differently, the owner of Frank, a young Maryland slave who escaped in 1789, stated that "when confronted his eye falls and discovers an uncommon wide space between the lid and the brow.[12]

Not all slaves, however, were prepared to display this outward sign of deference. This, of course, was particularly the case when the slave's well-being was under threat. One ex-slave reported that he had disconcerted buyers at a slave auction and avoided being sold by aggressively meeting the gaze of prospective bidders as they cast their eyes over him.[13] Other slaves habitually held their heads erect, meeting their masters' eyes with a direct stare, an assertive, even troubling characteristic that their owners were sure to remember when composing a runaway slave advertisement. Thus we read that "when speaking," the North Carolina slave John "looks you full in the face," that "when spoke to" and "if sober," the Maryland slave Bacchus "generally looks you full in the face," and that the bondsman Peter, who escaped from his Maryland owner in 1783, was in "no ways bashful," but was prepared to "look a person stedfast though guilty."[14]

Even slaves who assumed the apparently submissive down look could invest this gesture with ambiguous meanings. Dick, who made his escape from Baltimore in 1764, was described as having a "roguish down look," Peter, who ran from his Maryland owner in 1784, as having a "sneaking down look," and

Sam, who absconded in 1785, as displaying a "down impudent look." A Pennsylvania slave, described by his master as "a very bragging fellow, given much to flattery," had "a down designing look."[15] The down look, then, was no guarantee of easy compliance with planter authority. As many slave owners realized, this gesture could mask a slave's true nature and intentions. John, aged about thirty, who was owned by Virginia slaveholder Robert Daniel and ran away in 1779, may have had a "down look," but was also, his master declared, "very artful." Tom, a "young well set Negro Man," who went missing in 1778, had "a down look" but "when spoke to, leers with his eyes which are large and full," a disconcerting gestural combination, one would think. There is a sense of dissonance, too, in the descriptions of the runaways Moses, who had "a very swanky walk, with a down look, and sour countenance" and Abel, who displayed "a down look, unless when spoken to, and then has a smile on his countenance" and who had "but little to say, and is inclinable to be sulky and sullen, when angry." When captured, the Louisiana runaway William "had around his neck an iron collar with three prongs extending upwards," and "many scars on his back and shoulders from the whip," yet the obviously nonsubmissive William, too, was described as having "a down look."[16] But even where slaveholders recognized the down look as an ambiguous sign, they may not have suspected that the averting of the head and eyes, constituent elements of the down look, could possess, for African Americans, an added cultural significance.

The difficulties slaveholders had in "reading" black intentions must have been increased by the existence among slaves of gestural codes of which they were largely ignorant. In his discussion of Kongo influences on African-American artistic culture, Robert Farris Thompson states that *nunsa*, a "standing or seated pose with head averted, . . . is present in black America" and that the turning of the head to one side "signals denial and negation." Thompson continues:

> In 1977 I saw a black man from New Orleans counter accusations by turning his head to one side, with lips firmly pursed. . . . There are countless mirrors of this pose in Gullah country, especially when a black mother sharply rebukes her child. Steward writes that "the child purses the lips, turns his head to one side, and it stays there." A cognate expression was observed in colonial times [in the West Indies] by Charles William Day: "when Negroes quarrel they seldom look each other in the face. . . ." Annette Powell Williams summarizes an extension of this fundamental gesture in black United States: "an indication of total rejection is shown by turning one's head away from the speaker with eyes closed."[17]

Close examination of the runaway advertisements turns up examples of what may well have been similar instances of black resistance or contempt. The owner of Samuel, a Virginia slave who escaped in 1786, noted that "when spoken to, [he] often turns his head on one side, and shuts one of his eyes." The Virginia slave Jack, who ran away in 1766, "speaks plain for an African born, but avoids looking in the Face of them he is speaking to as much as possible." Osym, a new

Negro, about eighteen years of age, who absconded in 1766, was "inclin'd to squint or looking side-ways." And if, as previously suggested, the closing of the eyes was also a sign of dismissal, the gestures of other slaves may take on added meaning. Of Phill, a Virginia slave, his owner remarked that "when he speaks, or discourses with any person, [it] appears as if his eyes were almost shut," while Dinah, another Virginia slave, "keeps her eyes rather closed when speaking."[18]

Slaveholders and other white observers drew attention not merely to the way slaves directed their gaze but to the manner in which they moved their eyes. Caesar, a South Carolinia slave from the Ibo Country, was described as having "remarkably large rolling eyes," and, according to her master, "when spoke to," the "negro wench, Scisley" became "very huffy, and [was] remarkable in shewing the white of her eyes." Billy, who escaped in Virginia in 1776, exhibited "a remarkable turning of his eyes and winking, with some hesitation before he replies upon being spoken to" by whites.[19]

Here it is important to remember that runaway slave advertisements typically described the eye movements of slaves in a carefully circumscribed and in fact very constrained series of situations. Slave owners' comments were based on observations of their slaves' behavior while they were conversing with, or perhaps more correctly, listening to the instructions of, their owners. (Because of the limited nature of the surviving evidence, we have virtually no idea at all what sort of gestures or eye movements occurred when African Americans talked amongst themselves.) Judging by their language, many owners were never as aware as were their slaves of the dramaturgical nature of these everyday interactions, but the slaves, and any knowing audience of their compatriots who happened to be nearby, certainly realized that they were engaged in a performance, and one where the slightest misjudgment about how transparently they could display their attitude to whites could have the direst of consequences. The range of behavior detailed in the preceding two paragraphs indicates, perhaps, some ways in which slaves tested the limits of bondage, ways that allowed them to register what the owners would have labeled impudence but is more correctly characterized as dissent, frustration, and even contempt for white authority—and ways to do so with a minimal chance of retribution. What these white slave owners were observing was the lineal ancestor of a social signal that, in the second half of the twentieth century, would come to be called "rolling the eyes."[20] Of course, the power of slave owners, a power that many were remarkably uninhibited about exhibiting in all its visceral rawness, ensured that there were clear limits to slave actions. In most cases, whites compelled their slaves, however grudgingly, to obey their instructions in some degree or other, but nevertheless, this type of bodily language was important in allowing the slaves to fashion a psychic space within which African-American culture flourished.

If these eye movements directed at whites were intended to be difficult to read, the advertisements also depict bodily movements that were much less opaque. Such behavior clearly transgressed codes supposedly governing slaves' demeanor. Rather than appearing submissive, some slaves evidently adopted a prideful bearing, standing erect and walking in a forthright, confident manner. According to his Maryland owner, Sam, who ran away in 1779, had "a proud bold lofty carriage." Renah, a young Virginia slave woman who absconded in 1781, had "a brisk walk and lively carriage." Betty, a Virginia runaway, was also "proud in her Carriage," while Peter, who escaped in Maryland in 1783, "walk[ed] with a great air." Clem, from Maryland, who fled in 1771, was described by his master as having "a swaggering Air with him in his Walk," and the South Carolinia runaway, John, had "a strutting walk."[21] As with blacks who dressed in expensive clothing, those so described may have been testing society's boundaries, contesting white notions as to how a slave should look.

But as well as registering concerns that slaveholders would have regarded as legitimate, the runaway advertisements demonstrate a fascination on the part of the owners with the ways in which slaves' behavior differed from their own: indeed, it is possible to see whites grappling with the limitations of their language as they tried to capture the elusive physical movements of their missing human property. We can learn something from their attempts, but a more vivid and dramatic demonstration of kinesic differences between blacks and whites can be achieved if we turn to a different set of sources and examine the ways in which African Americans moved their bodies during musical performance, especially in dance. Given the importance of dance in African cultures, it is hardly surprising to find blacks continuing with this activity in the New World societies into which they were forcibly incorporated, but since whites' descriptions tend to be meager, it is hard to tell what forms such dancing took. Our concern, however, is not to identify various African and European dances or syncretic blendings between them, but to identify an "otherness" in the way blacks used their bodies in dance, and, beyond that, to understand its cultural significance.

One such difference, sometimes commented upon by white observers, related to the angular movement of major joints—elbows, knees, ankles. Peter Wood links this phenomenon to West African dance forms, particularly those associated with the Bakongo culture of the Congo River, and points out that such movements persisted in the dance motions of African Americans in the Sea Islands, a region to which many slaves from the Angola region were originally brought.[22] Writing from this area in 1862, schoolteacher Laura Towne described how blacks performing the religious dance known as the shout shuffled in a circle, "turning round occasionally and bending the knees" (a shuffling motion would, of itself, require that knees and ankles were bent). Benjamin Botkin, describing one version of the shout, noted that "one might shout acceptably by standing in one place, the feet either shuffling, or rocking backward or forward, tapping alternately with heel and toe, the knees bending." Again, Lydia Parrish pictured one shouter as giving "a stylized, angular performance," with "arms held close to her body, elbows bent at right angles." Wood writes of a slave song that called on dancers to "gimme de kneebone bent," an instruction that whites probably associated with the Christian requirement to bend the knee in prayer, but more probably related to the West African belief that "straightened knees, hips, and elbows epitomized death and rigidity, while flexed joints embodied energy and life."[23]

Another characteristic, one that often attracted comment from whites, was the emphasis in black dance on the lower body or pelvis. In his classic study of African "survivals" in African-American culture, Melville J. Herskovits noted that the European practice of couples dancing close, with their arms around each other, was regarded by Africans and relatively unacculturated West Indian blacks as "nothing short of immoral," while "the manipulation of the muscles of hips and buttocks that are marks of good African dancing" evoked, in whites, a similarly disdainful response.[24] Evidence gathered by Lynne Fawley Emery and Dena J. Epstein on the nature of black dance in the African diaspora supports Herskovits's contention that whites considered black dances obscene. Describing the Calenda, a dance that was very popular with West Indian blacks around the turn of the eighteenth century, Pere Labat noted how, in response to the drum beat, the lines of dancers would alternately "approach each other [and] strike their thighs together, . . . the men's against the women's" and then "withdraw with a pirouette," all the while using "absolutely lascivious gestures."[25] George Pinckard, who saw Barbadian slaves performing what was probably the Calenda early in the nineteenth century, protested that the dancers' "approaches" to each other, and "the attitudes and inflexions in which they are made," were "highly indecent."[26] Similar comments were made about the Chica, another dance greatly favored by West Indian blacks. In the late eighteenth century, Moreau de St. Mery, after noting the same alternating forward and backward movement by pairs of dancers, wrote that "when the Chica reache[d] its most expressive stage, there is in the gestures and in the movements of the two dancers a harmony which is more easily imagined than described."[27]

What whites apparently found alienating was the emphasis in black dancing on the lower body, or pelvis, as the axis and originator of movement. In this respect, black dance seemed to de-emphasize those aspects of the body that Europeans took as communicative, namely the arms and the legs (as, for example, in classical European ballet, which thinks of all movements in terms of the arrangement of limbs around an unchanging torso). Conversely, black modes of dancing seemed to emphasize those aspects of the body that Europeans preferred to repress or deny. Of course, during black dance the arms, legs, and feet were moved to some degree, but these motions seemed subsidiary, and were less highly esteemed. The Englishman Edward Long, having observed the movements of a female slave dancing in Jamaica in 1774, concluded that "in her paces she exhibits a wonderful address, particularly in the movement of her hips, and steady position of the upper part of her person." Long commented further that "the execution of this wriggle . . . is esteemed among them [Jamaican blacks] a particular excellence."[28] In 1790, J. B. Moreton, also describing black Jamaican dancers, considered it "very amazing to think with what agility they twist and move their joints," so that it seemed as though the dancers "were on springs or hinges, from the hips downward. . . . Whoever is most active and expert at wriggling," Moreton went on to say, "is reputed the best dancer."[29]

On the mainland, the most spectacular and most obviously "African" dances performed during the nineteenth century were those that took place at Congo Square in New Orleans. There, on Sundays, hundreds of African Americans, both slave and free, assembled to watch extravagantly dressed dancers perform to the accompaniment of drums, banjos, violins, and other instruments. Observing this spectacle in 1819, Benjamin Latrobe, who had been attracted to the square by "the most extraordinary noise, which I supposed to proceed from some horsemill, the horses trampling on a wooden floor," experienced only a profound sense of cultural alienation, his description of the festivities highlighting such things as the "incredible quickness" of the drumming, the "curious" African-style instruments, and the "uncouth" singing, which he assumed to be "in some African language. . . . I have never," Latrobe declared, "seen anything more brutally savage and at the same time dull and stupid."[30] Others, more observant of the dancers themselves, have left accounts that suggest a strong West Indian influence, a predictable enough development given the cultural links between New Orleans and the Carribbean and the fact that the Haitian Revolution of the 1790s and early 1800s had seen many planters migrate to the city, bringing their slaves with them. Recalling a Congo Square dance that he took to be the Bamboula, but that Lynne Fawley Emery suggests was probably the Calenda, Henry Castellanos wrote of "the ludicrous contortions and gyrations of the Bamboula," and "the vibratory motions of the by-standers, who . . . contributed to the lascivious effect of the scene."[31] Later, a correspondent from the *New York World* described a Congo Square dance in which "[the] women did not move their feet from the ground[, but] only writhed their bodies and swayed in undulatory motions from ankles to waist[, while the] men leaped and performed feats of gymnastic dancing."[32]

The influence of Catholicism and New Orleans's French and Spanish background had made the city somewhat tolerant of black cultural display, but elsewhere on the mainland a more restrictive attitude prevailed. Religious opposition to slave dancing increased from the early nineteenth century, particularly in the wake of the evangelical revivals of those years. Partly in response to this opposition, there grew up within the slave community a seemingly curious distinction between "dancing," which was considered to be sinful, and what Alan Lomax has called "holy dancing," which was not. Many white preachers condemned dancing of all kinds and did their best to persuade slaves to give it up. But, perhaps recognizing the virtual impossibility of forcing African Americans to remain quiescent in a musical setting, black ministers discriminated, disallowing only certain European practices, specifically those of permitting couples to embrace while dancing and the crossing of the feet while executing various dance steps.[33] "Us 'longed to de church, all right," former Louisiana slave Wash Wilson explained, "but dancin' ain't sinful iffen de foots ain's crossed. Us danced at de [hush h]arbor meetin's but us sho' didn't have us foots crossed!"[34]

The most famous of the holy dances was the Ring Shout, in which slaves shuffled counterclockwise in a circle to the accompaniment of hand clapping, foot stamping, and the rhythmic chanting of snatches of Protestant hymns. The description of "M. R. S.," who visited a school in Beaufort in 1866, is typical:

> After school the teachers gave their children permission to have a "shout." This is a favorite religious exercise of these people, old and young. In the infant schoolroom, the benches were first put aside, and the children ranged along the wall. Then began a wild droning chant in a minor key, marked with clapping of hands and stamping of feet. A dozen or twenty rose, formed a ring in the centre of the room, and began an odd shuffling dance. Keeping time to the weird chant[,] they circled round, one following the other, changing their step to quicker and wilder motions, with louder clappings of the hands as the fervor of the singers reached a climax.[35]

Though whites generally associated the shout with Christian religious observances, there was some skepticism on this point, as M. R. S.'s reference to the "wild droning chant" suggests. Laura Towne saw in the shout "the remains of some old idol worship," and declared that she had never seen "anything so savage. . . . They call it a religious ceremony," she told her parents in 1862, "but it seems more like a regular frolic to me." William Francis Allen, also a schoolteacher, seems nearer the mark. "Perhaps," he wrote in 1863, the shout was "of African origin, with Christianity engrafted upon it. . . . These people are very strict about dancing, but will keep up the shout all night. It has a religious significance, and apparently a very sincere one, but it is evidently their recreation—just as prayer meetings are the only recreation of some people in the North."[36] The shout seems like a typical African-American adaptation, retaining the ring formation, foot stamping, polyrhythmic clapping, and shuffling of African dance forms but blending them with elements from a religion to which slaves had by then been converted or encouraged to adhere.

The shout may have eliminated "sinful" foot crossing, but it is not at all clear that the emphasis on the lower body as the axis of movement had disappeared as well. Schoolteacher Harriet Ware told how her pupils moved round in a circular fashion, with their arms and feet maintaining the beat and "their whole bodies undergoing most extraordinary contortions." Though there is no direct reference to hip movements here, it is possible that this observer considered that subject too indelicate to mention. The great South Carolinia rice planter D. E. Huger Smith, who had frequently attended both "shoutings" and slave dances and declared himself "competent to describe" both, was, however, explicit. He was not at all sure that his carpenter John, appointed religious "leader" by the visiting Methodist minister, had been able to persuade the other slaves "entirely to accept 'shoutings' as a substitute for dances." In time with the "inspiring" religious music supplied by the onlookers, this slaveholder wrote, the shouters "dance[d] without any fancy steps, *but with an indescribable* motion of the hips."[37]

By Huger Smith's account, secular dances were "quite different." To the music of the fiddle, accompanied by sticks (beaten on the floor) and bones, black dancers performed their jigs. "The dusky swain would grip the hand of the darksome belle. One swirl of both bodies under the arch of their arms and then they fell apart and made their 'steps' face to face."[38] Despite religious constraints of various sorts, such secular dancing continued among the slave population and, as the recollections of former slaves show, was greatly enjoyed. "We used to git back in de end cabin an' sing an' dance by de fiddle till day break," Sally Ashton told her interviewer. "Sho' had one time, swingin' dem one piece dresses back an' foth, an' de boys crackin' dey coat-tails in de wind." Sometimes slaves would attend larger dances on a nearby plantation: "Musta been hundred slaves over thar," Fannie Berry recalled, "an' they always had de bes' dances." But "wasn't none of this sinful dancin' where yo' partner off wid man an woman squeezed up close to one another. Danced 'spectable, de slaves did, shiftin' 'round fum one partner to 'nother an' holdin' one 'nother out at arm's length." Nancy Williams told how courting couples would slip away to a cabin far out in the woods to dance to the music of fiddles, tambourines, banjos, and bones. "Whoops!" she declared, "Dem dances was somepin." She would be "out dere in de middle o' de flo' jes' a-dancin'; me and Jennie, an' de devil. Dancin' wid a glass o' water on my head an' three boys a-bettin' on me. I . . . didn't wase a drap o' water on neider. Jes' danced old Jennie down. Me'n de debil won dat night. One boy won five dollars off'n me." "I was ve'y wicked when I was young," Martha Showvely, another former slave, confided. "I'd rather dance den eat."[39]

The general impression we get from such descriptions is of complex movements rapidly executed. This impression is confirmed by the testimony of Silvia Dubois, a former slave who was interviewed in the 1880s. She had attended a dance recently only to find that levels of skill had seriously declined. "They had a fiddle and they tried to dance," she averred, "but they couldn't—not a damned one of 'em." The problem was that these present-day dancers possessed no steps. "You can't dance unless you have the step," Silvia Dubois declared, "and they were as awkward as the devil; and then they were so damned clumsy. Why, if they went to cross their legs, they'd fall down." In her own youth, she explained, "I'd cross my feet ninety-nine times in a minute and never miss the time, strike heel or toe with equal ease, and go through the figures as nimble as a witch."[40]

In Charles Dickens's famous description of the great black dancer Mr. Juba, performing in the 1840s in a cellar in the Five Points district in New York, the impression we gain is, once again, of a general vigor of bodily movements, of complex steps performed at lightning speed, but also of great physical flexibility and suppleness. Several couples had taken the floor, Dickens wrote, where they had been "marshalled by a lively young negro, . . . the greatest dancer known." The account continues:

> But the dance commences. Every gentleman sets as long as he likes to the opposite lady, and the opposite lady to him, and all are so long about it that the sport begins to languish, when suddenly the lively hero dashes in to the rescue. Instantly the fiddler grins, and goes at it tooth and nail. . . . Single shuffle, double shuffle, cut and cross-cut: snapping his fingers, rolling his eyes, turning in his knees, presenting the backs of his legs in front, spinning about on his toes and heels like nothing but the man's fingers on the tambourine; dancing with two left legs, two right legs, two wooden legs, two wire legs, two spring legs—all sorts of legs and no legs—what is this to him? And in what walk of life, or dance of life, does man ever get such stimulating applause as thunders about him, when, having danced his partner off her feet, and himself too, he finishes by leaping gloriously on the barcounter, and calling for something to drink, with the chuckle of a million of counterfeit Jim Crows, in one inimitable sound! [41]

As Lynne Fawley Emery has revealed, when Juba danced in London, his extraordinary physical virtuosity provoked incredulity. One eyewitness wrote that he had never seen such "mobility of muscles, such flexibility of joints, such boundings, such slidings, such gyrations, . . . such mutation of movement." Another critic wished to know how Juba could "tie his legs into such knots, and fling them about so recklessly, or make his feet twinkle until you lose sight of them altogether in his energy."[42]

Juba (William Henry Lane), of course, was an internationally famous dancer, quite exceptionally talented, but broadly similar descriptions by whites of other African-Carribbean or African-American dancers—descriptions emphasizing suppleness, flexibility, and rapidity of movement—can be found in contemporary accounts assembled by Emery and Epstein. Describing Jamaican dancers in 1790, J. B. Moreton thought it "very amazing to think with what agility they twist and move their joints:—I sometimes imagined they were on springs or hinges, from the hips downwards." Mainland slaves performing the Juba dance, William Smith wrote in 1838, displayed "the most ludicrous twists, wry jerks, and flexible contortions of the body and limbs, that human imagination can devine." The suppleness of blacks' bodies was associated with the free movement of the pelvis, the fluidity of black dancers' bodies contrasting, for instance, with what Levine refers to as the "stiffly erect" bodily position commonly assumed in European dance forms, but more was involved than this.[43]

As was the case with dances performed in the West Indies and at Congo Square, there is, in these white descriptions, a sense of cultural difference. Even if the steps black dancers were using were familiar to whites, those steps were being performed at different speeds, combined in different ways, and executed with different movements of the torso and limbs.[44] Even if slaves were performing European dances—the quadrille, the cotillion, the schottische, and so on—differences in style such as the rhythmic complexity, the persistent improvization, and the unusual body movements suggested that different cultural values underlay the performance.

In their classic article on African-American dance, John Szwed and Morton Marks point out that attempts to investigate this phenomenon are made difficult by the lack of visual or literary sources.[45] However, they go on to suggest that because the relationship between black dance and music is so intimate, an examination of the latter may throw considerable light on the former. In an attempt to follow this approach, we shall consider, now, the procedure known as "Patting Juba."

According to ex-slave Solomon Northup's description, "Patting Juba" was performed "by striking the hands on the knees, then striking the hands together, then striking the right shoulder with one hand, the left with the other—all the while keeping time with the feet." After noting that African Americans set much greater store than do whites on "the acquisition of a sophisticated rhythmic sensibility," Frank Kofsky has asserted that patting "initiated the young into the complex rhythmic patterns necessary for the creation not only of music but also of dance," a function that the Hambone game of more recent times also performs. Like "Patting Juba," from which it is derived, the Hambone game "teaches independence"—that is, the ability to execute simultaneous cross-rhythms with both arms, both legs, the head and the torso," which is not only a necessary precondition for the creation of jazz, for instance, but "an integral and fundamental aspect of Black dance." (To begin to suggest the difficulty of attaining "independence," James Lincoln Collier has written: "You can learn to pat your head and rub your stomach at the same time, but try doing it to different tempos, especially when somebody is beating a drum at yet a third tempo.")[46] Within the characteristic circle formation associated with black performance style, for instance, a basic or ground beat might be laid down by the rhythmic stamping of feet, but against this beat singers, clappers, drummers, other instrumentalists, or a dancer, through the use of his or her body, may set up counterrhythms that play against the basic beat. It is this rhythmic complexity that the black dancer manages somehow to express.

Studies of African performance style throw light on how this is done. After noting that West African dance, like West African music, is characterized by "multiple meter," Robert Farris Thompson cites Waterman's observation that "the [West African] dancer picks up each rhythm of the polyrhythmic whole with different parts of his body." Thompson quotes Bertonoff's finding that, when the Ewe of Ghana dance, "the various limbs and members, head, shoulders, and legs are all moving simultaneously but each in a rhythm of its own." Alan Lomax has uncovered the same connection, concluding, on the basis of his cross-cultural study of dance forms, that "African cultures lead all the rest in emphasis on bodily polyrhythm, where the shoulders and the pelvis erotically rotate and twist, often to two separate and conflicting meters."[47] Dances in which the performer simultaneously expressed, through the movement of hips, shoulders, arms, knees, and feet, multiple rhythms provided by other members of the group were bound to appear alien and complex to white observers. The African-American cultural preference for constant rhythmic variation must have served further to disorient white onlookers.

Though whites did not fully understand what they were seeing, one can discover in their writings descriptions of slave dancers or singers picking up the various rhythms of a polyrhythmic structure with different parts of the body. Describing dancers in Congo Square, Colonel James Creecy noted that "the most perfect time is kept, making the beats with the feet, heads, or hand, or all, as correctly as a well-regulated metronome." Frederika Bremer, who attended an evening service in an African-American church in South Carolina in 1850, described how the congregation "sang . . . with all their souls and with all their bodies in unison; for their bodies wagged, their heads nodded, their feet stamped, their knees shook, their elbows and their hands beat time to the tune." Alan Lomax has recently shown that this tradition survived in the Delta and is visible elsewhere in twentieth-century musical and dance performance. Describing the performance style of G. D. Young's fife and drum band, Lomax writes that "they capered without lifting their feet; their shoulders, belly, and buttocks separately twitched to the beat." Napoleon Strickland, another of the black folk musicians whose performances Lomax has been able to observe, was able to create "multipart rhythms" from a diddley bow, "play[ing] a different beat pattern with each hand—two against three, or six against eight—and lay[ing] in the melody on top of these." This, Lomax points out, in similar vein to Kofsky, is a complex and difficult process, but the black musician "manages [it] with ease, since from childhood he has practiced patting games like *juba* to make himself perfectly bilateral, as well as multileveled, so that he can do different things with his right and left sides, meanwhile moving his feet and middle body and shoulders to other beat patterns."[48] In black dance, the same kind of rhythmic dexterity is displayed.

The polyrhythmic, improvisatory, and physically vivacious nature of black dance does indeed reflect a more general cultural aesthetic. We argue elsewhere that as slave women became heavily involved in the production of cloth and clothing on nineteenth-century plantations, the design of these items began to display a different aesthetic, whose clashing colors and irregular patterning also informed the artistic design of African-American slave quilts.[49] Maude Southwell Wahlman and others have shown that this aesthetic is still found among twentieth-century black quilters. "If I have red," Leola Pettway, an Alabama quilt maker, explained to Wahlman, "I put a different color next to it. If I am scraping a quilt, I put different materials together." The quilts of Plummer T. Pettway, of Boykin, Alabama, Wahlman writes, conveyed a sense of "variety and movement." Colors were "place[d] . . . at uneven intervals, so that her patterns appear to be constantly shifting." The effect produced by differences in patterns, color strengths, and placements was one of "constant surprise."[50] We could note, here, the former South Carolinia slave Mary Scott's comment that she "could weave it [cloth] with stripes and put one check one way and nother strip nother way." We might also, perhaps, better understand some African Americans' apparent preference for what, to whites, seemed odd combinations of clothes, garments that "clashed" with each other, and whose color combinations seemed incongruous. As the African-American quilter Sarah

Mary Taylor explained to Wahlman, "I tries to match pieces like I'd wear clothes."[51]

The same aesthetic characterizes African-American music, as even whites seem to have intuited. The metaphors they used to describe black singing, for instance, frequently evoked images of textile design or quilt making. In 1870, Elizabeth Kilham, who had gone to the South as a teacher, pondered the nature of hymns that, originally created by whites, had been reworked by blacks to suit themselves. "Were they composed as a whole," she wondered, "with deliberate arrangement and definite meaning, or are they fragments, caught here and there, and pieced into a mosaic, haphazard as they come?"—a question that might equally well have been asked of an African-American quilt. To Texas schoolteacher William P. Stanton, his black students' hymns "seem[ed] to be a sort of miscellaneous patchwork, made up from the most striking parts of popular Methodist hymns." Endeavoring to describe the singing of companies of black soldiers as they marched along, Colonel Thomas Higginson, the white commander of the First Regiment, South Carolina Volunteers, wrote that "for all the songs, but especially for their own wild hymns, they constantly improvised simple verses, with the same odd mingling—the little facts of to-day's march being interwoven with the depths of theological gloom, and the same jubilant chorus annexed to all."[52]

Maude Southwell Wahlman has observed that "the unpredictable rhythms and tensions of Plummer T's [Plummer T. Pettway's] quilts [are] similar to those found in . . . other African-based black American arts, such as jazz," a comment that recalls Frederick Law Olmsted's observation that both the slaves' color sense and their music were related to an underlying sense of rhythm, one that was alien to Euro-American cultural forms.[53] In similar vein, Robert Farris Thompson has pointed to the correspondence between the "emphatic multistrip composition" of "the cloth of West Africa and culturally related Afro-American sites" and the "multiple meter" of "the traditional music of black Africa." Thompson also sees a "visual resonance" between the "rich and vivid suspensions of the expected placement of the weft blocks" in Mande or Mande-influenced narrow strip cloth and "the famed off-beat phrasing of melodic accents in African and Afro-American music." For Thompson, the deliberate clash of colors and patterns gives Mande textiles their sense of "vibrancy" and "aliveness"; for John Miller Chernoff, the "clash and conflict of rhythms" produces in African music precisely these same characteristics.[54]

The remaining link, with black dance, is not hard to forge. The relationship between dance and both African and African-American music is so intimate that probably these two forms of cultural expression should more correctly be considered one. Like African-American music and textile design, black dance is characterized by rhythmic complexity. It, too, prizes improvisation over predetermined form. As with black music, whether from the slave period or after it, and as is also true of black quilts and clothing, African-American dance conveys an impression of "aliveness" and "vibrancy," the "unpredictable rhythms and tensions" of the performer evoking a sense of "constant surprise."[55] Just as the clashing colors and irregular patterning of slave textiles and the multiple rhythms and irreproducible sounds of slave music jangled white sensibilities, so the movements of the black body in dance often seemed alien and unaccountably strange.

Under slavery, the black body was a contested site, a surface on which the struggle for dominance between master and slave was often quite visibly played out. We show elsewhere that blacks were sometimes able to exercise a surprising degree of control over the manner in which they clothed their bodies and styled their hair, but it was still the case that blacks' bodies could be branded, mutilated, penetrated by the owner, or bought and sold like any other piece of property.[56] "They 'zamine you just like they do a horse," a Mississippi slave woman complained. "They look at your teeth, pull your eyelids back and look at your eyes."[57] Some slaves may have managed to walk upright, presenting their bodies in a prideful manner, but many more were forced into awkwardness by injury or inadequate diet, by coarse, ill-fitting clothing, or by painful shoes. Runaway ads depict these men and women as shambling along, with bodies bent forward from years of unremitting toil. George, who absconded in Maryland in 1785, had a "very lubberly gait" and "stoop[ed] forward"; Bacchus, who ran away in Maryland in 1789, walked "inactively and awkwardly"; James Nicholas, who escaped in Virginia in 1772, walked "slow, and stoop[ed] in his shoulders"; Strephon, a South Carolinia runaway, had "a slouching clumsy Gait."[58] To all such negative representations of the black body, the black dancer presented a powerful counterimage, one in which African-American slaves could feel deeply satisfying pride. Contrasting the festive dancing of the whites, before whom, as a skilled slave violinist, he had often played, with that of ordinary plantation blacks, ex-slave Solomon Northup was moved to exclaim: "Oh, ye pleasure-seeking sons and daughters of idleness, who move with measured step, listless and snail-like, through the slow winding cotillon, if ye wish to look upon the celerity, if not the 'poetry of motion'—upon genuine happiness, rampant and unrestrained—go down to Louisiana and see the slaves dancing in the starlight of a Christmas night."[59] If the prideful way in which some slaves presented their bodies tested the limits of the system's tolerance and the subtleties of their eye movements allowed the transmission of social signals that whites could not understand, black dance allowed slaves to refigure emphatically their construction within an oppressive system as pure physicality and utility. By aestheticizing the black body, by putting its vitality, suppleness, and sensuality defiantly and joyously on display, the black dancer repudiated slavery's evaluation of the slave body as nothing but a brute physical laborer and constructed, for a time, a world of difference, sharply at variance with that which blacks were normally compelled to inhabit.

NOTES

1. Richard Henry Dana, Jr., *The Journal of Richard Henry Dana, Jr.*, ed. Robert F. Lucid, 2 vols. (Cambridge, Mass., 1968), II, pp. 625–27.

2. Ruth Edmonds Hill, ed., *The Black Women Oral History Project*, 10 vols. (Westport, Conn., and London, 1991), II, p. 123.

3. Many of the printed runaway advertisements have been collected in Lathan A. Windley, compiler, *Runaway Slave Advertisements: A Documentary History from the 1730s to 1790*, 4 vols. (Westport, Conn., 1983). Here we will cite the newspapers and then, in parentheses, the references to the Windley volumes. In this case the note should read: *Charleston South-Carolina and American General Gazette*, February 21, 1781 (Windley, *Runaway Slave Advertisements*, III, p. 577); *South-Carolina Gazette* (Timothy), November 7, 1775 (Windley, *Runaway Slave Advertisements*, III, p. 345).

4. Inga Clendinnen, *Aztecs: An Interpretation* (New York, 1991), p. 285; Frederick Law Olmsted, *The Cotton Kingdom: A Traveller's Observations on Cotton and Slavery in the American Slave States*, ed. Arthur M. Schlesinger (New York, 1953), p. 28 (emphasis added).

5. *Baltimore Maryland Journal and Baltimore Advertiser*, September 24, 1790 (Windley, *Runaway Slave Advertisements*, II, p. 418); *Annapolis Maryland Gazette*, June 20, 1771 (Windley, *Runaway Slave Advertisements*, II, p. 88; *Virginia Gazette or American Advertiser* (Hayes), May 27, 1786 (Windley, *Runaway Slave Advertisements*, I, p. 385).

6. Shane White and Graham White, "Slave Clothing in the Eighteenth and Nineteenth Centuries," in *Past and Present*, No. 148 (1995), pp. 149–86.

7. Richard L. Bushman, *The Refinement of America: Persons, Houses, Cities* (New York, 1992), pp. 70–74; Jonathan Prude, "'To Look Upon the Lower Sort': Runaway Ads and the Appearance of Unfree Laborers in America, 1750–1800," *Journal of American History* 78 (June 1991): pp. 129–30.

8. Laura Matilda Towne, *Letters and Diary of Laura M. Towne, Written from the Sea Islands of South Carolina, 1862–1884*, ed. Rupert Sargent Holland (Cambridge, 1912), pp. 176–77; Charles Ball, *Slavery in the United States: A Narrative of the Life and Adventures of Charles Ball, a Black Man* (New York, 1969 [1837]), p. 384.

9. Quoted in Bertram Wyatt-Brown, "The Mask of Obedience: Male Slave Psychology in the Old South," *American Historical Review* 95 (December 1988), p. 1248; quoted in Leon F. Litwack, *Been in the Storm So Long: The Aftermath of Slavery* (New York, 1980), pp. 64, 95.

10. Olmsted, *The Cotton Kingdom*, p. 459; C. Vann Woodward, ed., *Mary Chesnut's Civil War* (New Haven and London, 1981), and see also pp. 48,113–14, 233, 794; quoted in James C. Cobb, "Does Mind No Longer Matter? The South, the Nation, and the Mind of the South, 1941–1991," *Journal of Southern History* 57 (November 1991), p. 698.

11. Prude, "'To Look Upon the Lower Sort,'" p. 141.

12. *Savannah Georgia Royal Gazette*, March 1, 1781 (Windley, *Runaway Slave Advertisements*, IV, pp. 86–87); *Virginia Gazette* (Dixon and Hunter), March 23, 1776 (Windley, *Runaway Slave Advertisements*, I, p. 175); *Virginia Gazette* (Purdie) April 11, 1777 (Windley, *Runaway Slave Advertisements*, I, p. 258); *Baltimore Maryland Journal and Baltimore Advertiser*, June 16, 1789 (Windley, *Runaway Slave Advertisements*, II, pp. 390–91).

13. Cited in James Oliver Horton, *Free People of Color: Inside the African American Community* (Washington and London, 1993), p. 82.

14. *Edenton State Gazette of North-Carolina*, July 9, 1790 (Windley, *Runaway Slave Advertisements*, I, p. 459); *Baltimore Maryland Journal and Baltimore Advertiser*, December 11, 1789 (Windley, *Runaway Slave Advertisements*, II, pp. 399–400); *Baltimore Maryland Journal and Baltimore Advertiser*, August 15, 1783 (Windley, *Runaway Slave Advertisements*, II, p. 291).

15. *Virginia Gazette or American Advertiser* (Hayes), August 14, 1784 (Windley, *Runaway Slave Advertisements*, I, p. 362); *Annapolis Maryland Gazette*, July 8, 1784 (Windley, *Runaway Slave Advertisements*, II, p. 144); *Annapolis Maryland Gazette*, July 18, 1785 (Windley, *Runaway Slave Advertisements*, II, p. 154); *Pennsylvania Gazette*, July 28, 1748, in Billy G. Smith and Richard Wojtowicz, *Blacks Who Stole Themselves: Advertisements for Runaway Slaves in the Pennsylvania Gazette, 1728–1790* (Philadelphia, 1989), p. 28.

16. *Gazette of the State of South-Carolina* (Timothy and Boden), July 15, 1779 (Windley, *Runaway Slave Advertisements*, III, p. 370); *Baltimore Maryland Journal and Baltimore Advertiser*, November 10, 1788 (Windley, *Runaway Slave Advertisements*, II, p. 216); *Baltimore Maryland Journal and Baltimore Advertiser*, July 18, 1783 (Windley, *Runaway Slave Advertisements*, II, pp. 287–88); *Baltimore Maryland Journal and Baltimore Advertiser*, July 20, 1784 (Windley, *Runaway Slave Advertisements*, II, pp. 312–13); Ulrich B. Phillips, ed., *Plantation and Frontier 1649–1863*, 2 vols. (New York, 1962 [1910]), II, p. 88.

17. Robert Farris Thompson, "Kongo Influences on African-American Artistic Culture," in Joseph E. Holloway, ed., *Africanisms in American Culture* (Bloomington and Indianapolis, 1990), pp. 158–59.

18. *Virginia Gazette or American Advertiser* (Hayes), May 27, 1786 (Windley, *Runaway Slave Advertisements*, I, p. 385); *Virginia Gazette* (Rind), August 8, 1766 (Windley, *Slave Runaway Advertisements*, I, pp. 282–83); *South-Carolina Gazette* (Timothy), July 21 to July 28, 1766 (Windley, *Runaway Slave Advertisements*, III, pp. 257–58); *Virginia Independent Chronicle* (Davis), August 29, 1787 (Windley, *Slave Runaway Advertisements*, I, pp. 391–92); *Virginia Gazette and Weekly Advertiser* (Nicolson), April 17, 1788 (Windley, *Runaway Slave Advertisements*, I, p. 240).

19. *Charleston Royal Gazette*, September 21 to September 28, 1782 (Windley, *Runaway Slave Advertisements*, III, pp. 598–99); *Virginia Independent Chronicle* (Davis), August 8, 1787 (Windley, *Runaway Slave Advertisements*, I, p. 391); *Virginia Gazette* (Purdie), September 6, 1776 (Windley, *Runaway Slave Advertisements*, I, p. 253); *Baltimore Maryland Journal and Baltimore Advertiser*, September 24, 1790 (Windley, *Runaway Slave Advertisements*, II, p. 418).

20. On "rolling the eyes," see Kenneth R. Johnson, "Black Kinesics—Some Nonverbal Communication Patterns in Black Culture," in J. Dillard, ed., *Perspectives on Black English* (The Hague, 1975), p. 301.

21. *Baltimore Maryland Journal and Baltimore Advertiser*, August 10, 1779 (Windley, *Runaway Slave Advertisements*, II, p. 229); *Savannah Royal Georgia Gazette*, March 15, 1781 (Windley, *Runaway Slave Advertisements*, IV, p. 89); *Pennsylvania Gazette*, September 2, 1762 (Smith and Wojtowicz, *Blacks Who Stole Themselves*, pp. 58–59); *Baltimore Maryland Journal and Baltimore Advertiser*, August 15, 1783 (Windley, *Runaway Slave Advertisements*, II, p. 291); *Annapolis Maryland Gazette* (Timothy), June 20, 1771 (Windley, *Runaway Slave Advertisements*, II, p. 88) *South-*

Carolina Gazette (Timothy), January 1 to January 5, 1759 (Windley, *Runaway Slave Advertisements,* III, p. 169).

22. Peter H. Wood, "'Gimme de Kneebone Bent': African Body Language and the Evolution of American Dance Forms," in Gerald E. Myers, ed., *The Black Tradition in American Modern Dance* (American Dance Festival Program, Durham, N.C., 1988), pp. 7–8.

23. Towne, *Letters and Diary,* p. 20; Benjamin A. Botkin, *A Treasure of Southern Folklore* (New York, 1949), p. 658; Lydia Parrish, *Slave Songs of the Georgia Sea Islands* (Athens and London, 1992 [1942]), pp. 55–56; Wood, "'Gimme de Kneebone Bent,'" pp. 7–8.

24. Melville J. Herskovits, *The Myth of the Negro Past* (Boston, 1958 [1941]), p. 271.

25. Quoted in Lynne Fawley Emery, *Black Dance: From 1619 to Today* (Princeton, 1988 [1972]), p. 22.

26. George Pinckard, *Notes on the West Indies* (London, 1806), p. 266.

27. Quoted in Emery, *Black Dance,* p. 25.

28. Quoted in Dena J. Epstein, *Sinful Tunes and Spirituals: Black Folk Music to the Civil War* (Urbana and Chicago, 1977), p. 40.

29. Quoted in Epstein, *Sinful Tunes,* pp. 42, 45.

30. Edward C. Carter II, John C. Van Horne, and Lee W. Formwalt, eds., *The Journals of Benjamin Henry Latrobe, 1799–1820: From Philadelphia to New Orleans,* 3 vols. (New Haven and London, 1980), III, pp. 203–4.

31. Quoted in Emery, *Black Dance,* p. 163. Emery believes that this dance was probably the Chica.

32. Quoted in Emery, *Black Dance,* p. 165.

33. Alan Lomax, *The Land Where the Blues Began* (New York, 1993), p. 365.

34. George P. Rawick, ed., *The American Slave: A Composite Autobiography,* Series 1 & 2, 19 vols. (Westport, Conn., 1972), XVI, p. 198.

35. Quoted in Epstein, *Sinful Tunes,* p. 281.

36. Towne, *Letters and Diary,* p. 20; quoted in Epstein, *Sinful Tunes,* p. 284.

37. Elizabeth Ware Pearson, ed., *Letters from Port Royal Written at the Time of the Civil War* (Boston, 1906), pp. 292–93; D. E. Huger Smith, *A Charlestonian's Recollections, 1846–1913* (Charleston, 1950), pp. 31–32, (emphasis added).

38. Huger Smith, *A Charlestonian's Recollections,* p. 32.

39. Charles L. Perdue, Jr., Thomas E. Barden, Robert K. Phillips, eds. *Weevils in the Wheat: Interviews with Virginia Ex-slaves* (Charlottesville, 1976), pp. 14, 49, 316, 265.

40. C. W. Larison, *Silvia Dubois, A Biografy of the Slav Who Whipt Her Mistres and Gand Her Fredom,* ed. Jared C. Lobdell (New York, 1988 [1883]), pp. 59–60.

41. Charles Dickens, *American Notes and Pictures from Italy* (London, 1907), pp. 89–90.

42. Quoted in Emery, *Black Dance,* p. 188.

43. Quoted in Epstein, *Sinful Tunes,* pp. 42, 45; quoted in Emery, *Black Dance,* p. 96; Lawrence W. Levine, *Black Culture and Black Consciousness: Afro-American Folk Thought from Slavery to Freedom* (New York, 1977), p. 16.

44. Levine, *Black Culture,* p. 16; Roger D. Abrahams, *Singing the Master: The Emergence of African-American Culture in the Plantation South* (New York, 1992), pp. 98–100.

45. John F. Szwed and Morton Marks, "The Afro-American Transformation of European Set Dances and Dance Suites," *Dance Research Journal* 20 (Summer 1988), p. 29.

46. Solomon Northup, *Twelve Years a Slave*, ed. Sue Eakin and Joseph Logsdon (Baton Rouge and London, 1968 [1853]), p. 167; Frank Kofsky, "Afro-American Innovation and the Folk Tradition in Jazz: Their Historical Significance," *Journal of Ethnic Studies* 7, no. 1 (1979), pp. 5–6; James Lincoln Collier, *The Making of Jazz: A Comprehensive History* (London, 1991 [1978]), p. 6.

47. Robert Farris Thompson, "An Aesthetic of the Cool: West African Dance," *African Forum* 3 (1966) p. 91; Alan Lomax, "The Homogeneity of African-Afro-American Musical Style," in N. E. P. Whitten and John F. Szwed, eds., *Afro-American Anthropology: Contemporary Perspectives* (New York and London, 1970), p. 193.

48. Quoted in Epstein, *Sinful Tunes*, pp. 134, 204; Lomax, *The Land Where the Blues Began*, 329, 349.

49. White and White, "Slave Clothing in the Eighteenth and Nineteenth Centuries," pp. 158-59.

50. Maude Southwell Wahlman, *Signs and Symbols: African-American Quilts* (New York, 1993), p. 11.

51. Wahlman, *Signs and Symbols*, p. 16; Rawick, *The American Slave*, III, p. 82.

52. Quoted in Epstein, *Sinful Tunes*, pp. 276–77; Thomas Wentworth Higginson, *Army Life in a Black Regiment*, passim.

53. Wahlman, *Signs and Symbols*, p. 12; Olmsted, *The Cotton Kingdom*, p. 467.

54. Robert Farris Thompson, *Flash of the Spirit: African and Afro-American Art and Philosophy* (New York, 1984), pp. 207–10; John Miller Chernoff, *African Rhythm and African Sensibility* (Chicago, 1979), pp. 47, 96.

55. Thompson, *Flash of the Spirit*, pp. 207–10; Wahlman, *Signs and Symbols*, p. 12.

56. Shane White and Graham White, "Slave Hair and African American Culture in the Eighteenth and Nineteenth Centuries," *Journal of Southern History*, 61 (1995), pp. 45–76.

57. Rawick, *The American Slave*, V, p. 191.

58. *Annapolis Maryland Gazette*, March 24, 1785 (Windley, *Runaway Slave Advertisements*, II, p. 151); *Baltimore Maryland Journal and Baltimore Advertiser*, December 11, 1789 (Windley, *Runaway Slave Advertisements*, II, p. 399); *Virginia Gazette* (Purdie and Dixon), August 13, 1772 (Windley, *Runaway Slave Advertisements*, I, p. 118); *South-Carolina Gazette* (Timothy), October 13 to October 20, 1758 (Windley, *Runaway Slave Advertisements*, III, p. 166).

59. Northup, *Twelve Years a Slave*, p. 166. On the reconfiguration of the black body in the twentieth century, see bell hooks, "My 'Style' Ain't No Fashion," *Z Magazine* (May–June 1992), pp. 27–29; Robin D. G. Kelley, "'We Are Not What We Seem': Rethinking Black Working-Class Opposition in the Jim Crow South," *Journal of American History* 80 (June 1993), pp. 84–86.

4

Deadly Amusements: Spectacle Lynchings and Southern Whiteness, 1890–1940

Grace Elizabeth Hale

> This effort to keep the white group solid led directly to mob law. Every white man [and woman] became a recognized official to keep Negroes "in their places." Negro baiting and even lynching became a form of amusement.
>
> —W. E. B. Du Bois[1]

> Mobbism has degenerated to the point where an uncomfortably large percentage of American citizens can read in their newspapers of the slow roasting alive of a human being in Mississippi and turn, promptly and with little thought, to the comic strip or the sporting page. Thus has lynching become an almost integral part of our national folkways.
>
> —Walter White[2]

There were ice trucks at the Waco fire. The leader of the mob was a big white man, a driver for the Big Four Ice Company, and trucks were good to stand on if a late-coming spectator hoped to see over all the other people. Waco, a town with 40,000 inhabitants, 63 churches, and 10 colleges and universities in 1916, could, it seemed, get up quite an audience. In other, smaller towns, special excursion trains from more populated places had been bringing in spectators and increasing mob sizes since at least 1893. No special trains had been necessary here, however, to create the festive atmosphere lent these occasions by large, milling crowds. Towns also advertised and in a twisted form of town boosterism used the standard methods of promoting commerce, but telephones helped tremendously, speeding the circulation of news through a neighborly word of mouth. In the city with the ice trucks, the Raleigh Hotel, too, advertised, billing its lodgings as "ten stories of comfort and safety, sleep where life is safe, absolutely fire proof," where "Waco welcomes *You*." The focus of all this attention, a black man named Jesse Washington, did not have a room there, and the estimated 15,000 white folks—men, women, and children—who welcomed him instead to the Waco, Texas, jail, courtroom, and finally city square found his body very flammable indeed. The burning alive of Jesse Washington in 1916 was a peculiarly modern ritual. As the *Houston Chronicle* recounted with shame, "they did such a thing in the cultured, reputable city of Waco."[3]

It was an uneasy landscape, the early twentieth-century South, a small-town, small-city world of ice companies and beauty parlors, soda fountains, and gas stations. It was a world where people who went to church on Sundays watched or participated in the torture of their neighbors on other days. In the decades following 1890, many lynchings no longer occurred in places untouched by the technological advances of the larger world. Lynchers drove cars, spectators used cameras, out-of-town visitors arrived on specially chartered excursion trains, and the towns and counties in which these horrifying events happened had newspapers, telegraph offices, and even radio stations that announced times and locations of these upcoming violent spectacles. Although after the peak decades of the 1890s the number of lynchings decreased even in the South, the cultural impact of the practice became more powerful. More people participated in, read about, saw pictures of, and collected souvenirs from lynchings, even as fewer mob murders occurred.[4]

Yet not all southern lynchings fit this new and evolving pattern. More often, small groups of white men hunted down and shot or hung their African-American victims after an argument over the year-end sharecroppers' "settle" or to send a message to other timber or turpentine camp laborers not to demand any better. These lynchings in the night claimed many, many more victims than the open-air spectacles of torture that drew large crowds, like Jesse Washington's. And white violence against southern blacks was not limited only to lynchings—white men continued in more private settings to rape black women and assault African Americans for "reasons" ranging from black resistance and economic success to white hatred, jealousy, and fear. "Private violence," as W. J. Cash explained in 1941, stemmed from the same circumstances that made spectacle lynchings "socially defensible" from a southern white perspective: "to smash a sassy Negro, to kill him, to do the same to a 'nigger lover'—this was to assert the white man's prerogative as pointedly, to move as certainly to get a black man back in his place, as to lynch." Violence, after all, had been a chosen method of white empowerment since Jamestown.[5]

But something was new about lynchings in public, attended by thousands, captured in newspapers by reporters who witnessed the tortures, and photographed for those spectators who wanted a souvenir and yet failed to get a coveted finger, toe, or fragment of bone. As Cash understood, far more was at stake than putting African Americans brutally in their place, for "private violence" succeeded in limiting and often eliminating black political activity and achieving significant white control of black labor. Explanations of the practice of lynching in the twentieth century, however, have focused on the persistence of the "barbaric" practice of the past rather than its transformation, in the case of spectacle lynchings, into a peculiarly modern ritual. Southern whites, according to contemporary observers like H. L. Mencken and Arthur Raper and such present-day scholars as James McGovern and Joel Williamson, lynched African-American men and occasionally women in the absence of "modernity" because the South lacked a "modern" economy, a "modern" white male sexuality," or even a "modern" theater. Even Jacquelyn Dowd Hall, in the best analysis of lynching to date, saw the region's extreme racism existing in conflict with modernizing efforts. And while W. Fitzhugh Brundage and Edward L. Ayers have shown that lynching was central to the New South and particularly to the structuring of its labor markets in areas experiencing rapid increases in their African-American populations, they have focused mainly on the more common private lynchings and their role in the New South economy.[6]

African-American antilynching activists, too—some of whom had barely escaped lynchings themselves—saw lynching as central to the New South, and examined the function of violence in structuring a changing southern economy and culture. From Ida B. Wells, who founded both the study of lynching and antilynching activism, to Frederick Douglass, W. E. B. Du Bois, Mary Church Terrell, James Weldon Johnson, and especially Walter White, such blacks understood that ritualized violence by whites—what Terrell called "this wild and diabolical carnival of blood"—was central not only to the white economy but to white identity as well. But African-American activists were often ignored.[7]

"Lynch carnivals," as a popular book from the 1930s described them, were rituals increasingly bound up with the way southern whites shaped the practices of modern consumption to their own ends, communal spectacles of torture that helped ease white fears of a raceless consumer society even as they helped structure segregation, the policy that would regulate this new southern world. Spectacle lynchings brutally conjured a collective, all-powerful whiteness even as they made the color line seem modern, civilized, and sane—and thus publicly resolved the race, gender, and class ambiguities at the very center of the culture of segregation. Spectacle lynchings were about making a racial difference in the New South and about ensuring the separation of all southern life into whiteness and blackness even as the very material things that made up southern life were rapidly changing. Racial violence was modern.[8]

Despite the roots of an expanding consumer culture outside the South, then, Coca-Cola was not the only consumer item invented within the region. White southerners made another, more important contribution to the rapidly evolving forms of leisure in twentieth-century America: they modernized and perfected violence as entertainment, what Du Bois chillingly described as a new and yet grisly form of white southern amusement. And like all cultural forms, lynching spectacles evolved a well-known structure with a sequence and pace of events. Beginning with a chase or jail-attack opening, the well-choreographed events proceeded through a prelude of public identification of the captured African American by the alleged white victim or the victim's relatives, announcement of the upcoming event to draw the crowd, and site selection and preparation. The main event built from a period of mutilation—often including castration—and torture to extract confessions and entertain the crowd to a climax of slow burning, hanging, or shooting. There followed a frenzy of souvenir gathering and display of the body and the collected parts.[9]

In a perverse twist on regional exceptionalism, lynchings of all kinds became fixed in the southern and national imagination as the dominant form of southern white violence against blacks. News of midnight shootings and hangings by small groups of white men circulated among both white and black southerners even when not reported in local papers. Hearing that "the white folks" quietly shot his classmate's brother, Richard Wright later recalled: "the white brutality that I had not seen was a more effective control of my behavior than that which I knew. The actual experience would have let me see the realistic outlines of what was really happening, but as long as it remained something terrible and yet remote, something whose horror and blood might descend upon me at any moment, I was compelled to give my entire imagination over to it." Since southern blacks rarely attended public lynchings, their knowledge of all these extralegal killings remained paradoxically remote and perhaps fantastic even as brutality struck close at hand. Yet in the twentieth century, spectator lynchings became the most widely known form of white violence against southern blacks even as less public lynchings claimed many more victims. Cash declared that by 1900, the white South had developed a lynching habit. Walter White lamented that by the 1920s, interest in the practice of lynching had spread far beyond the region in which mob murders were most likely to occur and "mobbism has degenerated to the point where an uncomfortably large percentage of American citizens can read in their newspapers of the slow roasting alive of a human being in Mississippi and turn, promptly and with little thought, to the comic strip or sporting page. Thus has lynching become an almost integral part of our national folkways." The distance was not far, then, between titillation and disgust, a white southern amusement, an African-American tragedy, and a new national pastime.[10]

But just how did a practice of quiet vigilante justice become a modern public spectacle, a narrative of astonished interest more than horrified concern, a national folkway? Consumer culture, spreading from the northeast across the country in the late nineteenth and twentieth centuries, created the possibility of a new kind of public, a much more heterogeneous group of shoppers, diners, travelers, vaudeville buffs and moviegoers, sports fans, and visitors to local, regional, and national fairs. In the North, as the historian David Nasaw has argued, segregation excluded African Americans from an emerging world of urban public amusements, denying them access to fair midways, amusement and baseball parks, and vaudeville and movie theaters. Yet segregation alone did not meld these new heterogeneous crowds into a white public. The spectacle of

African-American otherness was also required. Thus whites of all backgrounds could gawk at the "Dahomeys" in exhibits of "Darkest Africa," or "dunk the nigger" at Coney Island, and cheer on a black man's lynchers in the racist film *Birth of a Nation*.[11]

In the North, then, segregation and the spectacle of black otherness made a mass audience for the new purveyors of commercial entertainments and other new mass products. For southern whites, however, creating a new white public was both more difficult and, many believed, more necessary. There segregation and spectacle lynching made what Du Bois referred to as a new white "amusement" also a new southern order. Segregation strengthened racial boundaries without denying southern whites and blacks who could afford consumer products access to them, allowing white-owned businesses to sell African Americans, say, Coca-Cola, and protect white supremacy all the while. For southern blacks must, while enjoying their purchases, swallow their pride along with their soda. They could only publicly consume goods within spaces marked, whether labeled "for colored" or not, as clearly inferior. Yet making a spectacle of lynching disrupted the commonality of even this spatially divided experience of consumption. Only whites could experience the amusement of a black man burned. In a grisly dialectic, then, consumer culture created spectacle lynchings, which in turn became a southern way of enabling the spread of consumption. The violence helped create both a white consuming public and the structure of segregation in which consumption could take place without threatening white supremacy.[12]

Widely circulated newspaper stories, as Walter White understood, were central to the power of these new spectacles. Though thousands of white southerners witnessed and participated in lynchings as the twentieth century unfolded, the majority of Americans learned about these events from newspapers and to a lesser extent from books, pamphlets, and radio announcements. Those spectators who attended the lynching or later viewed the body or examined a display of "souvenirs" were affected as well by the narratives constructed by reporters to describe and explain these events. Beginning in the 1890s, representations of spectacle lynchings increasingly fell into a ritualistic pattern as the narratives constructed by witnesses, participants, and journalists assumed a standardized form. Spectacle lynchings, then, became more powerful even as they occurred less frequently, because the rapidly multiplying stories of these public tortures became virtually interchangeable.[13]

As a dominant narrative evolved and circulated more widely, innovations added in a particular lynching were easily spotted and picked up by subsequent mobs. The grisly dialectic began in the 1890s as newspaper coverage grew, crowds increased, and lynch mobs adapted the rituals of public executions to the needs of vigilantism and racial control. As James Elbert Cutler found in the first academic investigation of lynchings, published in 1905, before 1890 magazines ignored the subject entirely, while local newspapers printed small, sparse accounts. Three events in the early 1890s, however, initiated the early development of spectacle lynchings. The March 14, 1891, lynching of eleven Italian immigrants accused of aiding in the murder of the New Orleans police chief brought international attention to mob murder in the South. The enraged Italian government condemned the action and demanded indemnities. In May, before the fervor had faded, another public lynching in Louisiana occurred as a large crowd of whites tortured and burned an African American named Tump Hampton in St. Tammany Parish. Significantly, publicity generated by the Italians' murder spilled over onto the lynching of a black southerner. The founding event in the history of spectacle lynchings, however, was the 1893 lynching of Henry Smith in Paris, Texas, for the alleged rape and murder of three-year-old Myrtle Vance.[14]

Smith's murder was the first blatantly public, actively promoted lynching of a southern black by a large crowd of southern whites. The specially chartered excursion train, the publicly sold photograph, and the widely circulated, unabashed retelling of the event by one of the lynchers modernized and made more powerful the loosely organized, spontaneous practice of lynching that had previously prevailed. From 1893 on, railroad companies could be counted on to arrange special trains to transport spectators and lynchers to previously announced lynching sites. Some trains advertised in local papers, thus assuring that even small towns could turn out large crowds. Even after automobiles cut into the railroads' business, a 1938 commentator found that "modern trainmen, schooled in the doctrine of service," helped "in an informative way" by relaying news of upcoming lynchings to train passengers and townspeople "all along the rail lines."[15]

As important as the innovation in transportation, however, was the publication of the first extensive account of a lynching. In what was perhaps the most detailed account of a lynching ever written from a lyncher's point of view, the pamphlet *The Facts in the Case of the Horrible Murder of Little Myrtle Vance, and Its Fearful Expiation, at Paris, Texas, February 1, 1893* initiated a new genre of lynching narrative—the author as eyewitness and, in this case, participant.

This anonymous lyncher-as-reporter implicated the entire white community in the public torture and murder that had recently occurred: "From the first it was a clear case of temporary insanity of a whole populace, the moral and social shock for the time eclipsing every vestige of temperance in dealing with the culprit." And "populace" did not mean simply white men. Though the photographer focused on the scaffold, labelled with a large sign proclaiming "JUSTICE," the size of the crowd prevented the author from getting close to the action. The photograph, more a picture of the mob than of the victim, depicts a mass of spectators, including white women and children. From the earliest spectacle lynchings, then, white women were active participants in these events—hardly the passive, alleged victims that fueled white men's fury. The story of lynching as the entire white community in action, using savagery to protect "southern" civilization, was born.[16]

But lynchings never went unchallenged by African Americans and a few brave whites. Even as the dominant narrative of lynchings developed, antilynching activists beginning with Ida B. Wells worked to subvert the story, believing that by revealing the false accounts and empty justifications, they would expose the immorality and end the violence. The lynchings they and later white liberals described became a hybrid sort of spectacle lynching as well, as their stories circulated publicly and bumped against the narrative most white southerners had learned by heart. Thus the violence occurred and the story was written within a never-ending dialectic—the pushing and pulling at the boundaries of the racialized yet shifting spaces of segregation as culture.

If the lynching of Henry Smith marked the beginning of the transformation of the practice from quiet vigilante justice to modern public spectacle, Sam Hose's murder in Palmetto, Georgia, in 1899 made an isolated event into a new and horrifying pattern. The alleged crimes, the chase, and the lynching occurred in and around Palmetto, Newnan, and Griffin—small southern towns like any others yet within forty miles of Atlanta. Easy access to train and telegraph lines ensured that the lynching of Hose would be an "event," not just in the rural Georgia piedmont but in the self-proclaimed capital of the New South as well. The Hose murder added a key innovation—local and regional newspapers took over the publicity, promotion, and sale of the event and began the development of a standardized, sensationalized narrative pattern that would dominate reporting of spectacle lynchings through the 1940s.[17]

"DETERMINED MOB AFTER HOSE; HE WILL BE LYNCHED IF CAUGHT" began the story in the Atlanta *Constitution* on April 14, 1899. The best men were in the mob, proud and unmasked, the cream of "a half dozen counties." "Driven . . . almost to a frenzy" and vowing "never to give up the chase," these fine citizens, however, remained "perfectly cool" and would, the Atlanta papers assured readers, do what had to be done "as thoroughly and as orderly as though nothing unusual was involved." From the first, local and regional papers never doubted that the African American would be tracked down by the mob and killed, and the large black letters gave an eerie certainty to an act of violence that had previously been both anticipated and feared. After all, the entire white community was behind these best men, not really a mob, the *Journal* stressed, but more of a crowd. Sam Hose's alleged crimes had "closed the store doors in the towns and stopped the plows in the country," as white men, women, and children sought the "the fiendish beast."[18]

The white folks in Palmetto believed that on the previous night Sam Hose, a laborer on Alfred Cranford's farm, had taken an axe and split open the skull of the respected white farmer and then injured his children and raped his wife. "Whatever death is most torturous, most horrifying to a brute, shall be meted out," boasted one of the lynchers, "let him burn slowly for hours." Apparently no death was too horrifying for the large numbers of white spectators the newspaper announcements and specially chartered trains from Atlanta were certain to bring as soon as Hose was captured. The telegraph lines could transmit the definite time and place. Hose's fate had already been decided by the papers ten days beforehand, and as mobs sifted the countryside, ransacking black houses, black farms, and black sections, the days grew hotter, the reading audience larger, and chances that the torture and murder would provide white amusement more certain. On April 23, a Sunday afternoon in Newnan, Georgia, it was done.[19]

But the finale was still ten days away when the Atlanta papers began developing the story, and they needed more than the repetitive details of the chase to hook their audiences. Mrs. Cranford, the wife of the murdered man and the alleged victim of rape herself, provided the most exciting copy in those early days, but attempts to use her as both subject and object of the story exposed the gendered tensions at the center of spectacle lynchings. Granting interviews with reporters from both the *Journal* and the *Constitution*, she demanded an active role in planning the lynching, expressing a desire to witness Hose's torture and death and a preference for a slow burning. She was, in fact, the source of all that was known about Hose's attack on her family.[20]

Yet could a white woman play so important and public a role in a ritual that both brought out and created the white community, that made whiteness? With their desire for authenticity and gore, the papers pointed their spotlights at Mrs. Cranford. She had only claimed the power to shape the story presented by the brightness of her sudden "fame." The press was determined to place Mrs. Cranford onto the pedestal. She was no longer a good and common farm wife but now a woman of "refined parentage." As a "lady," Mrs. Cranford was doubly savaged by the "black beast" rapist. Proclaiming that "death would have been mercy," the reporters related the very details of the rape that she alone could have given them. Just as white women both helped in the chase and cheered on the "best men," it was Mrs. Cranford's account of Hose's crimes that initiated the spectacle lynching, as the papers transformed her from active participant to passive victim. But in the end, Hose was murdered in Newnan, and her wish to see the lynching and for the spectacle to take place in Palmetto was ignored.[21]

The small group who had captured Hose took him to Griffin on the regular Macon-to-Atlanta train early that Sunday morning. The papers played up the festive atmosphere as the railroad, eager to please and keep this special traffic separate from the other passengers, provided an excursion train to take Hose and the fast-growing mob to Palmetto. The papers reported that "it was marvelous how the news spread and thousands came here to satisfy their curiosity and to take part in the lynching." Other trains, too, were en route for the lynching, and officials of the Atlanta and West Point Railroad estimated they sold 1,000 tickets and that stowaways stole 500 more spaces.[22]

While the papers insisted that the mob escorting the captured Hose was an orderly, determined "crowd," reports stressed that at every step these good citizens feared some crazed outsider would shoot the prize and deny them their fun. Afraid, ironically, that Hose would be killed, they lynched him at Newnan, still ten miles from Palmetto, just after church let out. Receiving word quickly by telegram, the papers had special correspondents at the scene, and the Monday editions detailed the cutting off of Hose's ears, his castration, and a very slow burning. The reporters went to great lengths to "civilize" the mob, saying, "the crowd was cool and went about its work carefully and almost with a system." Another paper pronounced "absolute order and decorum." An ex-governor of the state, W. Y. Atkinson, bragged that although he had not prevented the lynching, he had succeeded in persuading them to move the lynching out of Newnan's town square and away from the white women and children, and that "the crowd was a marvel of coolness and determination and . . . remarkably orderly."[23]

The reporters even went so far as to praise the unusually great courage of the victim, that he did not flinch as he marched to the stake or cry out as his legs slowly burned. "I stood as close to the flames and the writhing figure in their midst as the heat would permit," the *Journal's* reporter revealed as he described Hose "battling in the flames with the wildest superhuman energy": "now he was twisting around the tree, now biting at the back of the pine, jumping and springing and twisting and fighting for every inch of life, kicking the embers with his dangling legs, blood vessels bursting, eyes protruding, but not a word, not a tear, but, oh God, the horror of his face." The stronger and more manly the victim, the greater the glory of the mob that defeated him.[24]

But certain images threatened to break through the narrative of a calm avenging white civilization—images of "frenzied men" and "delirious delight," of an old white-haired man screaming "God bless every man that had a hand in this" and "thank God for vengeance," and of a mingling of white and black blood as men rushing to cut off pieces of Hose's body, cut the hands of their friends instead. The barbarism of the trophy gathering in particular exploded any claim of white deliberateness and calm. Mob members had collected some body parts, the choice ears and penis and fingers cut off before the fire, and many spectators afterwards turned "souvenir seekers," rushing in to push back the still hot coals and hack up the body, cutting out the heart and other internal organs, fighting quicker onlookers for the most cherished prizes. The *Journal* reported "men scrambled and fell over each other in their mad haste to secure something that would be a memento to the horrible tragedy. And everything that had any bearing on the occasion was grabbed and pocketed, even the ashes were picked up in handkerchiefs and carried away in triumph. Men left the scene bearing huge chunks of burned wood, limbs of the tree which was made the stake, pieces of bone, and revolting and bloody segments of skull." A market for souvenirs quickly developed, as spectators too far away from the burning bargained with luckier men and purchased at "inflated prices" their own keepsakes of that glorious day. In the process of giving its readers the sensationalized details of the spectacle, the papers blurred if not obliterated the fine distinction between a ritual of civilization taming savagery and actual savagery itself. If indeed "the whole male community seemed to be a unit," what that unit accomplished did not seem as clear as many southern whites wanted to think.[25]

Afterwards, the crowd broke up and went home, and those souvenirs also traveled, ending up in dusty mason jars in crossroad stores, on the mantels of farmhouses, in the homes of some of those best men. At least one relic made it to Atlanta. Though W. E. B. Du Bois did not write his alternative narrative of the aftermath of Hose's lynching until decades afterward, this "souvenir" certainly extended the reach of the horrifying spectacle:

A Negro in central Georgia, Sam Hose, had killed his landlord. I wrote out a careful and reasoned statement concerning the evident facts and started down to the Atlanta *Constitution* office, carrying in my pocket a letter of introduction to Joel Chandler Harris. I did not get there. On the way the news met me: Sam Hose had been lynched, and they said his knuckles were on exhibition at a grocery store farther down Mitchell Street, along the way I was walking. I turned back to the University. I began to turn aside from my work. I did not meet Joel Chandler Harris nor the editor of the *Constitution.*[26]

The Hose lynching signaled a turning point for Du Bois, a transformation in his own thinking on the "race problem" generally and racial violence particularly. The display of Sam Hose's knuckles, he claimed, irrevocably changed his life. Having recently reconstructed the African-American experience for an international exhibition, Du Bois was robbed of access to the newspaper of his own city and brought to his knees by a white southerner's display of the meaning of blackness.[27]

The lynching of Jesse Washington in the City Hall square of Waco, Texas, in 1916 mimicked the pace and structure of events in the Hose lynching. Though early reports did not so assuredly predict a lynching beforehand, the Waco papers presented the details of Lucy Fryar's murder and rape in the standard sensationalized pattern. The doctor reported that she had been surprised by her attacker, killed by the first blow, and ravished while dead. And yet one report followed the dominant narrative and stressed how the highly respected white woman had struggled valiantly against her violator. In the lynching narrative, even the corpse of the white woman recoiled from the black man's lust. The Waco *Semi-Weekly Tribune* provided a "Chronology of the Crime," and though the lawbreaking referred to was the rape and murder of "Mrs. Lucy Fryar," this summary of events culminating in the eighteen-year-old African American's lynching provided as accurate an outline of the ritual of southern spectator lynchings as had ever been published.[28]

By 1916, however, the newly formed National Association for the Advancement of Colored People added a collective black voice to the national dialogue about whiteness. In the case of Jesse Washington, the NAACP had an investigator, a white woman named Elizabeth Freeman, at the scene within days. She discovered that a photographer, in what became a standard part of these spectacles, went to the lynching to create his own souvenir business. It seemed Gildersleeve—he put his name on the photographs—knew something would happen and set up his camera and equipment down at City Hall ahead of time. Tipped off by telephone, he arrived in time to get pictures even before the mob lit the fire. Quickly printing the photos as postcards, he sold them for ten cents a piece. Ten cents, after all, was significantly cheaper than the five dollars that by day's end Washington's teeth were reportedly fetching and less even than the links of the chain that were trading for a quarter. No one, it seemed, was selling the more coveted body parts. But the key difference in the burning alive of Jesse Washington was that the NAACP got the pictures. Perhaps Gildersleeve was a sexist—he charged Freeman, posing as a suffrage activist, five times his regular price.[29]

Many of the good people of Waco had apparently sensed danger in such graphic photographs. The pictures revealed the City Hall Square spilling over with people and the lighting of a black man on fire. They showed the body burning, burnt and charred beyond human resemblance, and white boys smiling at the ash. The mayor and sheriff hesitated, not wanting in the weeks after to circulate the pictures further by giving them to outsiders. The photographs could subvert the story they wanted told about Waco when they circulated beyond the approving context of the souvenir-seeking crowd. Erasing the fine line local newspapers constructed between civilized ritual and savage spectacle, the pictures appeared widely in the weeks afterward—provoking regional and national condemnation and subverting the often recycled story of the white community in action. The narrative of white unity would not hold.[30]

As the Smith, Hose, and Washington lynchings have demonstrated, then, innovations like trains and cars, telegraphs and telephones, and cheaper newspapers and photographs could expand and strengthen the power of each incident as easily as they increased white condemnation. And *Birth of a Nation*, shown widely through the end of the decade, merged the twentieth-century spectacle lynching with Reconstruction-era violence, producing a spectacle of lynching for the entire nation. The symbolic reunion of North and South that the racist film captured so vividly and to such popular acclaim echoed the political reconciliation evident in the election of the southerner Woodrow Wilson president in 1912 and the segregation of Washington, D.C., during his first term. By the time of America's entrance into the Great War in 1917, Wilson realized, as George Creel, his chair of the Committee on Public Information bluntly stated, the need to "weld the people of the United States into one white hot mass instinct," and the president borrowed *Birth of a Nation* imagery to celebrate another American ride to the rescue. The spectacle of African-American otherness created white unity and gave birth to the nation. Whether most Americans rationally agreed with the film's distorted interpretation of the Civil War and Reconstruction mattered little.[31]

The lynching of Claude Neal in Marianna, Florida, in 1934 signaled the end of the gruesome southern practice of spectator lynchings. There were a few other bestial murders of black men and women afterward—the burning to death of two black men with gasoline blow torches in the town square of Duck Hill, Mississippi, in 1937 stood out for its barbarity across the entire history of southern white racial violence. But the Neal lynching, unfolding against the background of Scottsboro, the Alabama arrests and convictions of nine young African Americans for the alleged rape of two young white millworkers, was different.[32]

Claude Neal was lynched in an isolated backwoods in rural northern Florida instead of in broad daylight in the center of a southern city. The details of the lynching, which had occurred at the hands of the approximately one hundred white men who had taken turns torturing Neal over ten hours, did not appear in the press. The NAACP, however, sent Howard Kester, a young white liberal associated with the Committee on Economic and Racial Justice, to Marianna to do undercover work. Kester was "to get all the gruesome details possible together with any photographs of the body, crowd, etc." By late November the NAACP had published Kester's report, the widely circulated *The Lynching of Claude Neal*. At last, the details of perhaps the most chillingly brutal lynching to date were made public. The NAACP had adroitly made the torture and murder of Claude Neal into a spectacle.[33]

After Neal, the myth of lynching as the story of an entire white community in action, using savagery to protect southern civilization, was done. The NAACP and other organizations also began using photographs and grisly descriptions of lynched black men on petitions circulated for signatures in support of federal antilynching legislation and on postcards mailed out to raise funds to combat racism. The lynching spectacle, then, had given way to the growing antilynching crusade's attempt to make a spectacle of lynching. Lynching may have remained a white southern pastime, but it became a much more private sport. If the nation wanted to look at or read about the mutilated and murdered bodies of blacks, it would have to sign the petition.[34]

NOTES

I would like to thank Fitzhugh Brundage and Nancy MacLean for comments on an abbreviated version of this paper given at the 1993 Southern Historical Meeting in Orlando, Florida. I would also like to thank David Levitt, T. J. Jackson Lears, Eliza McFeely, Lynn Ponce de Leon, and Dee Garrison.

1. W. E. B. Du Bois, "Georgia, Invisible Empire State," *The Nation*, 120 (January 21, 1925), 63–67.

2. Walter White, *Rope and Faggot: A Biography of Judge Lynch* (New York, 1929), p. viii.

3. On the Washington lynching, see the series of letters between Elisabeth Freeman, NAACP investigator, Waco, Texas, and NAACP head Roy Nash, New York, New York, dated May 21–29, 1916, and undated (the description of the Waco Hotel is taken from Freeman's stationary letterhead); ten black-and-white photos, some made into postcards, taken by Gildersleeve of the town and of the lynching; "The Waco Lynching," a typed report by Elisabeth Freeman, NAACP investigator sent to Waco; a copy of Jesse Washington's official confession; and the local newspaper clippings: "Negro Confesses

to Terrible Crime at Robinsonville," *Waco Times-Herald*, May 9, 1916; "Negro Burned to a Stake in the Yard of City Hall," *Waco Semi-Weekly Tribune*, May 17, 1916; "Who Will Cast the First Stone?" *Waco Morning News*, May 24, 1916. An NAACP press release, "Waco Horror Stirs to Action," quotes a now unavailable *Times-Herald* article, probably May 16, 1916. Quote from "The Horror at Waco," *Houston Chronicle and Herald*, May 16, 1916. All of these sources and clippings from nonlocal papers cited in the following notes are in the NAACP Papers, Part 7, Series A, the Library of Congress, Group I, Box C–370 and Microfilm Reel 19. See also James M. SoRelle, "'The Waco Horror': The Lynching of Jesse Washington," *Southwestern Historical Quarterly* 86 (April 1983), pp. 517–36. See also "The Waco Horror," editorial, special supplement to the *Crisis*, 12 (July 1916), 1–8.

Freeman claimed that her informants admitted 15,000 spectators at the lynching originally and then reduced this number as they became suspicious. When she left, the crowd numbered only 500. See her report, p. 20. Newspaper accounts give many different estimates of crowd size. The photographs, however, demonstrate that the crowd was extremely large and numbered in the thousands.

4. A form of violence with a long history in America, lynchings have nevertheless occurred within vastly different social and economic spaces and asserted widely varying cultural meanings. For the declining practice of lynching whites after 1900, see W. Fitzhugh Brundage, *Lynching in the New South, Georgia and Virginia, 1880–1930* (Urbana, Ill., 1993), pp. 86–102.

See NAACP Papers, Part 7, "The Anti-Lynching Campaign, 1912–1953," Series A, "Anti-Lynching Investigation Files, 1912–1953," for the NAACP's extensive case files. These records contain news clippings and lynching studies dating back to 1885, but the case files begin in 1912. See also case studies provided in White, *Rope*, pp. 23–39; James Weldon Johnson, "The Practice of Lynching: A Picture, the Problem, and What Shall Be Done about It," *Century* (November 1927): pp. 65–70; Arthur F. Raper, *The Tragedy of Lynching* (Chapel Hill, 1933), pp. 59–440; Frank Shay, *Judge Lyunch: His First One Hundred Years* (New York, 1938), pp. 153–204. See also W. E. B. Du Bois, *Dusk of Dawn: An Essay Toward an Autobiography of a Race Concept* (1940), reprinted in W. E. B. Du Bois, *Writings* (New York, 1986), pp. 602–3, 716-39; and W. J. Cash, *The Mind of the South* (1941; rpt. New York, 1991), pp. 43–45, 116–23, 170, 299–310, on the changing practice of lynching in the South.

5. On contemporary sources on African-American women and the ever-present threat of rape by white men, see Du Bois, "Damnation of Women," in *Darkwater: Voices from within the Veil* (1920; rpt., Millwood, N.J., pp. 163–86; and White, *Rope*, pp. 62–66; Cash, *Mind*, pp. 118–19.

6. For the modern economy argument, see Raper, *Tragedy*, pp. 3–40, and James R. McGovern, *Anatomy of a Lynching: The Killing of Claude Neal* (Baton Rouge, 1982), pp. 1–41. For an argument about white male sexuality, see Joel Williamson, *A Rage for Order: Black/White Relations in the American South since Emancipation* (Oxford, 1986), pp. 98–126. For the argument about a lack of movie theaters, see H. L. Mencken, "The Sahara of the Bozart," *New York Evening Mail*, November 13, 1917. Jacquelyn Dowd Hall, *Revolt against Chivalry: Jesse Daniel Ames and the Women's Campaign against Lynching* (New York, 1974), pp. 129–57. See also Edward L. Ayers, *The Promise of the New South: Life after Reconstruction* (New York, 1993), pp. 155–59.

7. Cash, *Mind*, p. 115; Ida B. Wells, *On Lynchings: Southern Horrors; A Red Record; Mob Rule in New Orleans* (New York, 1969), and *Crusade for Justice: The Autobiography of Ida B. Wells* (Chicago, 1970), pp. 18–20; Frederick Douglass, *Why Is the Negro Lynched?* (Bridgewater, England, 1895); W. E. B. Du Bois, "Georgia," "Jesus Christ in Texas," in *Darkwater*, pp. 123–33, *Dusk*, pp. 602–3, 716–739, and "Lynchings," *The Crisis* (August 1927); Mary Church Terrell, "Lynching from a Negro's Point of View," *North American Review* 178 (June 1904). pp. 853–68, quote, p. 865; James Weldon Johnson, *Lynching: America's National Disgrace* (New York, 1924), and "The Practice of Lynching," pp. 65–70; and Walter White, *A Man Called White* (1948; rpt., New York, 1969), pp. 39–58.

8. Spectator lynchings claimed at least three African-American victims outside the South, in Marion, Indiana, where two men were lynched, and in Coatesville, Pennsylvania. See White, *Rope*, pp. 36–37; Raper, *Tragedy*, pp. 387–406; and Dennis B. Downey and Raymond M. Hyser, *No Crooked Death: Coatsville, Pennsylvania, and the Lynching of Zachariah Walker* (Urbana, Ill., 1991); The "popular book" is Shay, *Judge Lynch*, pp. 149, 168–204.

9. On contributions of early cinema to violence as entertainment, see Miriam Hansen, *Babel and Babylon: Spectatorship in American Silent Film* (Cambridge, Mass., 1991), pp. 1–20. However, with lynchings, at least for the thousands of white spectators and participants, the violence was unmediated.

10. Quotes, Richard Wright, *Black Boy*, p. 190 and White, *Rope*, p. viii. For African Americans as members of lynch mobs and as spectators at lynchings, see Shay, *Judge Lynch*, pp. 82–83, and Brundage, *Lynching in the New South*, pp. 45, 178–79. For lynching as southern exceptionalism, see Cash, *Mind*, p. 118, and Brundage, p. 3.

11. See David Nasaw, *Going Out: The Rise and Fall of Public Amusements* (New York, 1993), pp. 72–79, 92–94. On consumer culture, see Richard Wrightman Fox and T. J. Jackson Lears, *The Culture of Consumption* (New York, 1983); Lizabeth Cohen, *Making a New Deal: Industrial Workers in Chicago, 1919-1939* (Cambridge, 1990), pp. 99–158; and Warren Susman, *Culture as History: The Transformation of American Society in the Twentieth Century* (New York, 1984).

12. I develop this argument more explicitly in "For Colored, for White: Bounding Consumption in the South, 1890–1940," (Paper delivered at the American Historical Society Meeting, January 1995, Chicago, Illinois).

13. On the swift standardization of the lynching ritual, see Joel Williamson, *The Crucible of Race: Black–White Relations in the American South since Emancipation* (New York, 1984), pp. 184–85.

14. For the history of lynching and its development out of frontier vigilantism, regulator movements, and the violence inherent in slavery, see Cutler, *Lynch Law*, pp. 41–154; and John Ross, "At the Bar of Judge Lynch: Lynching and Lynch Mobs in America" (Ph.D. diss., Texas Tech University, 1983), pp. 1–27.

15. Sources on the 1893 lynching of Smith include, Anon., *The Facts in the Case of the Horrible Murder of Little Myrtle Vance, and Its Fearful Expiation, at Paris, Texas, February 1, 1893* (Paris, 1893) unpaged; Cutler, *Lynch Law*, p. 228; Shay, *Judge Lynch*, p. 92; Williamson, *Crucible*, pp. 185–87, and Ross, "Bar," p. 28. For the quote on modern trainmen, see Shay, p. 92.

16. *The Facts in the Case*, unpaged. See also the photographs of the Smith lynching in the Pictures of Lynchings file, the Division of Prints and Photographs, Library of Congress. Though the victims of lynch mobs do not often live to tell their stories, at

least two accounts of lynchings have been written by men who have escaped from lynch mobs. See Irenas J. Palmer, *The Black Man's Burden; or the Horrors of Southern Lynchings* (Olean, N.Y., 1902); and James Cameron, *A Time of Terror* (Milwaukee, 1982). See also Raper, *Tragedy*, pp. 387–406, on the 1930 lynching in Marion, Indiana, from which Cameron escaped.

17. Newspaper sources on the Hose lynching include the *Atlanta Constitution*, April 14, 1899, pp. 1–2, and April 24, 1899, pp. 1–2; the *Atlanta Journal*, April 15, 1899, pp. 1, 3, and April 24, 1899, pp. 1, 3; the *Macon Telegraph*, April 24, 1899, p. 1 and April 25, 1899, p.6; the *Birmingham News*, April 24, 1899, p.1; and the *New York Times*, April 25, 1899, p. 2. See also Williamson, *Crucible*, p. 204; Brundage, *Lynching in the New South*, pp. 34, 82–83; and Mary Louise Ellis, "'Rain Down Fire': The Lynching of Sam Hose," (Ph.D. dissertation, Florida State University, 1992). See Mary Church Terrell, "Lynching," pp. 859–60, for-African-American antilynching activists' efforts to challenge white southerners' descriptions of Hose's crimes. See also the *New York Age*, June 22, 1899.

18. *New York Age*, June 22, 1899. Quotes are from *Atlanta Constitution*, April 14, 1899; *Atlanta Journal*, April 15, 1899.

19. *Atlanta Journal*, April 15, 1899.

20. Ibid.

21. Ibid.

22. *Atlanta Constitution*, April 24, 1899, and *Atlanta Journal*, April 24, 1899. The quote is from the *Constitution*. On the details about the trains from Atlanta, see the *Constitution*, p. 2.

23. The first quote is from the *Atlanta Constitution*, April 14, 1899. The rest are from the *Atlanta Journal*, April 15, 1899.

24. *Atlanta Journal*, April 15, 1899.

25. All quotes from the *Journal* except the last one, which is from the *Constitution*. On a market for lynching "souvenirs," see the *New York Tribune*, as quoted in Shay, *Judge Lynch*, p. 109: "Those unable to obtain the ghastly relics directly, paid more fortunate possessors extravagant sums for them."

26. Du Bois, *Dusk of Dawn*, pp. 602–3.

27. *Waco Times-Harold*, May 9, 1916; *Waco Semi Weekly Tribune*, May 17, 1916; *Waco Morning News*, May 24, 1916. From this point on, Du Bois turned away from his academic work and toward activism, leaving his life as a scholar for the editorship of the *Crisis* and a more direct battle with the evils of racism. See David Levering Lewis, *W. E. B. Du Bois: Biography of a Race, 1868–1890* (New York, 1993), pp. 226–27.

28. See local newspapers quoted in note 3.

29. *Waco Semi-Weekly Herald Tribune*, May 17, 1916; Elisabeth Freeman report, pp. 15, 14, 21.

30. Freeman report, pp. 15, 21. The ten photographs NAACP acquired are in the Lynching Pictures file, NAACP Collection, lot 10647-4, the Division of Prints and Photographs, Library of Congress. See also the local newspapers quoted in note twenty-seven and "The Horror at Waco," *Houston Chronicle and Herald*, May 16, 1916; "The Background of Lynching," *San Francisco Bulletin*, May 16, 1916.

31. Creel quoted in Rogin, *Sword*, p. 230. The NAACP stepped up its investigations of lynchings in the decade following 1910 and published its important antilynching book, *Thirty Years of Lynching*. On the fight for the Dyer Anti-Lynching Bill, see Walter White, *A Man Called White*, p. 42, and Robert L. Zangrando, *The*

NAACP Crusade against Lynching (Philadelphia, 1980), pp. 51–71. For the most recent and forceful argument that modernization, urbanization, and technological advances were responsible for the decrease in the practice of lynchings, especially after 1934, see McGovern, *Anatomy of a Lynching*.

32. On the Duck Hill, Mississippi, lynching, see NAACP Papers, Part 7, Series A, Group 1, Box C-360, and Reel 13; White, *A Man Called White*, pp. 123, 172; and Shay, *Judge Lynch*, pp. 247–48. On Scottsboro, see Dan T. Carter, *Scottsboro: A Tragedy of the American South* (Baton Rouge, 1969); James Goodman, *Stories of Scottsboro* (New York, 1994); White, *A Man Called White*, pp. 125–133; and Walter White, "The Negro and the Communists," *Harper's Magazine* 164, December 1931, pp. 62–72.

33. Walter White to Howard "Buck" Kester, October 31, 1934 (quote); Howard "Buck" Kester, Nashville, to Walter White, November 1, 1934; and Howard "Buck" Kester, to Walter White, November 7, 1934, NACCP Papers. See also Kester's report, published by the NAACP as a report by a "southern white university professor whose entire life has been spent in the South and whose family for generations has occupied high rank there." NAACP, *The Lynching of Claude Neal* (New York, 1934) p. 1. The NAACP also publicized the Neal lynching through extensive press reports, examples of which are NAACP, "Florida Officials Ignored NAACP Plea to Halt Advertising Lynching," (n.d. but after October 27, 1934), and "NAACP Investigator Says Secret Interracial Romance Was Basis of Florida Lynching," (n.d. but after November 16, 1934), in NAACP Papers, Part 7, Series A, Group 1, Box C-341 and Reel 4. McGovern, *Anatomy of a Lynching*, pp. 126–30.

34. See NAACP Part 11, Series B, Reel 28, for an example of a petition with two photographs of the bodies of lynch mob victims circulated by the NAACP and the American Society for Racial Tolerance. See the Pictures of Lynchings from the NAACP archives, Division of Prints and Photographs, Library of Congress, for a postcard with a picture of a lynch mob victim circulated to raise funds for the NAACP.

5

Who Were the Victims of Lynchings? Evidence from Mississippi and South Carolina, 1881–1940

Terence Finnegan

In recent years historians have returned with renewed enthusiasm to the task of explaining lynching in the South. Many explanations of lynching combine old interpretations with new twists on the "crisis" in late-nineteenth-century southern race relations that engendered the ferocity and barbarity of widespread lynching. Recently, Edward Ayers has argued that lynching typically occurred in rural, sparsely populated parts of the South, which had few towns, weak law enforcement, and little contact with more progressive parts of the region. This interpretation is reminiscent of those of earlier scholars, like James Elbert Cutler, Earl Fiske Young, and Arthur Raper, but Ayers also argues that lynching was a key tool in the repertoire of white supremacy.[1] Lynchings were infrequent, according to Ayers, where blacks and whites lived in close proximity with one another, presumably because regular contact and a shared past helped the two races better understand one another. But lynching was rampant where whites encountered "strange niggers" who had no roots in a community, who were transient, and who had little appreciation for the niceties of southern race relations.[2]

Lynching was more than an outgrowth of the fears that whites had of black criminality. Lynching typically was not the result of any "crime" committed by blacks but of violent conflict between blacks and whites that resulted from the inequities of the southern racial system. White fears of black transients and sexual offenders no doubt did much to fan the flames of lynching, but the root cause was the daily discord that existed among black and white southerners who knew and worked with one another. The dynamic behind lynching was not so much an extralegal effort to quash black criminality, but rather a visceral reaction to the intransigence and resistance of southern black workers to the daily manifestations of white supremacy.

The typical black lynching victim was far from an outcast in southern society. Most black victims were agricultural workers, primarily tenants, who had frequently lived and worked in the same area for years. Often these victims were accused of some crime against their landlord or supervisor. Over 60 percent of all black lynching incidents in Mississippi and South Carolina involved African-American agricultural workers.[3] As one might expect in two rural states, no significant difference existed in this regard between Mississippi and South Carolina (in the former, 62 percent of black victims were agricultural workers; in the latter, 63 percent). In slightly less than 90 percent of the agricultural lynchings for which information is available, whites accused tenants of committing a crime against their employer or some member of their employer's immediate family. Murder or assault accounted for over 50 percent of all the crimes charged against agricultural victims. In contrast to the stereotype, rape or attempted rape was cited in only about 15 percent of the lynching incidents that involved agricultural workers.

The next largest group of black lynching victims was nonfarm workers, from blacksmiths to stevedores and sailors. Nonfarm black victims were involved in about 19 percent of lynching incidents in Mississippi and in 20 percent of lynching incidents in South Carolina. As was the case with agricultural workers, whites typically lynched nonfarm workers for allegedly committing some crime against their employer. Murder and assault-related crimes accounted for approximately 42 percent of the alleged causes of lynching incidents that involved African-American nonfarm victims.

Unlike agricultural lynching incidents, however, alleged rape and other women-related crimes were the justification in almost 37 percent of nonfarm lynching incidents. Whites feared some working-class blacks, especially itinerant workers who seemed to have little regard for the niceties of white racial etiquette. Seminomadic black laborers, such as those who toiled in isolated lumber and turpentine camps, lived in a separate, isolated rural society. White anxiety over these drifters resulted in a greater percentage of lynching incidents for rape and female-related transgressions among nonfarm workers (36.8 percent) than among agricultural workers (22.5 percent).[4]

But despite the belief among whites that lynching was aimed primarily at "undesirable" elements, black criminals or outlaws were the victims in only about 11 percent of African-American lynching incidents. Victims in this category included persons who supposedly belonged to an organized band of criminals, convicts, ex-convicts, and persons wanted for various crimes. In Mississippi over 13 percent of black lynching incidents involved criminals, but in South Carolina the figure was only about 3 percent. This may have been because of the frontierlike conditions that existed in some Mississippi regions (such as the Piney Woods, where over one-third of black lynching victims were purported outlaws or criminals) and a greater sense of judicial efficacy that existed in South

Carolina. Murder-related crimes topped the reasons for lynching black criminals, being cited as the cause in about 45 percent of lynching incidents. The next most frequent charge against black "outlaw" victims was rape. Anecdotal evidence suggests that outlaw victims typically had no apparent connection with the person they were accused of harming, which reinforces the notion that outlaw victims were more distant from white society than were other black lynching victims.

But lynch mobs did not confine their work to the marginal or most oppressed blacks; another small but important group of victims were professional men and landowners. Blacks who had professional or supervisory positions were lynched in about 3.5 percent of black lynching incidents, as were members of the black agricultural elite—landowners. Whites often perceived these victims as being openly defiant of white racial etiquette; not surprisingly, most victims in this category were lynched in retaliation for murder and assault-related crimes or for no crime at all. South Carolina had more professional or landowning black victims than did Mississippi (13.3 percent and 5.5 percent respectively). The greater percentage of black landowners in South Carolina than in Mississippi probably accounts for this difference.[5] African-American landowners were somewhat underrepresented as lynching victims—probably because they had more personal autonomy and less contact with whites than did African-American tenants.

Although some scholars have suggested that blacks rarely challenged their white employers, evidence from Mississippi and South Carolina indicates otherwise.[6] The accounts of lynchings involving agricultural workers are filled with descriptions of African Americans being lynched for injuring or killing their employers during disputes and disagreements of all kinds. Whites lynched agricultural victims not simply because they were black, but because they dared to challenge (often physically) the superior social position of their white landlord or supervisor.

In July 1903, for example, Cato Garrett, a young black tenant from Mississippi's Natchez District, killed a popular and "well-connected" planter named Harry Stout. Garrett had argued with Stout about placing a mule in a meadow, and when words came to blows, Garrett stabbed Stout in the heart with a small pen-knife. Although authorities convened a special grand jury to ensure that Garrett would receive a speedy trial, three days after the killing fifteen of Stout's friends took Garrett from a law officer and hung him on a small road near the scene of the killing. No arrests were made.[7]

Frank De Loache and his son John were two tenants lynched in the Inner Coastal Plain region of South Carolina in December 1905 after they were accused of killing an "influential and prosperous" farmer named Hayne Craddock. Craddock had come to De Loache's cabin with two other black tenants to collect a ginning debt. When the elder De Loache refused to pay, Craddock assaulted him. The one-armed De Loache called for his son John to help, and when John De Loache promptly appeared with a gun, a struggle ensued, and Craddock fell dead with a wound in the back. The news of the killing spread quickly, but the local magistrate managed to arrest the De Loaches before a mob could form.

Unfortunately for the De Loaches, the magistrate chose to lock them in an outhouse on the Craddock place and leave them overnight in the care of a constable. The next morning, a large crowd of Craddock's angry friends and relatives had gathered at Craddock's farm. The constable was utterly incapable of preventing the subsequent lynching even though some whites admitted that Craddock may well have been killed by the two black tenants who had accompanied him to De Loache's cabin. After the constable allowed some of the mob to beat the De Loaches for a half hour or so, some of the white men present argued against a lynching. But others insisted that "this is a white man's country and we ain't going to let it go just so." Around 11:30 A.M. the constable finally wired for help, but by noon the two De Loaches were dead, shot to death near a little stream some two hundred yards from a road. The failure of authorities to protect the De Loaches prompted South Carolina Governor D. C. Heyward to launch an official investigation. Eventually seven "prominent" farmers were arrested in connection with the lynching. The *Charleston News and Courier* admitted that a conviction was unlikely but insisted that "the fact is being established in the public mind that the lyncher has to fight for his life and liberty." No doubt the *News and Courier* was correct when it claimed that "every man, woman, and child within a ten mile radius" of the lynching knew who the lynchers were, but on the day of the hearing all but one of the state's witnesses were black. All seven men arrested were eventually released because of insufficient evidence.[8]

African-American tenants routinely resisted the attempts of white employers to impose their will on work arrangements, crop settlements, monetary matters, freedom of movement, or interpersonal relations, which resulted in scores of lynchings that grew out of these disputes.[9] Whites felt compelled to act not because they doubted the ability of the legal system to impose an acceptable punishment nor to salvage the honor of a moral degenerate; instead, they believed that if they did not lynch these tenants that "no white man who had wronged a Negro would be safe." If African-American tenants had not been resisting their landlords in myriad ways, such fear would have been unwarranted. Numerous contemporary observers, including NAACP activists James Weldon Johnson, William Pickens, and Walter White, believed that white landlords' exploitation of African-American farm laborers was the fundamental cause of lynching.[10] In essence, many lynchings resulted from the refusal of African Americans to submit to the indignities of white racism.[11]

The correlation between the demand for labor and lynching incidents is a moderately strong .35, meaning that, in general, as tenants spent more time in the fields they were more likely to be lynched. This is consistent with the notion that lynching often stemmed from work-related disagreements that tenants had with their landlords.[12]

When tenants worked less, as in midwinter and especially in the month of August, fewer lynchings occurred. The decline in lynchings during October and November, the peak time for cotton harvesting, probably resulted from the improved position that tenants found themselves in at this time of year. Landlords may have been more accommodating around harvest time, lest their laborers leave and allow the cotton to rot in the fields.

The increase in lynchings in December probably resulted from the "settling-up" that usually occurred at the end of the season. Such was the case with tenant Robert Motely, who labored on a cotton plantation in the Mississippi Yazoo Delta.[13] When Motely objected to the settlement offered by prosperous planter R. W. Silvey, Silvey attempted to horsewhip Motely. After Silvey kicked Motely in the face several times, Motely's brother William shot Silvey, mortally wounding the planter. William Motley escaped, but Robert Motely was not so lucky and was jailed at Lambert. The night after the incident an armed mob broke into the Lambert jail and hung Motely. The problem for whites in the postbellum South was that black tenants were not the submissive slaves that supposedly had contentedly worked the land before the war.[14]

The unwillingness of whites to accept the culture of freedom that blacks dreamed and hoped for brought about the "crisis of the New South," which involved a widening chasm of suspicion between whites and blacks born after slavery. In stark contrast to the loyal and peaceful slaves of antebellum lore, many whites now detected a "new sort of black character: the 'desperado' or 'bad nigger'" in the late-nineteenth-century South.[15] Unlike the beloved, docile, infantile darky, whom whites thought they knew so well, "bad niggers" scoffed at the pretensions of white caste, authority, and honor.

No African-American worker generated more fear and suspicion among whites than the itinerant laborer, who was an "outsider" to both the black and white communities. The slavelike status of many black manual workers made them the target of derision even among African Americans. The criminal background of some laborers and the rather unsavory moral conditions that prevailed in many of the camps, moreover, exacerbated the stereotypical fears of whites.[16] Indeed, the unexpected appearance of a strange African-American worker could sometimes send ripples of fear through a white community. If such a worker attacked, threatened, or scared a white woman, his fate was often death.

Consider the fate of the stranger, Willie Spain, who came to Badham, South Carolina, in late August 1906. The twenty-one-year-old Spain had arrived from North Carolina to work in the lumber industry. Spain had been able to secure only intermittent employment with the Dorchester Lumber Company, however, and one afternoon he was seen running from the house of the lumber company store manager, S. L. Connor, who briefly struggled with Spain but was unable to subdue him. Spain had apparently intended to rob the residence but was frightened away by the screams of Connor's eleven-year-old daughter. A posse captured Spain within two hours and turned him over to the custody of Sheriff

M. M. Limehouse. Spain was in jail all of a half hour before a mob came to lynch him. The pusillanimous Limehouse allowed a mob to take Spain from the jail without resistance before he wired the governor for assistance.[17] After a perfunctory identification by the girl, the mob mutilated Spain's body with so many gunshots that it was beyond recognition.[18] Working-class African-American lynching victims were the only social group accused of attacking more females than males, further evidence of the paranoia that whites felt toward many nonfarm black workers.

Young African-American strangers accused of scaring or attacking white women, however, were not the only blacks who engendered fear in whites. Jordan Parker, for instance, was a "hard case" living near Purvis in Mississippi's Piney Woods region.[19] The sixty-five-year-old Parker was the youngest of four brothers, all of whom died under violent circumstances. Two of Parker's brothers had reportedly been killed after the war by former Confederate soldiers who claimed that the brothers had robbed their homes while they were away. A third brother had allegedly been a robber who operated around the Pearl River swamp. After a series of robberies, whites organized a manhunt for the brother, who was shot to death at his hut.

The white community living around Poplarville and Purvis feared Parker. Local lore had it that he had helped murder eleven men fifteen years previously and then sent them adrift down the Pearl River, each bearing a card marked "Free Ticket to Hell." Five years later, a brother of one of the men whom Parker had killed shot Parker and left him for dead. But Parker survived the incident and became a recluse, supporting his family through hunting and fishing.

In mid-December 1884, a New Orleans and Northeastern train killed one of Parker's pigs, prompting him to send a claim to the railroad for $2.25. When the railroad failed to promptly compensate him, whites claimed he became enraged and made it known that he would "ditch" a train. Three days before Christmas, a New Orleans and Northeastern train with about one hundred persons aboard derailed on a curve about a mile north of Purvis. A white engineer and a black fireman were scalded to death.

On Christmas day Parker was arrested and jailed at Poplarville. News of the arrest spread quickly, and a large crowd was present for the hearing. Although a number of Purvis's "most respectable" citizens testified against Parker, the state had little conclusive evidence, so the judge decided to send the case to county court in Marion, some forty miles distant.

That night, however, a mob of thirty-five unmasked men rammed a rail through the jail door at Poplarville while the guards inside were ostensibly sleeping. Around 3 A.M. the mob boarded a southbound train with Parker in tow. As the train proceeded south toward Picayune, the mob tortured Parker with a red hot poker, applying it to his sides and hands. The train stopped at an abandoned sand pit about ten miles south of Poplarville, where the mob tied him to a pine tree in plain view of the tracks and shot him to death. Pinned to his breast was a flyleaf that read, "This is the train wrecker who wrecked the train on Dec. 22. Tried by Judge Lynch and sentenced to death. This should be a caution to all other train wreckers." The "respectable" citizens of Purvis and Poplarville remained silent about the lynching, no doubt relieved that such a threatening black man had been given his due. Needless to say, no effort was made to prosecute the deceased engineer's friends, who were widely believed to have been responsible for the lynching.

If not in direct conflict with employers themselves, other black nonfarm workers were in harm's way simply because of labor tensions within the white community or because they held jobs whites wanted. Most conspicuous in this regard were rail workers. When workers struck the Illinois Central railroad in the fall of 1911, for instance, the company hired black strikebreakers, who immediately became the targets of violence.[20] The railroad was unable to operate its shops at McComb, Mississippi, until Governor Earl Brewer ordered over four hundred national guardsmen to McComb to maintain order. To protect the African-American workers, the railroad built a stockade around its shops and opened a commissary inside so that strikebreakers would not need to venture out.

Some of the black workers were locals, however, who returned home each evening. One evening in early January 1912, a group of African-American workers was returning to their homes in nearby Summit when white strikers fired on them. Two of the black workers were killed and one was mortally wounded. Six striking white workers were eventually charged with the crime, but a grand jury indicted only two of them. At the trial of one of the defendants, on March 1912, the state presented eyewitness testimony from two of the African-American workers, who identified the defendant as a member of the mob. Nevertheless, the jury deliberated for less than a half hour before returning a verdict for acquittal. The strike had divided the white community, with African-American workers caught between the company's interests and those of the white workers. Exasperated by the acquittal, the trial judge, who was in sympathy with the railroad, observed despairingly that the "material progress" of Mississippi would continue to be slow as long as such crimes were "hidden out or winked at by many of our [white] citizens."[21]

If many whites feared or loathed nonfarm black workers, they were often positively terrified of African-American felons and "outlaws." The crime wave that plagued the rural South in the last quarter of the nineteenth century helped change "the dominant image of blacks in the white mind . . . from inferior child to aggressive and dangerous animal."[22] The fear of black outlaws led many whites to regard lynching as a positive good. A young white female teacher from the eastern piedmont of South Carolina, for example, wrote her fiancee about the laudatory activities of a lynch mob that hanged five notorious black "bandits." The woman was "overjoyed" at the lynching, saying that "the negroes deserved worse punishment." Far from acting rashly, the lynchers had, according to the white teacher, viewed the matter from "all sides" before deciding on a "wise" and "proper punishment" for the "desperate" band of outlaws.[23]

Such "wise and proper punishment" was unfortunately quite routine in some parts of Mississippi and South Carolina. In Mississippi's Old Natchez region, for instance, at least seven outlaws or convicts were lynched in less than thirty months in the early 1890s.[24] Two of these lynching incidents involved gangs of thieves, who had allegedly committed a series of crimes over an extended period of time. Smith Tooley and John Adams, for example, were lynched in July 1892 at the Vicksburg courthouse after whites accused them of a series of robberies and one murder.[25] The sentiment against Tooley and Adams was so strong that the governor ordered the Warren County Light Artillery to guard the jail at night. On the night of July 5, however, a mob of over six hundred men stormed the jail, which was surrounded by a brick wall twenty feet high. The Warren County Light Artillery had a gatling gun and could have easily dispersed the mob, but, as one observer noted, "it was useless to expect them to fire upon their relatives and friends," and only the first lieutenant reported for duty. The mob used a huge pole to ram the jail gate and was inside the jail in about fifteen minutes. Not wanting to act "rashly," the mob interrogated each of the victims for about an hour and even had a secretary record their statements. When it became apparent that the two victims continued to talk only to forestall their deaths, some of the mob began to clamor for the lynching to commence. Both men were hanged in the courthouse yard before an excited crowd, although those in charge of the hanging supposedly remained calm. Ida B. Wells-Barnett later claimed that white men who profited from the goods that Tooley and Adams had stolen had organized the lynching out of fear that they would be exposed.[26]

Even more terrifying than a marauding band of thieves was an African-American convict who allegedly committed some heinous crime while free from prison. Many of these lynching victims were prison "trusties" who, because of their willingness to help discipline other prisoners, enjoyed special privileges, which sometimes included leaving the camp or jail. Lawson Patton was a trusty lynched at Oxford, Lafayette County, in Mississippi's Pontotoc Hills region in September 1908.[27] Home of the University of Mississippi, Oxford was one of the more enlightened towns in Mississippi at that time.[28] Patton was a habitual offender who had run a "blind tiger" drinking establishment for years. Although Patton frequented the Oxford jail on a regular basis, he did not have a reputation for being impudent or disrespectful toward whites. One of the white prisoners in the Oxford jail was a tenant named McMillen, who had been convicted the previous June of resisting arrest. The man's wife and three children lived on a nearby farm, and McMillen was in the habit of sending his wife messages through Patton.

In the early afternoon of September 8, 1908, Patton delivered a message to Mrs. McMillen from her husband, but remained on the farm until the woman ordered him to leave. Patton was apparently drunk at the time, perhaps because the evening before he had paid his fine and had been released from jail. In any event, Patton and Mrs. McMilllen argued, and when a daughter went to investigate she found her mother dead, with her throat slashed from ear to ear.

The local sheriff quickly organized a posse that included practically the entire white male population of Oxford. A running chase ensued in which Patton was shot at some one hundred times. Although wounded several times, Patton probably would have escaped had not two boys with shotguns filled his back with buckshot and held him at bay. Patton was brought to town under heavy guard and placed in jail. The bloodied and weakened Patton presented a "bestial appearance" as the mob paraded him through the streets. Almost immediately the town was full of armed men and boys who openly talked of lynching him. When Judge W. A. Roane realized that a lynching was imminent, he tried to persuade the mob to disperse. Roane promised the crowd that Patton would be given a speedy trial when the county court convened in a week. The Reverend W. S. Spruggins from the local Methodist church also spoke, urging the mob to go home. Following Roane's plea for restraint, however, former U.S. Senator W. V. Sullivan delivered a sensational harangue demanding Patton's immediate execution. Later, when questioned about his actions, Sullivan revealed the white community's sense of outrage that a black man would dare commit such a crime. "I led the mob," Sullivan proclaimed, "and I'm proud of it. I directed every movement of the mob, and I did every thing I could to see that he was lynched. Cut a white woman's throat! And a negro! Of course I wanted him lynched. I saw his body dangling from a tree this morning, and I'm glad of it."[29]

The Lafayette County jail was perhaps the strongest in Mississippi, but after Sullivan's speech the mob set about their task with determination. After rushing the jail and breaking through the front doors, the mob used chisels and sledgehammers to break open the steel doors. The sheriff concluded that resistance was pointless and abandoned the jail so that he would not be forced to give up his prisoner. After two hours of work the mob broke through a massive steel door to the cheers of hundreds outside the jail. Their elation was short-lived, however, when the mob discovered that yet another steel door stood between them and Patton. The mob then decided it would be faster to break through the brick walls of the prison, but this tedious work had to be done on ladders. It took the mob another three hours to penetrate the prison walls. Hundreds of men helped in the work, and reinforcements were brought in on the Illinois Central railroad. "It is doubtful if ever before in the history of mobs," said one reporter on the scene, that "there has been a more systematic and long-continued assault made on a jail or door than has been witnessed by hundreds of Lafayette, Marshall and Yallobusha citizens here tonight." All the while, none of those in the crowd tried to disguise themselves in any fashion. Actively participating were all types of white male citizens, both men and boys, blacksmiths, artisans, and farmers. Business and professional men of all kinds (with the notable exception of ministers) eagerly watched the mob capture Patton and lynch him. The following day, Judge Roane, a group of ministers, and eighteen other citizens all condemned the lynching. Nevertheless, the coroner's jury decided that Patton had been killed by parties unknown. Most in Oxford seemed "satisfied with the actions of the mob," who had once again made perfectly clear to the African-American community the harsh, brutal realities that buttressed white supremacy.[30]

The most offensive crime an African-American convict could commit, of course, was rape. The 1928 New Year's Eve burning of Charley Sheppard, a trusty from the Parchman Prison Farm who had allegedly killed a prison guard and then kidnapped and raped the man's daughter, attracted the largest crowd to ever witness a lynching in either Mississippi or South Carolina.[31] The forty-one-year-old Sheppard was serving a twenty-year sentence for manslaughter before he supposedly beat and stabbed to death J. D. Duvall, a carpenter sergeant at the prison farm. The powerfully built Sheppard said he cut the fifty-five-year-old Duvall's throat because Duvall had beaten him for returning late from a leave of absence. After killing Duvall, Sheppard abducted one of Duvall's eight children, an eighteen-year-old daughter named Ruth.

For three days, over one thousand armed men scoured three counties in search of Sheppard (he had released the girl after twenty-four hours). Sheppard was eventually found on the plantation of Miss Laura Mae Keeler, where Sheppard's brother Tom was a tenant. Because Keeler feared mob violence, she had Tom Sheppard brought to her house the night before his brother arrived. When a cook on the plantation found Charley Sheppard in one of the tenant cabins, Keeler notified authorities of his whereabouts and asked that armed guards and bloodhounds be sent to aid in Sheppard's capture.

Not wanting to see Sheppard lynched, however, Keeler thought better of the matter and decided to talk to Sheppard herself before a mob arrived. Unarmed, Keeler went to the cabin Sheppard was hiding in, and he agreed to give up if Keeler turned him over to the sheriff. Sheppard told Keeler that he would "shoot it out" if Keeler did not take responsibility for his safety. Miss Keeler then went back to the house and told the armed men who had already arrived that she was going to escort Sheppard to the sheriff. Amazingly, the men reluctantly agreed and sent another convict trusty and a white man from Jackson to accompany Keeler.

Keeler and Sheppard started for the sheriff early in the morning and took back roads to avoid the many posses in the area. But word spread quickly of Sheppard's capture, and shortly after noon an armed mob of at least fifty cars, led by one of Duvall's brothers, stopped Keeler's car near Cleveland and demanded that Sheppard be turned over to them. Realizing it was futile to resist, Keeler pleaded that the mob relinquish Sheppard to authorities.

The mob toured the countryside to allow every possible person to see Sheppard and "visited several negro camps in which Sheppard's impending fate was described with warnings to the blacks." At Lombardy a makeshift platform was constructed in front of the May Brothers' store, from which Sheppard confessed to his alleged crimes. All the lights of the store were turned on Sheppard to allow the crowd to see him. Word of Sheppard's impending burning at one of the prison farm gates was sent out "by all possible means throughout the countryside." Thousands of cars joined a silent parade to Camp 11, where Sheppard had released Ruth Duvall some days earlier and now was to be burned. So many cars converged on the scene that every gas station in the area was drained of fuel.[32]

By early evening six thousand people had gathered at the site of the burning. When Sheppard finally arrived, mob members methodically built a huge wood pyre. As the bound and strapped Sheppard lay on the wood, mob members doused the pile with gasoline that participants had carried to the scene in all types of containers. Fearing that Sheppard might die from the gas fumes, some in the mob stuffed his nose and mouth with mud. The burning was delayed several minutes when it was learned that Duvall's son and brother-in-law were on their way to the scene. When they arrived, the two men were taken to the front of the crowd and given the honor of shooting Sheppard if he tried to escape.

Shortly before the pyre was lit, a "wild-eyed" mob member "leaped atop the pile of wood, straddled the negro's body and cut his ears off with a pocket knife." This was the only bodily mutilation reported against Sheppard. The burning began about quarter past seven. The crowd gasped in amazement as the flames shot high in the air. Women shrieked with terror as Sheppard "twisted and fought his ropes, cursing his captors and white people generally."[33] As Sheppard roiled back and forth in the flames, he finally rolled completely off the pile of wood. When Sheppard tried to get to his feet, some of the mob raised their guns but were stopped by others who argued that Sheppard should suffer as much as his life would allow. Some of the mob quickly tossed Sheppard back on the pyre and poured fresh cans of gasoline on the burning bier. Some witnesses claimed Sheppard continued to fight the ropes which bound him for forty-five minutes before finally succumbing to the flames.

When the burning was over, souvenir hunters carried off body parts. The next morning Sheppard's skull and other body parts were seen strewn along the roadside; those who took them had apparently been sickened by the odor. The man who had cut off Sheppard's ears, however, proudly displayed them at a gas station in Drew the following day. As for the authorities, they had, in the words of Governor Theodore Bilbo, "neither the time nor the money to investigate 2000 people."[34]

Whites also lynched landowning or even prominent, wealthy blacks for not "knowing their place" in white society. Whites were more sensitive to the actions of successful blacks and would often seize on any excuse to eliminate the good fortune of those deemed privileged. The case of the African-American postmaster Frazier Baker is a good example of how successful African Americans could be lynched not for any alleged crime but simply because their status contradicted white notions of black inferiority.

Lake City, South Carolina, a "white man's town," had fewer than a dozen black residents, none of whom owned "a foot of land" within the corporate limits of the city. Hence white residents were shocked in September 1897 when Baker, a forty-year-old "coal black" schoolteacher and Colored Farmer's Allianceman from Florence County, was appointed postmaster of Lake City. E. H. Deas, the black deputy collector of internal revenue for South Carolina, had recommended Baker for the job, but trouble began almost immediately after Baker assumed office. Whites complained that Baker was "uncivil, ignorant, and lazy." They noted that under the previous, white postmaster there had been three mail deliveries per day, but that Baker managed only one.[35]

Baker did reduce service, but only after whites repeatedly tried to mob him. In December 1897 a postal inspector was sent to investigate the trouble. When the inspector recommended that the office be closed, whites burnt the post office to the ground in January 1898, hoping that Baker would be forced to resign since no white person would rent the government space in town. Seeking to ensure Baker's safety, the U.S. Postmaster General ordered Baker to restrict mail delivery to daylight hours. After the government acquired an old schoolhouse in the "suburbs," however, some of the racial tension evidently dissipated, because Baker felt safe enough to send for his wife and six children in early February. But local whites were determined to remove Baker from office at any cost, and a week or so after his family arrived they resolved to kill him. A few days before his death Baker had received new threats on his life, which he reported to Washington.[36]

Late on the night of February 21, 1898, Baker awoke to find the post office (which doubled as the family's residence) in flames. He gathered his family and told his son, Lincoln, to sound the alarm; but as soon as the boy opened the door shots rang out. Realizing the danger, Baker dragged his son back from the door, screamed at the lynchers, and ran back and forth in the small room praying for God's deliverance. When the flames became unbearable, Baker and his family started again for the door, but before he opened it a bullet struck and killed his two year-old daughter Julia. As Baker opened the door a barrage of bullets greeted him, and he fell backward on his wife's lap, dead. In the confusion Lavinia Baker was also shot in the arm, but she somehow managed to gather her panicked family and they crawled out of the house and hid in some nearby bushes. Two of the younger children escaped unharmed, but three older children received serious gunshot wounds. The family remained in Lake City for three days after the lynching, during which time they received no medical treatment for their injuries.[37]

The cowardly attack on the Baker family elicited condemnation from all quarters. Governor William Ellerbe called the lynching "the worst incident that had happened in the state in years." The Augusta (Georgia) *Chronicle* opined that the lynchers had "placed themselves beyond the pale of sympathy, even of the bitter opponents of negro office-holding." Although the *Chronicle* accused Washington of the worst folly for "trying to force upon a community a public official who was repugnant to the people," it noted that "an unacceptable postmaster does not furnish justification for the murder and massacre of women and children." The Columbia *Record* recommended that every ringleader in the lynching should be hanged and said that "the lives and the property of colored citizens are as dear to them as those of white citizens are to them, and they should be protected in their enjoyment."[38]

The occasional lynching of African-American women provides additional evidence that the practice punished blacks who advocated or sought social equality. Women were victims in at least twenty-six lynchings in Mississippi and South Carolina. Over half of the African-American women lynched died with their husbands, sons, or lovers, who had usually been accused of murdering a white man. But of those black women lynched alone, only one-quarter were accused of a murder-related crime. Some scholars have suggested that white men found black women less threatening than black men, but African-American women were also lynched for challenging the white caste system.[39] In early 1881, for example, whites in the western piedmont of South Carolina lynched an old black woman for allegedly burning the barn of a prominent planter. In July 1894 whites lynched a black woman in Simpson County, Mississippi, allegedly for inciting a race war. A white posse from the Yazoo Delta brutally beat and shot a black female tenant named Jennie Collins, a mother and longtime resident of the area, after she refused to allow them to search her cabin.[40]

Although mobs that lynched African-American women were condemned by many whites, the brutal nature of their actions often evoked a defensive response from local whites. In December 1895 whites lynched a black man and his mother in South Carolina's Outer Coastal Plain. Broxton Bridge was a heavily black township of Colleton County that whites claimed had been beset by a recent crime wave. After a local white church was robbed of a Bible and some furniture, some white men apparently decided to make an example of young Isham Kearse, who was suspected of committing several robberies and of burning a store. When four prominent white men, including a doctor, learned that Kearse was staying at his mother Hannah Walker's house near Broxton Ford, they enlisted the aid of two other white men who knew Kearse.

The mob encountered Isham on the road to his mother's and immediately "arrested" him. They put a rope around his neck, tied him to a buggy, and dragged him two miles to a ferry, where they waited for two other mob members to retrieve Hannah Walker and Isham's seventeen-year-old wife Rosa. When the women arrived, the mob stripped the three naked and whipped them with an old buggy trace. Isham and his mother were beaten so badly that a physician later described their bodies as "pulpified."[41] Rosa Kearse, who had recently had a baby, was also beaten from head to foot, but she survived the attack. The next morning Isham's body was found at the scene of the whipping. One hundred yards away, his mother's body was found lying on top of a log in a pool of water about knee deep. Rosa Kearse managed to crawl home, but was in critical condition.

The savageness of the lynching elicited widespread condemnation from many of South Carolina's white papers.[42] But some local whites reacted bitterly to these criticisms, saying that in the months before the lynching a wave of arson had engulfed the area. Homes, tenant houses, barns, stables, gin houses, sawmills, stores, and crops had all been mysteriously burned. In addition, at least six white men had been allegedly stabbed or shot by blacks. "Notwithstanding all these crimes," wrote one irate resident, "only one negro has suffered. Numerous warrants have been sworn out, but never served from the simple fact that the fellows wanted could not be found." Local white residents had even petitioned the governor to end the crime wave, but had received no reply.[43]

Governor John Gary Evans, nephew of one of South Carolina's most notoriously racist politicians, reacted by assigning a state detective to investigate the murder of Isham Kearse. The subsequent report indicated that the lynchers had been after Kearse for some time and attributed the lynching to "pure cussedness." In time, four white men from "four of the largest and most respectable families" in the state were tried for the murder of Hannah Walker but were speedily acquitted.[44]

African-American women were victims in only about 3.5 percent of all lynchings, but over 11 percent of all incidents that involved documented torture had black women victims. All lynchings were barbarous, and the murder of women by mobs was certainly no exception. Whites lynched black females infrequently, but when they did so they often intended the incident to be a vicious reminder about the unrestrained mandates of white supremacy. The desire to send a brutal message to the African-American community probably explains why over 80 percent of lynching incidents that involved black females in Mississippi and South Carolina occurred in majority black regions. The extraordinary depravity exhibited in many lynchings of African-American females showed, according to Walter White, how "the race problem in this country has resolved into the saving of the bodies of blacks and the souls of whites."[45]

In the predominantly rural states of Mississippi and South Carolina, caste conflict was most prevalent in the landlord-tenant relationship, which explains why the majority of African-American lynching victims were agricultural workers. African-American farm workers regularly challenged the injustices of their white oppressors, and this often led to violent conflict. When a black man got the better of a dispute with his white employer, whites often responded with a lynching in the hopes of eliminating future affronts to white supremacy; hence lynchings became an integral feature and a routine occurrence in the white caste system of the South. Black workers outside the agricultural sector were also at risk for lynching. The itinerant, isolated, and bawdy working conditions of many African-American laborers invoked suspicion and fear among the white population. These African Americans seemed particularly threatening to whites, which explains why black nonfarm laborers were lynched more often for alleged sexual crimes than were black agricultural laborers. African Americans who had achieved some success in southern society were also the occasional target of lynch mobs. These individuals were often lynched for maintaining their dignity in the face of white harassment or simply because their position in society was an affront to some whites. In extraordinary circumstances, whites even lynched

African-American women, often with untamed brutality, so as to reinforce the notion that every member of the black community would be held accountable for the "undisciplined freedom" that prompted African Americans to resist the everyday manifestations of racial oppression.

NOTES

1. For the older interpretations see James E. Cutler, *Lynch Law: An Investigation into the History of Lynching in the United States* (New York, 1905); Earl F. Young, "Relation of Lynching to the Size of Political Areas," *Sociology and Social Research* 12 (March–April 1928); pp. 348–53; and Arthur F. Raper, *The Tragedy of Lynching* (Chapel Hill, N.C., 1933); Edward L. Ayers, *The Promise of the New South: Life after Reconstruction* (New York, 1992), pp. 156–59.

2. Ayers, *The Promise of the New South*, pp. 156–157.

3. For the majority of lynching victims, no information about their societal status is available. Consequently, my conclusions must be interpreted with caution. Nevertheless, I was able to identify the societal status of about 38 percent of all lynching victims in Mississippi and South Carolina.

4. W. Fitzhugh Brundage, *Lynching in the New South: Georgia and Virginia, 1880–1930* (Urbana, Ill., 1993), pp. 81–82; Edward L. Ayers, *Vengeance and Justice: Crime and Punishment in the Nineteenth-Century American South* (New York, 1984), pp. 236–43; Nollie Hickman, *Mississippi Harvest: Lumbering in the Long-Leaf Pine Belt, 1840–1915* (Oxford, 1962), p. 139.

5. Loren Schweninger found that in 1890, for example, 21 percent of black farmers in South Carolina were landowners, while only 13 percent of black farmers in Mississippi were the same. Loren Schweninger, *Black Property Owners in the South, 1790–1915* (Urbana, Ill., 1990), p. 164.

6. Brundage, *Lynching in the New South*, p. 122.

7. *New Orleans Daily-Picayune*, July 7, 8, 1903.

8. *Charleston News and Courier*, December 27, 28, 29, 1905, and February 3, 4, 5, 8, 1906.

9. Among the lynching incidents that grew out of strained landlord-tenant relations, at least forty-seven involved the murder or attempted murder of a landlord or overseer (or a relative of the same) by a tenant.

10. Walter White, "An Example of Democracy in Mississippi," Ms, National Association for the Advancement of Colored People Papers, Series A, Reel 13, Frames 1155–1163, Library of Congress. James Weldon Johnson, "The Practice of Lynching," *Century* 115 (November 1927), pp. 65–70; Walter White, *Rope and Faggot* (New York, 1929), chap. 5; William Pickens, *Lynching and Debt Slavery* (New York, 1921); Herbert Shapiro, *White Violence and Black Response: From Reconstruction to Montgomery* (Amherst, Mass., 1988), pp. 198–99.

11. The information on labor requirements is taken from Warren C. Whatley, "Southern Agrarian Labor Contracts as Impediments to Cotton Mechanization," *Journal of Economic History* 47 (1987), pp. 68–69. The major cotton producing regions included are the Black Prairie, Old Natchez, and Yazoo Delta regions from Mississippi and the three piedmont regions (eastern, upper, and western) along with the Inner Coastal Plain

from South Carolina. For further information on these regions, see Terence Finnegan, "'At the Hands of Parties Unknown': Lynching in Mississippi and South Carolina, 1881–1940" (Ph.D. diss., University of Illinois, 1993), chap. 1.

12. If lynching incidents were unrelated to labor demand, the correlation would have been O; if, on the other hand, lynching incidents had varied exactly with labor demand, the correlation would have been 1. The correlation was obtained by computing the *Pearson's r* between the average number of black lynching incidents (perpetrated by white mobs) per month and the average labor requirements per month to cultivate an acre of cotton. Long ago James Elbert Cutler noted the relationship between field work and lynching in his classic study, *Lynch Law*. Cutler hypothesized that the decline in lynching during August resulted from the black custom of attending religious revivals during that month, while the increase in December was possibly related to the "indulgence in excesses" among African Americans celebrating Christmas. See Cutler, *Lynch Law*, p. 165.

13. Information on this lynching can be found in NAACP files, series A, Reel 13, Frames 1000–1001.

14. This was, of course, the same reason that whites had hung slaves in the antebellum South. On slave hangings and honor-related violence among blacks, see Ayers, *Vengeance and Justice*, pp. 136, 234; on blacks being lynched for rejecting the constraints of the white caste system, see George Wright, *Racial Violence in Kentucky, 1865–1940: Lynchings, Mob Rule, and "Legal Lynchings"* (Baton Rouge, 1990), p. 10; and White, *Rope*, pp. 103–5.

15. Ayers, *Vengeance and Justice*, p. 231.

16. Ibid., p. 243; Brundage, *Lynching in the New South*, p. 114–15. Hickman, *Mississippi Harvest*, pp. 148–50.

17. Limehouse's conduct met with some scorn even among whites. Some local ruffians apparently took delight in chiding Limehouse for his cowardice. One Thomas Harley, for instance, who had been tried and convicted in absentia for assault because Limehouse had refused to arrest him, informed the *Dorchester* (S. C.) *Eagle* that he would have surrendered but was afraid "that I would have been lynched by a mob as others have been while in the custody of Limehouse." See Jack Mullins, "Lynching in South Carolina, 1900–1914" (M.A. thesis, University of South Carolina, 1961), pp. 55–57.

18. For details concerning Spain's lynching, see *Charleston News and Courier*, August 24, 25, 26, 1906.

19. Accounts of Parker's life and lynching can be found in *New Orleans Daily-Picayune*, December 28, 29, 1884.

20. Information on the strike and the lynching can be found in *New Orleans Daily-Picayune*, January 18, 20, 22, 30, 1912; February 1, 16, 1912; March 1, 1912. Also see *U.S. Congress, Senate, Commission on Industrial Relations Report and Testimony* (64th Cong., 1st sess., 1915–1916), S. Doc. 28, 9714–9715.

21. Jacquelyn Dowd Hall, *Revolt Against Chivalry: Jessie Daniel Ames and the Women's Campaign Against Lynching* (New York, 1979), p. 133.

22. Ibid. On the late-nineteenth-century crime wave, see Ayers, *Vengeance and Justice*, pp. 169–184.

23. Letter from unknown female teacher (Bissie) to W. L. McKeown, April 15, 1887, uncatalogued, South Caroliniana Library, University of South Carolina, Columbia.

24. In the early years of the twentieth century, the Piney Woods region of Mississippi experienced a similar outbreak, in which five convicts (one was an ex-convict) were lynched in slightly less than forty months from October of 1904 to December of 1907. For details, see *New Orleans Daily-Picayune*, October 9, 1904; August 5, 1905; October 22, 1906; December 16, 1907.

25. *New Orleans Daily-Picayune*, July 6, 1892.

26. Ida B. Wells-Barnett, *On Lynchings: Southern Horrors, a Red Record, Mob Rule in New Orleans* (New York, 1969), p. 24.

27. The account of Patton's lynching is drawn from *New Orleans Daily-Picayune*, September 9, 10, 1908; *New York Times*, September 9, 10, 1908; and letter from W. A. Roane to E. F. Noel, September 13, 1908, Record Group 27, Volume 209, Folder 158, Mississippi Department of Archives and History, Jackson.

28. Lafayette County was, of course, William Faulkner's home. He undoubtedly knew of the Patton lynching, especially since a brother of one of his classmates participated in the mob. Faulkner's famous character Joe Christmas is at least partially based on Lawson Patton. See Jean Mullin Yonke, "William Faulkner as a Moralist and Cultural Critic: A Comparison of His Views with Those of Historians and Social Scientists" (Ph.D. diss., University of Kansas, 1981), p. 194.

29. *New York Times*, September 10, 1908.

30. *New Orleans Daily-Picayune*, September 10, 1908.

31. Information on the Sheppard lynching can be found in NAACP files, Series A, Reel 13, Frames 740–749; 1038–1039.

32. Jackson (Miss.) *Daily News*, January 1, 1929.

33. Ibid.

34. *New York World*, January 2, 1929.

35. *Charleston News and Courier*, February 22, 23, 24, 25, 26, 27, 28, 1898; April 12, 1899.

36. Ibid., April 14, 1899.

37. Ibid., February 27, 1898; July 2, 1898.

38. Ibid., February 26, 1898.

39. John Dollard, *Caste and Class in a Southern Town*, 2nd edition (New York, 1949), pp. 289–90; Brundage, *Lynching in the New South*, pp. 80–81.

40. *New York Times*, April 18, 1881; *New Orleans Daily-Picayune*, July 25, 1894. See also NAACP, Series A, Reel 13, Frames 371–401.

41. *Charleston News and Courier*, December 24, 1895.

42. *Charleston News and Courier*, December 7, 1895; December 18, 1895; December 26, 1895.

43. *Charleston News and Courier*, January 9, 1896.

44. *Charleston News and Courier*, February 25, 1896.

45. *New York Times*, January 3, 1927.

II

SOUTHERN HISTORY THROUGH LIFE HISTORY

6

Thomas Thistlewood Becomes a Creole

Trevor Burnard

> Sir, A Good Ship and easy gales have at last brought me to this part of the New World. New indeed in regard of ours, for here I find everything alter'd. . . .
>
> Britannia rose to my View all gay, with native Freedom blest, the seat of Arts, The Nurse of Learning, the Seat of Liberty, and Friend of every Virtue, where the meanest swain, with quiet Ease, possesses the Fruits of his hard Toil, contented with his Lot; while I was now to settle in a Place not half inhabited, cursed with intestine Broils, where slavery was establish'd, and the poor toiling Wretches work'd in the sultry Heat, and never knew the Sweets of Life or the advantage of their Painful Industry in a Place which, except the Verdure of its Fields, had nothing to recommend it.[1]

One question often asked, seldom answered, is whether there is such a thing as a colonial psychology. Do only certain people go to colonies and are they changed when they get there?[2] Many scholars have agonized and theorized over "the shock of the new," the impact of new lands and new peoples on the European imagination. Few have gone on to speculate on what happens next, when the traveler is turned into a native, or a native of sorts. In this essay I wish to examine the life of one European-turned-native—Thomas Thistlewood of Lincolnshire, England, and Westmoreland, Jamaica—in order to explore the development of a colonial and a racially oppressive psychology. Adaptation to a new land is always a mixture of inheritance and experience.[3] Usually, historians concentrate on inheritance: Here I would like to turn our attention to the effect of experience in what Edward Brathwaite calls the creolization process.

Brathwaite calls creolization the single most important factor in the development of Jamaican society. He defines this process as "a cultural action—material, psychological, and spiritual—based upon the stimulus/response of individuals within the society to their environment and—as white/black, culturally discrete groups—to each other." Through this cultural action an immigrant becomes a Creole—a Creole being a combination of two Spanish words that together mean a committed settler, one identified with the area of settlement, one native to the settlement though not ancestrally indigenous to it.[4]

The culture of Jamaican whites was, by the mid-eighteenth century, a creole culture with a way of life essentially dissimilar from the metropolitan model of England. The environment—both physical and social—was radically different, and new immigrants had to learn to adapt. It was not an immediate process: as Brathwaite notes, if all Jamaican Creoles were colonials, it does not follow that all colonials in Jamaica were creolized.[5] Yet the power of West Indian society to mold newcomers was strong. However oddly constructed West Indian society might appear in England, it took little time for the English coming to the islands to be caught up in a system that seemed internally logical and perfectly natural. The historian J. B. Moreton observed of people creolized to the slave tropics that "imperceptibly like wax softened by heat, they melt into their manners and customs." Soon, not only native but immigrant whites demonstrated "passions and sensations" far "different" from those experienced "in colder regions."[6]

The most unfamiliar custom for English immigrants was the institution of slavery, an institution that, although essential to white prosperity on the island, was a source of constant friction and fear. Slavery in one of the most complete slave societies in human history—slaves composed nearly 90 percent of the population by 1750—shaped every aspect of Jamaican life and was an institution that every immigrant had to come quickly to terms with on arrival in the island.

White immigrants quickly absorbed prevailing Jamaican racial lore. On arrival, it is clear from contemporary accounts, Europeans were shocked by the brutality of Jamaica's slave system. A small few never overcame their distaste for slavery, but most became inured to an institution that did not exist in Britain and to a view of Africans that saw them as inherently and biologically inferior.[7] Even if a person did not have an especially negative view of blacks prior to arrival, he or she soon adhered to prevailing white racial views concerning them. At the very least, whites became convinced that slavery was a necessity for production in a hot climate. As Reverend John Venn explained in a letter written after eleven years' residence in Jamaica: "The thing that shocks a Stranger Most, and in which this country differs from England more than in Climate is the Slavery in which the poor Negroes are held. I wish it were otherwise, but as white People cannot support the labour of the Field, and are not to be had if they could, and Negroes cannot be hir'd, nor will work except by Compulsion, if the European will have Sugar, Rum, Spices, etc., they must permit Slavery in the Colonies."[8]

Thistlewood does not seem to have been especially biased against African Negroes, even if he was capable of considerable brutality toward them.[9]

Certainly, he does not evince the virulent racism against blacks that is so graphically evident in the work of planter and historian Edward Long. Explicitly racist statements are rare in Thistlewood's diary. Early on in his stay, twenty days after accepting a position as estate keeper, he expostulates in frustration that his slave charges are "a Nest of Thieves and Villains" and, more interestingly, in May 1751 he describes a custom of Africans of picking off head lice and eating them as behavior paralleled by monkeys. These are the only two entries in his diary that explicitly refer to blacks as being biologically inferior. Nevertheless, if less of a racist than one might expect, Thistlewood is far from being an abolitionist: he never questions except once, and then in the most oblique way, the rightness of slavery, and quickly agrees with prevailing white conceptions about the rightful places of whites and blacks in Jamaican society. One of the aims of this chapter is to explore how an immigrant could learn prevailing racial ideology in an extremely racially oppressive society to such an extent that he could become an oppressor himself.[10]

Thomas Thistlewood was a very ordinary man who lived a very ordinary life, first in England and then in Jamaica, where he died in 1786. We would know nothing about him except for the fact that he assiduously kept a daily diary that has been fortuitously preserved. This diary contains about 10,000 pages of closely written manuscript that allows us to trace the outlines of Thistlewood's every day life in ways impossible for almost any other colonial in Britain's eighteenth-century empire.

Thistlewood is of interest for many reasons beyond the mere survival of his diary. Most important, he is a representative of a significant group in colonial society that has been seldom noted in colonial historiography: ambitious immigrants from England of middling status who emigrated to the prosperous but deadly British Caribbean sugar islands or to the North American mainland. Those whom we know most about, usually through their diaries, were people like William Byrd, Landon Carter, and Thomas Jefferson of Virginia—wealthy, literate, politically prominent, native-born Americans.[11] Yet a large percentage of people in most colonies, and an overwhelming percentage in the British West Indies, where death and disease continually decimated both the white and black populations, were immigrants, usually of relatively humble status. Their main aim in moving far from home and loved ones was to attain a modicum of prosperity and a comfortable sufficiency in lands that they hoped resembled their native country.

What do we know about Thistlewood prior to his arrival? In some ways he was not the typical immigrant to the eighteenth-century Caribbean. That mythical typical immigrant was a man in his early twenties, arriving as an indentured servant. He would have left his native village or hamlet for London or Bristol or Glasgow, but this trip would have been his first trip outside of Britain. Thistlewood was older than usual—twenty-nine when he left for

Jamaica in 1750—of higher status than customary for immigrants to the New World, being of solid yeoman stock with a number of substantial relatives in Lincolnshire; and was an experienced traveler, having spent the years between 1746 and 1748 as purser of supercargo on a ship owned by the East India Company. As such, he traveled to India, and, significantly for his future decision to go to Jamaica, to the Portuguese slave society at Bahia in Brazil. Most important, Thistlewood was well educated and intellectually curious, an avid reader, and a dedicated amateur scientist and botanist. The conventional wisdom about early Jamaica is that it was an intellectual wasteland, where learning was at a low ebb, "the office of a Teacher is look'd upon as contemptible" and where "the Generality seem to have a greater Appreciation for the modish Vice of Gaming Than the Belles Lettres."[12] Reading Thistlewood's diary casts doubt on such aspersions, but it is likely that Thistlewood was unusual in the range of intellectual activities that he enjoyed.

If he was not the quintessential immigrant, he was hardly atypical. As Douglas Hall notes, although Thistlewood was not one of the crowd, "his account of his own activities and of the activities of others display[s] no great disparities of behaviour" from that noted in observers' renderings of Jamaicans and their society. If older, he was not much older than the norm; if of higher status on arrival than the ordinary indentured servant, his status was not that of the Jamaican plantocracy; if intellectually curious, his opinions and his demonstrated actions were nothing if not conventional. In short, Thistlewood seems to be an ordinary man of the Enlightenment, with a magpie curiosity but little originality, either in his planting endeavors or in his social ideas. There is no indication that Thistlewood ever questioned the status quo; he seems to have been firmly attached to the maintenance of white dominance in the island and willingly accepted the authority of great planters in politics and society, and he appears to have been accepted and liked by most whites in his neighborhood after he had established himself as a reliable long-term resident.[13]

We have no independent assessments of Thistlewood as a man, but we can begin to discern some of his personality, character, and quirks from the terse comments he made in his diary. He was, even for an eighteenth-century man living before Freud, singularly unrevealing about his feelings and motivations. He was seldom reflective about himself or even about others. Unlike Samuel Pepys or the Virginian Landon Carter, Thistlewood did not write a diary as a way of venting emotions that could not be released during the day. Thistlewood's diary was mostly an aide-mémoire—a combination of diary, work journal, account book, and personal cyclopedia.

Nevertheless, a picture of Thistlewood's character and interests can be drawn from his diary entries. As one would expect from an immigrant willing to transplant himself to a heavily slave society in which whites were outnumbered by African slaves, Thistlewood was confident in his ability to look after himself physically—several times in his first few years in Jamaica, Thistlewood had to forcefully overcome slaves who attacked him—and mentally, as he dealt with both slaves under his care and whites in his local community. He was sure of his abilities and talents, as can be seen in his determination to forge the best possible deal for himself as an overseer, and expected others to recognize those abilities. He could be prickly when he thought he was being taken advantage of—there are numerous examples where Thistlewood stood up for his rights even when confronting supposed superiors. Thistlewood became, on his own terms at least, a successful colonial, well respected, integrated into local society in his parish of Westmoreland, and comfortably well-off. It might be presumed that this moderate success was due in part at least to his particular personality and that the traits Thistlewood possessed—self-confidence, a feisty independence when required, gregariousness combined with a capacity to cope by himself, and a sanguine temperament that never questioned the rightness of slavery and white superiority—were requisite necessaries in the colonial personality.

Thistlewood had never been to Jamaica before he left England in 1750, but he would have had some inkling of what to expect from his previous travels, from contacts that he made in 1748 and 1749, people who had experience in Jamaica, and, quite probably, given his taste for reading, from published accounts of Jamaica. Like any other eighteenth-century Englishman, he could have gone elsewhere. Shortly after arriving in Jamaica, Thistlewood noted that while "Virginia and the Carolinas were much troubled with Ague and Fever," Pennsylvania was reputed to be a "delightful countrey." Thistlewood need not have confined himself to British colonies: on September 18, 1751, he noted, immediately after accepting a position as an overseer, that if he had "not done this, [he] would have gone to Hispaniola . . . to have learnt to make Indico." As a calculating man whose clear aim in moving to the colonies was to accumulate wealth and attain independence from the control of others, he would have come to Jamaica only after assessing the advantages and disadvantages of residence in Britain's tropical island outpost.[14]

If Thistlewood had read a book on what life was like in Jamaica, the most current would have been Charles Leslie's *A New and Exact Account of Jamaica*, published in Edinburgh, probably in 1740. This was written very much as a guide for new arrivals, being composed as a series of letters home from one such. The type of comments about Jamaica are typical of most other descriptions made about mid-eighteenth-century Jamaica. It is not too unreasonable a leap, therefore, to assume that Thistlewood would have received the sort of advice that Leslie offered potential emigrants.

Leslie was less than enthusiastic about many aspects of life in Jamaica, but there was enough in his book to whet a reader's appetite. In particular, he emphasized how much opportunity there was in Jamaica, which he described as "a Constant Mine, where Britain draws prodigious riches."[15] Much of that wealth went to rich planters, but with lots of free land, an entrepreneurial culture, a constant thirst for relatively highly paid white servants, heavy employment for skilled tradesmen, and many opportunities outside sugar to make money, an immigrant who behaved well could do excellently. The high likelihood of finding a comfortable sufficiency would have been music to Thistlewood's ear. He would also have been gratified to discover that, if learning was at a low ebb, the white people of Jamaica were renowned for their hospitality and that gentlemen at least lived in "a very gay Manner" and were "perfectly Polite and have a Delicacy of Behaviour which is exceeding taking." He would also have noted Leslie's deprecating comments about Jamaica's clergy and churchgoing in the island without concern. Thistlewood was to trouble the church little with his presence in his first decade in Jamaica—he attended service only once in the 1750s and then only as part of his militia duties.[16]

Thus, if Thistlewood was interested in going to an island of "Grand Appearance" where people "live well, enjoy their Friends, drink heartily, make Money, and are quite Careless of Futurit," then Jamaica was a good choice. There were some risks, however. The most significant problem for whites in Jamaica was that the island had a well-deserved reputation as a death trap. Leslie's first glimpse of native Jamaicans revealed them to be "all sickly," with "muddly" complexions, wan color, and meager bodies, and he noted that "Death deals more in this Place than another," with a "Revolution of lives in this Island" every seven years and "that as many die in that space of time as perfectly inhabit it."[17]

Yet, Thistlewood would have learned from Leslie, there were ways by which precipitate death could be overcome. One particular eighteenth-century fear concerned white skin in a torrid climate.[18] Leslie disliked the climate, arguing that the sultry sun made the place sickly. But in a letter written in 1751 to the Bishop of London, the Reverend John Venn, a resident of Jamaica for eleven years, portrayed the evils of Jamaica's climate as less terrible than usually represented. Some constitutions, he admitted, cannot be supported in Jamaica. "People of a florid complexion" should stay home as should people with "weak frames, plethoric habits, or gross bodies." But others "have their Health very well and live to a great Age."[19] Thistlewood confirmed for himself that people could live to a great age in Jamaica immediately on arrival in Kingston, when he met William Cornish, a sprightly eighty-one-year-old, whose health, Thistlewood noted, "was based on drinking mostly water & chocolate for 37 years." He also met Venn's immediate supervisor, the Reverend William May, long-serving rector of Kingston since 1722. Both men were living examples that men could live to old age in Jamaica.[20]

What he would have learned from both men was that to maintain excellent health in the tropics meant temperate living. It was an article of faith among educated Jamaicans that most deaths of whites were caused by intemperance. As Leslie put it, the "Death of Thousands can be ascribed to nothing less than intemperance. . . . If newcomers were more careful to live moderate, and abstain from the Use of Spiritous Liquors, they might live as happily and free from Diseases as anywhere else."[21] Thistlewood heeded such advice. Clearly the high mortality of Jamaica was of concern: two days after arrival, he noted in conversation with a doctor that "of 150 passengers brought over 16 months ago,

122 were dead." Mortality among new arrivals who had not been "seasoned" was extraordinarily high: David Galenson estimates that up to 40 percent of bookkeepers died within three years of arrival in Jamaica. Thistlewood was aware of how precarious life was in this deadly climate. In 1752, for example, he witnessed the arrival and then sudden demise of a Scottish bookkeeper on the estate he ran. Thomas Christy arrived on June 21 and was dead by September 1, 1752.[22]

Thistlewood was more careful than Christy, whom he privately considered to be intemperate in diet and drink. The opposite was true of Thistlewood. For a white Jamaican, he lived very moderately indeed, taking especial care with what he ate and drank, particularly on first arrival on the island. Moreover, he was solicitous about his bodily functions, carefully noting any abnormality, and very cautious in relation to Jamaica's notorious climate—exposure to the sultry sun was reckoned by eighteenth-century physicians to be fatal to Europeans. It took Thistlewood five years to forget himself: on October 3, 1755, he noted that having stood in the field in the sun a long time, he had contracted a fever, a fever that persisted for nearly a month. Even after considerable residence in Jamaica, an immigrant could still make beginners' mistakes. After five years, Thistlewood was not fully creolized, at least according to current climatic theories.[23]

Another danger Leslie would have alerted Thistlewood to would have been hurricanes and earthquakes. Leslie considered these natural phenomena as bringing more fear to Jamaicans than even slave revolts or the legendarily avaricious court officials. Natural disaster was and remains a great risk in the Caribbean. In 1692 Jamaica suffered the greatest natural catastrophe in colonial American history when the flourishing town of Port Royal was leveled to the ground by an earthquake. In the 1720s and again in the 1780s, a series of hurricanes devastated the island, killing many and destroying massive amounts of property. Thistlewood was to experience a major hurricane very soon in his sojourn in Jamaica, on September 11, 1751. He was amazed and excited as well as terrified by this strange, frightening yet exhilarating experience, and wrote a good deal in his diary describing the "strange havoc" wrought by this very Caribbean event.[24]

Yet experiencing a hurricane was not sufficient to make Thistlewood a Creole. Nor was staying alive, comprehending the native flora and fauna, nor calculating how best to make a living—all of which were of considerable concern to him, especially in his first two years in Jamaica. Quickly Thistlewood adapted to the strange climate (within nine months of arrival, he considered himself "somewhat inured to ye heat of ye Country"), adjusted himself to the different plants and animals in Jamaica, and began to enjoy hunting and fishing for some of the more appetizing specimens. Moreover, he had absorbed sufficient conventional wisdom about the best occupations to enter into that by September 1751, he had achieved a position as overseer at William Dorrill's sugar plantation. Initially worth £60 per annum, by 1754 Thistlewood increased this salary, by dint of demonstrated competence and hard bargaining, to £80 per annum, with a built-in bonus. Thistlewood nevertheless only truly became a Creole when he began to master the intricacies of white/black behavior in this peculiar society.[25]

What would Thistlewood have known about Jamaican race relations before arrival? If he had read Leslie, he would have absorbed the following facts and racial lore. As everyone knew, whites were heavily outnumbered by African slaves. Although Leslie admitted that there was always a danger of slave revolts, whites managed to maintain order through extremely brutal treatment of slaves in custom and law, the severity of which Leslie considered to be justified from the vast racial imbalance on the island. Slave laws were particularly draconian by the standards of British America, and were designed entirely for the benefit of whites. If a Negro attacked a white, he or she would be punished by branding, torture, or death. Thistlewood would have realized even prior to arrival that the clearest division in Jamaican society was between all whites and everyone else and that Jamaican society was constructed solely for the benefit of the former. White solidarity was the primary value that held Jamaican society together, although, as Thistlewood was to discover, there were cracks in that supposedly impregnable edifice.

In his first year in Jamaica, Thistlewood learned a good deal about both African slaves and Jamaican whites. He realized very soon that he was in an African country. Six days after arrival, he wandered with a companion to the west in Kingston "to see Negroes diversions—odd Musick motions etc.—The Negroes of each nation by themselves." By July 17, 1750, Thistlewood was on a cattle estate in western Jamaica, the only white, with forty-two slaves under his care. Much of his first year was spent solely in the company of Negroes: between November 1750 and February 1751, he saw other white people no more than three or four times. By this latter date, he had begun to understand African customs a little more fully. By the time of his first Christmas in Jamaica, he could distinguish between "Creolian, Congo and Coromantee Musick and dancing."[26]

He had begun also to understand how a white should behave toward blacks and had come to realize how much the maintenance of white dominance in the island rested on naked force. Twelve days after arriving in Westmoreland parish, his future employer, Mr. William Dorrill, meted out justice to "runaway Negroes," whipping them severely and then rubbing pepper, salt, and lime juice into their wounds. Three days later, Thistlewood witnessed Dorrill receiving a dead runaway, cutting off his head and sticking it upon a pole while burning his body. Going to the local town of Lacovia on October 1, he witnessed an even more graphic example of white might exercised through summary force when he "Saw a Negroe fellow named English . . . Tried [in] court and hang'd upon ye 1st tree immediately (drawing his knife upon a White Man) his hand cutt off, Body left unbury'd." In mid-July 1750, less than two weeks after becoming estate keeper on Florentius Vassall's Vineyard estate, he watched his first employer, the scion of one of the richest and most distinguished families on the island, give the leading slave on the estate, Dick, a mulatto driver, "300 lashes for his many crimes and negligences." Given these examples from his betters, it is not surprising that Thistlewood also maintained his authority through the heavy application of force. By July 20, 1750, already convinced that his slaves were "a Nest of Thieves and Villains," he had whipped his first slave, and by August 1, he was prepared to give Titus, a slave who harbored a runaway, 150 lashes.[27]

Thistlewood also discovered in his first year in Jamaica other ways in which whites and blacks interacted. One such relationship was financial. Much of Jamaica's internal economy was in the hands of slaves and free blacks. Edward Long estimated that this group held up to 20 percent of the island's circulating currency, and Thistlewood quotes William Dorrill as saying that "by a very good computation, the Negroes in this parish lye out near 20 thousd pounds pr: ann:." On the same day that Thistlewood saw William Dorrill desecrate the body of a dead runaway, he also engaged in commerce with slaves—buying clothes from a Negro girl and giving, presumably in return for money, an old coat to "a negroe fellow."[28]

A more important relationship between black and white, at least as far as Thistlewood was concerned, was sexual. Sex was the one area in which Thistlewood was immoderate in his appetite. He had enjoyed a hearty sex life in England with prostitutes, servants, the wife of a former friend, and with a Lincolnshire woman, Bett Mitchell, whom it seems he wished to marry.[29] Sex was a subject that continued to interest him after he came to Jamaica, Thistlewood being as much devoted to the theory of sex as to its practice. He worked out customary Jamaican sexual practices very early on. When meeting the elderly but sprightly William Cornish on April 27 in Kingston, he noted that Cornish "keeps a genteel mulatoo girl."[30] Thistlewood would have been certain to note that living openly with slave or free mulatto concubines brought no social condemnation, and indeed was expected behavior. It is noteworthy that Thistlewood made no attempt to marry a white woman during his stay in Jamaica but confined his attentions solely to black women.

He also noted in his diaries prurient items of sexual curiosity. On June 26, 1750, he recorded an anecdote by Mr. Dorrill about a Negro girl who had both a white and a black lover and who conceived mulatto and black twins. Three weeks later, when on the Vineyard estate, he noted that one slave woman, Phoebe, wanted to shave her private parts—a clear hint to Thistlewood that "some in Jamaica are very sensual."[31] His appetite whetted by lurid tales, Thistlewood began sleeping with slave women. From four slave partners in 1750, Thistlewood expanded to eleven in 1751 and to similar numbers for the next five years. Sleeping with slaves under his care was clearly a perk of office that he greatly relished, and may have been a major attraction of life in Jamaica for unattached young male immigrants.

By the end of his first year, therefore, Thistlewood could have been forgiven for thinking that he was well on the way to becoming a Creole. Yet there was still much to learn, as Thistlewood was to discover. Beneath the surface reality of complete white dominance and utter black subservience, Jamaican life was much more complex than either Thistlewood or later historians have realized.

The first complexity that Thistlewood needed to master after he had been "seasoned" to Jamaica was the character of white social relations. Thistlewood saw little of whites while working at Vineyard estate, but his social contacts greatly increased after he became overseer on Egypt estate in September 1751. In part, this was because Egypt was more conveniently located than the remote Vineyard estate, but the main reason seems to have been that Thistlewood was beginning to be accepted by established white settlers as a person of some importance.

Most interpretations of Thistlewood and his diary dwell only in passing with Thistlewood as a member of white society in Westmoreland Parish. Every historian to date who has examined the diary has used it primarily as a marvellous entrée into the complicated human relations between master and slave. Yet it is a mistake to downplay Thistlewood's connections with other whites in order to focus on his relations with blacks. It is true that Thistlewood spent much time among blacks and fashioned complex relations with them. Nevertheless, if he lived among and with blacks, he identified very much with whites and socialized heavily in their company. From around 1752 onward, Thistlewood was involved in a constant round of visiting and mixing with fellow whites. Only rarely did he spend more than two or three days without white company. More important than just the extent of contacts between whites was the extent to which the character of individual white relations both secured white dominance and allowed opportunities for individual blacks to gain small advantages.[32]

Commentators on Jamaican society in the eighteenth century attributed white safety in part to tribal divisions within African-born slave communities and in part to the strict discipline and tribal unity of whites on the island. Certainly, viewed from the perspective of new African slaves or unseasoned white employees, whites seemed to be the strongest and most unified tribe in the colony. Slaves were cowed by the threat, often realized, of white violence, a violence certain to be raised if blacks dared to attack a white person. They were also kept in check by an elaborate system of passes that controlled movement, and they were officially denied access to arms. Whites were required to serve in a militia whose main purpose was to prevent slave rebellion. Moreover, from the 1730s, whites had come to an agreement with their principal domestic enemy, the maroon communities in the Jamaica interior, in such a way that the maroons became white allies rather than threats to white security.

Seen from the inside, by resident whites, the white tribe also seemed very powerful. Unlike contemporary European society, there were remarkably few divisions within white Jamaican society, and there were a number of rules of behavior that solidified white unity. The only important ethnic division was between Christian and Jews. The latter were well represented in Jamaica, having arrived there in the late seventeenth century, and they had prospered. Yet Jews were only partially included within white society. Thistlewood was by no means as hysterically anti-Semitic as historian Edward Long, but he clearly differentiated between Jews and other whites, seldom mentioning them by name but commenting on their strange customs and making occasional hints that he distrusted Jews and thought them rapacious.[33]

There were, of course, considerable class divisions within white society, particularly between large planters, salaried employees, and servants, but what is remarkable is less the recognition of those divisions by local whites than the relatively narrow gap between each group. White society in the West Indies was characterized by a striking equality and freedom, which impressed all observers.[34] The historian Bryan Edwards commented on this informality and friendliness in his usual perceptive way:

> It appears to me that the leading feature is an independent spirit and a display of conscious equality throughout all ranks and conditions. The poorest White person seems to consider himself nearly on a level with the richest, and emboldened by this idea approached his employer with extended hand, and a freedom, which, in the countries of Europe, is seldom displayed by men in the lower orders of life towards their superiors. It is not difficult to trace the origin of this principle. It arises, without doubt, from the pre-eminence and distinction which are necessarily attached even to the complexion of a White Man, in a country where the complexion, generally speaking, distinguishes freedom from slavery.[35]

Thistlewood was not a great planter and spent most of his time among people of his own middling station—fellow overseers, surgeons, ship captains—but he did have considerable contacts both with his social superiors and with his social inferiors. As soon as he arrived in Westmoreland, he met the wealthy William Dorrill, who not only welcomed him but lent him a horse and offered him a job in two months' time. He developed a friendship with the plain-speaking, rather coarse, but very rich Tom Williams, whose lurid tales clearly delighted Thistlewood. He even caught the attention of the leading man in the district, Colonel James Barclay, who on December 10, 1751, called on Thistlewood and, to Thistlewood's gratification, told him that he had been appointed a highway surveyor. Less than a month later, Barclay invited Thistlewood to his house for dinner, in itself a measure of Thistlewood's acceptance into local society.[36]

It was also a signal example of one of the principal values that governed white social relations. Jamaican whites prided themselves on their generosity and especially on their hospitality. Every commentator noted this as a feature of eighteenth-century Jamaican society. It is clear that extending to visiting whites hospitality—food, lodgings, occasionally the loan of transport—was expected behavior for Jamaican whites. Such gestures were extended to Thistlewood when he arrived on the island and when he traveled outside his district; he extended the same hospitality to whites when they passed by his residence. Whites from every social station, from great planter to indentured servant, could expect, when they visited another white, to be put up for the night and fed. Thistlewood records a constant stream of visitors to his place, all of whom expected to be entertained. Indeed, the presumption of hospitality was so strong that it erased all distinction between locals and travelers.[37]

Hospitality was not just an important value: it served a crucial role in uniting all ranks of white society. Just as all white men were required to help in the protection of the island through serving in the local militia, so whites were obligated to acknowledge the importance of having a white skin in a society predicated on white dominance, by giving other whites special favors. To be white in Jamaica was to be in certain respects equal to all other whites, regardless of wealth or status. Through the custom and practice of hospitality, Jamaican whites acknowledged the special tribal status of whites. In order to protect themselves from the overwhelmingly numerically dominant black majority, whites needed to know that they were all members of a privileged community that also had shared communal duties. Generous hospitality was evidence of that community membership.

The ideal was to present white society as an impregnable fortress into which blacks, free or slave, could not enter. That undoubtedly is how Thistlewood would have seen white rule in his first year in Jamaica. Yet within this seemingly seamless structure of white dominance, there were fissures deep enough to allow enterprising blacks niches of opportunity. Learning how to deal with these fissures if you were a white or exploit them if you were black was essential in becoming a Creole.

There were three flash points within white society and one from within black society that posed a danger for whites. The flash points within white society developed not from ethnic, class, or political divisions—that would have spelled disaster for white rule in the islands as it was later to do in the 1790s in St. Domingue—but from the clash of individual personalities.

The first way in which white solidarity could be diluted arose from the fiery temper of most creole Jamaicans, especially great planters. As Thomas Jefferson noted, being the master of adult slaves from childhood breeds an imperious personality.[38] Jamaicans, especially rich, native-born Jamaicans, were notorious for their proud demeanor and quick touchiness. Violence was meant to be directed solely against blacks, but whites, inured to acting violently, could not always stop themselves from confronting fellow whites. Dorrill once told Thistlewood that "in this Country, it is highly necessary for a Man to fight once or twice, to keep Cowards from putting upon him." Whites were quick to respond to threats of violence if their will was thwarted, as Thistlewood had discovered a month prior to Dorrill's comment, when he had a fierce argument with his employer, Florentius Vassall, about his service conditions. Vassall swore that "if he should receive such an other letter from me as my last, he would make Blood flow about my face," to which Thistlewood boldly answered that "he must not wait for another but do it now if he thought proper."[39]

Vassall desisted, and Thistlewood eventually had very good relations with him, though not while in his employ. But the quarrel would have undoubtedly weakened Thistlewood's authority among his slaves, especially when two days later Vassall told the head slave, Dick, to "obey Mr Mortimer in everything the same as himself and look upon him as his Master." Blacks were supposed to be subservient to all whites, but in practice could play one white off against another.[40]

Quarrels between masters and underlings are endemic in all societies. But there were some quarrels that were peculiar to Jamaica. One of the greatest advantages of moving to the Caribbean was manifold chances for sex. White men constantly availed themselves of black and mulatto women, much to the dismay of their white marital partners and, no doubt, their black paramours.[41] During the first years of residence in Jamaica, Thistlewood fully exploited this situation—he engaged in sexual congress with a large proportion of eligible female slaves on both Vineyard and Egypt estates.

Problems arose, however, when a man became attached to one particular slave. One of the advantages for white men, supposedly, of black or mulatto women in Jamaica was their inconstancy and their ready availability. This advantage became a decided disadvantage when attempting to lay sole claim to an individual mistress, as inconstancy precluded fidelity. There was a definite pattern to Thistlewood's philandering. First, there was an initial period of promiscuous experimentation. Next came a semimonogamous relationship with a single slave (Marina at Vineyard, Negro Jenny at Vineyard 1751–1753, and finally Phibbah, who became his de facto wife and who bore him his son and heir), although with more than occasional forays to other slaves.

Thus, Thistlewood, like most white Jamaicans, became attached to a single slave, Phibbah, who, not surprisingly, was favored over all other slaves. Thistlewood's relationship with Phibbah was extraordinarily complex and puts the lie to depictions of relations between white men and black women as being based solely on sexual exploitation. Phibbah was more beneficiary than victim of Thistlewood's attentions. White solidarity could never be complete, because a large percentage of white men were compromised through their involvement with colored mistresses. Thistlewood was an obvious example, but a better illustration of how sexual involvement with blacks could complicate and weaken relations between whites can be seen by looking at the love life of Thistlewood's subordinate on Egypt estate, the bookkeeper William Crookshanks.

Crookshanks, like Thistlewood, was an immigrant with connections and some means who arrived recommended by John Cope at Egypt estate on May 16, 1754, "to learn the plantation business." Like Thistlewood, he partook freely of the sexual delights available for young white men, and like Thistlewood, although more quickly than his immediate supervisor, he suffered the consequences of those delights. By the June 5, Crookshanks had "a dose of the clap," an occupational hazard for Jamaicans that Thistlewood had already experienced several times in his first four years on the island. Venereal disease was endemic in the island, with one doctor claiming that up to four-fifths of the populace had their lives shortened by unwise sexual adventurism. To a degree, having gonorrhea and having to undergo the excruciating after-effects of both illness and remedy was an essential part of the "seasoning" process.[42]

Like Thistlewood, William Crookshanks became drawn to a single slave. By late 1754, he had become attached to Myrtilla, a slave belonging to Thistlewood's neighbor. Myrtilla miscarried a child in mid-February 1755 that Crookshanks thought was his but which Thistlewood unkindly believed should have been attributed to Salt River Long Quaw, a slave. Thistlewood, who had an uneasy relationship with Crookshanks, made a number of derisive comments about the younger man's infatuation with Myrtilla. He strongly suspected that she took advantage of Crookshanks, pretending illness to get out of work, and he disapproved of Crookshanks allowing his passion for his slave to get in the way of both his financial interests and, more important, his friendship with other whites.[43]

Sex and sexual jealousy could lead to a deterioration in relations between whites, thus weakening the fabric of white solidarity. It was in sexual matters that the distinctions of social hierarchy were most apparent. Slaves, after all, were property, and those who owned such property had rights, including sexual rights, that they were not unwilling to lay claim to. Crookshanks found that out with Myrtilla. His love was owned by his friends William and Elizabeth Mould, and although they were willing to allow Crookshanks to hire Myrtilla for a year (a bad bargain for Crookshanks, since it cost him £20 and Myrtilla earned him just £15.15s), they insisted on reclaiming their property after the year's lease was up. Moreover, they punished Myrtilla for her infractions by putting her head in a yoke. This led to what Thistlewood described as an extraordinary scene: Crookshanks hysterically abused the Moulds before repenting, going down on his knees "begging their pardons etc."[44]

Clearly Crookshanks had damaged his position in white society by excessive concern for a slave and, more important, by questioning the authority of whites over their slave property. Crookshanks also caused trouble for himself through his relationship with Phibbah, Thistlewood's mistress. At first, the relationship was cool. Thistlewood recounted, with apparent approval of his mistress's sauciness, an argument between the two on July 30, 1754. Crookshanks was drunk and "abuse[d] Phibbah in a strange Billingsgate language—She answer'd him pretty well." The next day saw Crookshanks "out of humor . . . he is so affronted at Phibbah." In all likelihood, he was also affronted at Thistlewood, who took Phibbah's side rather than the side of his tribal partner.[45]

The coolness between Phibbah and Crookshanks soon gave way to affection, and perhaps to more than affection. By December 15, Thistlewood was having words with William and Phibbah "about their Familiarity."[46] Because Crookshanks was his subordinate, this was a situation that Thistlewood could control. He also could take action against equals, such as his predecessor, John Filton, whom on April 22, 1752, Thistlewood caught with Phibbah, presumably in flagrante delicto. Thistlewood discharged Filton from the plantation, thereafter bearing a particular animosity against him, and gave Phibbah seventy lashes.[47] But Thistlewood was powerless to stop the advances toward Phibbah of his employer, and Phibbah's owner, John Cope. By October 1754, Thistlewood was quarreling frequently with Phibbah about Cope, arguments that did not succeed in their purpose, as a year later Thistlewood noted that he "suspected Phibbah with JC." The remedies employed by Thistlewood against Filton and Crookshanks were to no avail in this case: Phibbah was Cope's property, and interfering with a man's right to property, human or otherwise, was impossible. But Cope's predations could not have endeared him to his employee, thus weakening white solidarity. Even worse, Phibbah's attachment to Cope must have complicated her existing relationship to Thistlewood, quite probably to Phibbah's advantage.[48]

Tribal solidarity and property rights often collided and made white-white and white-black relations more complex than they at first seemed. A white was supposed to be superior to all blacks, and his authority over blacks was meant to be unchallenged, protected by fierce laws and strongly held customs. Moreover, a white was seemingly entitled to deal with blacks on his property in any way that he saw fit. Yet conflict between whites often arose when a man's authority to control events in his patch of designated authority clashed with the property rights of another.

We can see this by examining the interactions between Thistlewood and his social superior, Colonel Barclay. As noted above, Thistlewood was gratified when Barclay appointed him as a surveyor and invited him to dinner—it showed that he was an accepted member of society. Even more satisfying was the occasion on April 15, 1753, when, meeting Barclay on the road, Barclay told him that "he would do his business for him." Thistlewood had seemingly caught the attention and gained the patronage of the most powerful man in the parish. Yet these harmonious relations were soon disturbed by Thistlewood's insistence on establishing his mastery on his own estate. On May 11, 1753, Thistlewood caught Colonel Barclay's slaves fishing on a river on his property and soundly whipped them. Barclay was irate at another man usurping what he believed was his privilege alone, and threatened Thistlewood that he would whip Thistlewood himself if this reoccurred—as it did in early November 1753 and on January 2, 1754. Barclay did not whip the stubborn overseer, but he did exact revenge. In the past, Thistlewood had missed militia exercises without penalty, but when he did not go to a mustering on October 19, 1753, Barclay moved to fine him—unfairly, in Thistlewood's opinion. Clearly, Barclay was sending a message to Thistlewood that his authority was not to be challenged.[49]

The fiery temper of Jamaican planters and their touchy insistence on their unchallenged rights over their property was a major fissure within white tribal solidarity that was often exploited by slaves. Thistlewood had received an early indication of how slaves could manipulate whites in December 1752, when he repeated a conversation that he had with his leading slave at Egypt, Quashe, who told him that he "should not eat much more meat here!" Thistlewood asked him if he meant to poison or murder him, to which Quashe replied, "neither, but he intended to invent some great lie and go and tell his master to get me turned away." There is no doubt that such stratagems often succeeded.[50]

Quashe's bold statement was all the more disturbing because it followed one of the crucial events that truly made Thistlewood a Creole. Although it is a grave mistake to underestimate the enormous coercive powers that whites had in Jamaica, blacks were in the majority and occasionally tested their luck against white force. Whites not only had to fight occasionally to prove they were not cowards; they had to fight to defend themselves from slaves. Thistlewood found this out for himself on several occasions in his first year at Egypt estate. On four occasions—twice in February and twice in December—Thistlewood had to restrain slaves by force. In three of the four episodes, Thistlewood was trying to prevent a slave from running away. On the fourth, however, two days after Christmas, Thistlewood had the bad luck to encounter a runaway slave, Congo Sam, who endeavored not just to resist but to murder his master with a machete.[51] Thistlewood managed to conquer his assailant, but to his chagrin, the Egypt slaves stood by and refused to help. Eventually, one slave, London, did assist but then allowed Congo Sam to escape. It was only after two white gentlemen fortuitously passed by that Thistlewood was able to quash Sam's murder attempt.[52]

Here was reality with a jolt. Slaves might be cowed by white power, but on occasion individual slaves would resist, and when they did resist, they would be supported, tacitly if not actively, by other slaves. On such occasions, the coercive powers of white society would not be enough. From this time onward, if not before, Thistlewood could have been in no doubt that he was part of a vulnerable, outnumbered minority among a hostile enemy majority. Individual slaves occasionally killed (Thistlewood notes several examples of premature death for whites occasioned by black assaults or suspected poisonings), and all the ferocious slave laws of Jamaica could not stop such killings. This realization was significant in the creolization process. It could be argued that to become a Creole one had to survive assaults and that one was not truly a Creole until one had experienced the full horror of a major slave revolt. By that reckoning, Thistlewood was not fully creolized until July 1760, when whites in Westmoreland began to wreak cruel vengeance on slaves involved in the large-scale revolt of May–June 1760 that goes by the name of Tacky's revolt.[53]

I would argue, however, that Thistlewood was truly a Creole well before this. There are a number of events which might signal Thistlewood becoming a Creole. Perhaps he became a Creole merely after surviving a year in Jamaica's hot climate—most did not survive. Perhaps he became a Creole after surviving a hurricane, the most formidable national phenomenon of the Caribbean. Perhaps we can date his creolization to Colonal Barclay's invitation for dinner. That signaled his acceptance into local white society. Perhaps he became a Creole when he stopped his relentless philandering and settled down, more or less, into a permanent relationship with a black slave mistress, Phibbah. Perhaps he only became a Creole after withstanding the assault by Congo Sam that nearly cost him his life.

The event, however, that I would like to pick as the most appropriate symbol of Thomas Thistlewood's becoming a Creole occurred early in 1756, nearly six years after his arrival in Kingston. On Saturday, January 3, 1756, Thistlewood rode east to nearby Hertford and there bought, for £43:12:8, an Ebo boy of 16 whom he named Lincoln. At the next militia exercise, he proudly took this new acquisition with him. This purchase was a very important moment in Thistlewood's sojourn in Jamaica, and his fellow militiamen would, no doubt, have recognized it as such. To truly be a white Creole in Jamaica, one needed a stake in society. Land was best, but the first step toward becoming a landowner was to become a slaveholder. By owning a slave, Thistlewood signaled his intention to stay on the island. He also gave final evidence to local blacks that he too had joined the oppressor class.

By now Thistlewood would have learned many of the nuances of life in Jamaica. He would have discovered, as all do who read his diaries, that beneath the surface reality of heat, hospitality, tribal solidarity, and racial oppression that characterized society on the island, there were deeper and much more complex undercurrents. It required several years of immersion into this very complicated society to start to understand that the stark realities so apparent on first arrival were not always as simple as they seemed. By 1756, Thistlewood had begun his long journey of comprehension. Now a slaveowner, he had become an oppressor. It was time to discover the next steps in establishing a Jamaican identity.

NOTES

1. [Charles Leslie], *A New and Exact Account of Jamaica* (Edinburgh, n.d. but probably 1740]), pp. 1, 14. From other evidence it seems certain that Charles Leslie is the author.

2. For a provocative attempt to answer this question, see Octave Mannoni, *Prospero and Caliban: The Psychology of Colonization* (New York, 1956).

3. Jack P. Greene and J. R. Pole, eds., *Colonial British America* (Baltimore, 1984) pp. 15–16.

4. Edward Brathwaite, *The Development of Creole Society in Jamaica, 1770–1820* (Oxford, 1971), pp. xiv, xv, 296 (quote).

5. Ibid., p. 100.

6. Sheila Duncker, "The Free Coloureds and their fight for Civil Rights in Jamaica 1800-1830," (unpublished MA Thesis, University of London, 1960), p. 231. J. B. Moreton, *Manners and Customs of the West Indian Islands* (London, 1790), p. 78.

7. [Leslie], *A New Account of Jamaica*, p. 41. See the extraordinary anon., *An Essay Concerning Slavery and the Danger Jamaica Is Exposed to from the Too Great*

Number of Slaves (London, 1746) for an impassioned argument that free Negroes should be encouraged because free labor was much superior to coerced.

8. Reverend John Venn to Bishop Sherlock, June 15, 1751, General Correspondence, Jamaica, Volume 18, pp. 45–52, 46 (quote), The Fulham Papers in the Lambeth Palace Library, American Colonial Section.

9. Thistlewood's diaries are among the Monson MSS at the Lincolnshire County Records Office, Lincoln, England (Monson Vol. 31, items 1–37). Each volume covers a single year. I simply give a date for all citations to the diary. See Gordon Lewis, *Main Currents in Caribbean Thought: The Historical Evolution of Caribbean Society in Its Ideological Aspects* (Baltimore, 1983), and Edward Long, *The History of Jamaica*, 3 vols. (London, 1774, rpt. 1970), II, pp. 351–505, esp. pp. 353–56.

10. Monson 31/1, July 20, 1750 (quote), 31/2, May 20, 1751, 31/8, July 17, 1757.

11. One exception is the journal/memoirs of William Morally, an indentured servant in the late-eighteenth-century middle colonies. Susan Klepp and Billy G. Smith, eds., *The Infortunate: The Voyage and Adventures of William Morally, an Indentured Servant* (University Park, Pa., 1992).

12. [Leslie], *A New Account of Jamaica*, pp. 36–38.

13. Douglas Hall, *In Miserable Slavery: Thomas Thistlewood in Jamaica, 1750-1786* (London, 1989), p. xvii. In summary, I would agree with Douglas Hall that generalizations based on the Thistlewood diaries are more likely to be reliable than not.

14. Monson 31/1, Sat., June 2, 1750 (quote); September 18, 1751. The type of immigrant suited to Jamaica is well described by William Burke in 1777: "[Jamaica] Suits those of a fiery restless temper, willing to undertake the severest labour, provided it promises but a short continuance, who loves risk and hazard . . . and who puts no medium between being great and being undone." William Burke, *An Account of the European Settlements in America* (London, 1777), 2 vols. I, p. 106. For the significance of independence as a primary value of white society in British North America and the British Caribbean, see Jack P. Greene, *Imperatives, Behaviors, and Identities* (Charlottesville, Va., 1992), pp. 9, 20–29, 188–90.

15. [Leslie], *A New Account of Jamaica*, p. 353.

16. Ibid., p. 28.

17. Ibid., pp. 50–51. Death was a real risk in the Caribbean. For a preliminary investigation into the demographic chances of white survival in early Jamaica, see Trevor Burnard, "A Failed Settler Society: Marriage and Demographic Failure in Early Jamaica," *Journal of Social History* 28 (1994), pp. 63–82.

18. Karen Ordahl Kupperman, "Fear of Hot Climates in the Anglo-American Colonial Experience," *William and Mary Quarterly* 41 (1984), pp. 213–40.

19. Reverend John Venn to Bishop Sherlock, June, 15, 1751, Fulham Papers in the Lambeth Palace Library , Vol. 18, pp. 45–52.

20. Monson 31/1, Friday, April 27, 1750, Tuesday, May 1, 1750. Cornish, in fact, lived until he was ninety.

21. [Leslie], *A New Account of Jamaica*, p. 51.

22. Monson 31/1, Thursday April 26, 1750; 31/3, June 21–September 1, 1752. David W. Galenson, "British Servants and the Colonial Indenture System in the Early Eighteenth Century," *Journal of Southern History* 44 (1978), pp. 44–45.

23. Monson 31/6, October 1755.

24. Monson 31/2, September 11–14, 1751.

25. Monson 31/2, January 11, 1751; September 18, 1751; 31/5, September 12, 1754.

26. Monson 31/1, April 29, 1750; December 25, 1750.

27. Monson 31/3, May 15, 18, 1750; 31/1, July 16, 20, 1750, August 1, 1750, October 1, 1750.

28. Long, *History of Jamaica*, I, p. 537; Monson 31/3, December 26, 1752, Monson 31/1, May 18, 1750.

29. It is very possible that Thistlewood emigrated to Jamaica as a consequence of this rebuff. He was clearly depressed by the rejection, citing Ecclesiastes 7:28 on May 1, 1749, a month after the event: "One man among a thousand have I found, but a woman among all these have I not found." In all likelihood, Thistlewood's failure to marry Bett Mitchell was not just a matrimonial failure but doomed his efforts to enter into farming in his native Lincolnshire. Monson 31/1, May 1, 1749.

30. Monson 31/1, April 27, 1750.

31. Monson 31/1, June 26, July 17, 1750.

32. A number of historians have used the Thistlewood diaries to examine slave life in Jamaica. Besides Hall, *In Miserable Slavery*, see Owen A. Sherrard, *Freedom from Fear: The Slave and His Emancipation* (London, 1959), pp. 85–97; J. R. Ward, "A Planter and His Slaves in Eighteenth-Century Jamaica," in T. C. Smout, ed., *The Search for Wealth and Stability: Essays in Economic and Social History Presented to M. W. Flinn*, (London, 1979), pp. 1–20; Philip Morgan, "Three Planters and Their Slaves: Perspectives on Slavery in Virginia, South Carolina, and Jamaica, 1750–1790," in Winthrop D. Jordan and Sheila L. Skemp, eds., *Race and Family in the Colonial South*, pp. 68–76, and Michael Mullin, *Africa in America: Slave Acculturation and Slave Resistance in the American South and the British Caribbean, 1736–1831* (Urbana, Ill., 1992), pp. 79–88.

33. For references to Jews by Thistlewood, see, inter alia, Monson 31/1, May 1, 1750, May 7, 1750; 31/2, December 7, 1751; 31/3, January 21, 1752; 31/4, February 29, 1753.

34. Elsa Goveia, *Slave Society in the British Leeward Islands at the End of the Eighteenth Century* (New Haven, 1965), pp. 212–15.

35. Bryan Edwards, *The History, Civil and Commercial, of the British Colonies in the West Indies*, 3 vols. (London, 1801), II, pp. 7–8.

36. Monson 31/1, May 3, 1750; 31/2, July 17, 1751, December 10, 1751, January 1752, March 19, 1752.

37. In the first three months of 1752, for example, Thistlewood entertained white strangers on at least five occasions. Monson 31/3, January 24, February 19, February 25, March 11, March 28, 1752.

38. Thomas Jefferson, *Notes on the State of Virginia*, ed. William Peden (Chapel Hill, 1955), pp. 162–63.

39. Monson 31/2, July 21, 1751; May 24, 1751.

40. Thistlewood was one of the very few people invited to attend Vassall's funeral in 1778, and was the only person not a great planter. Hall, *In Miserable Slavery*, pp. 256–57. Monson 31/2, May 26, 1751.

41. See, e.g., the many quarrels between John and Mary Cope in 1754 and 1755, many seemingly occasioned by John Cope's attachment to Thistlewood's mistress, Phibbah. Monson 31/5, November 22, 1754. Monson 31/6, February 9, March 17, April 19, June 15, 1755. Mrs. Cope had much reason to doubt her husband, who, by Thistlewood's account, often expected to have slaves provided for him while at Egypt. See Monson 31/6, August 13, 1755; Monson 31/7, May 2, 1756.

42. Monson 31/5, April 15, 1753 (quote), May 7, 16, 1754.

43. Monson 31/6, February 13, 23, 1755, October 15, 1755.

44. Monson 31/7, February 24, 1756.

45. Monson 31/5, July 30, 31, 1754; December 15, 1754.

46. Monson 31/5, December 15, 1754.

47. Monson 31/3, April 22, 1752. Thistlewood had not yet taken up with Phibbah at this stage.

48. Monson 31/3, April 22, 1752, April 15, 1753.

49. That this was deliberate is clear from an earlier entry by Thistlewood that Mr. Dorrill had told him that "Colonel Barclay has promised to fine me severely if ever I miss Exercise at Savanna la mar for whipping his Negroes." Monson 31/4, February 14, 1753, May 11, 1753, 1754, January 2, 1754.

50. Monson 31/3, December 27, 1752.

51. The Christmas season was notorious for increases in slave assaults against whites. See Robert Dirks, *The Black Saturnalia: Conflict and Its Ritual Expression on British West Indian Slave Plantations* (Gainesville, Fla., 1987).

52. Monson 31/3, December 27, 1752.

53. Thistlewood sometimes suspected that he was being poisoned as well: "Not above quarter of hour in bed before took with a Violent vomiting and purging, extreme Sick, tho' very well before, Suspect Poison." Monson 31/4, January 6, 23, 1753. In this case, Thistlewood was let down by his fellow whites, who, to Thistlewood's amazement and anger, acquitted Sam.

7

Doing God's Service: Adelbert Ames and Reconstruction in Mississippi

Warren A. Ellem

The story of Adelbert Ames (1835–1933) has as its central theme the growth of a Republican conscience. It is essentially the story of a Union officer who united the cause of his country with his own ambition as he rose through the ranks from lieutenant in his first battle, Bull Run, in May 1861 to brevet major general by the end of the war. It is the story also of a man who came, through his commitment to the Union, to accept the cause of freedom for the slave. From that commitment to freedom, Ames was led by his experiences to confront the elusive third war aim proclaimed by a minority, the equality of rights of the slave, a commitment that American society as a whole deferred.[1] Ames did not begin as the freedmen's advocate, though he rejoiced in the death of slavery. His experiences in North Carolina and South Carolina after the war, as the process of Reconstruction developed haltingly, awakened him to the depth of southern white enmity against federal authority and against the freedmen. As Congress implemented the Civil Rights Act and the Reconstruction acts and initiated the fourteenth and fifteenth amendments, Ames aligned himself with the Congress. In many respects, Ames's developing thoughts and reactions mirrored that of many northerners during and after the war as they reacted to southern behavior and President Johnson's policies on Reconstruction. Overseas in Europe during 1866–1867, Ames followed keenly the course of Reconstruction. When he returned to America, it was as a lieutenant colonel in the regular army from August 1867. His duty was to implement the Reconstruction acts in Mississippi, which he did under General Alvan Gillem (Andrew Johnson's friend) before taking command himself and enforcing federal authority vigorously.

In other respects, however, Ames was radicalized by his experiences beyond the commitments society was prepared to make. The very fact that it took his military and political work in three southern states (North Carolina, South Carolina, and Mississippi) to educate him to the extent of the task undertaken by Reconstruction reflected the limits of northern understanding of that task. As Reconstruction developed in the South, and particularly in Mississippi, Ames's commitment to Reconstruction came to center increasingly on the freedmen. Perhaps later than many in coming to accept black suffrage and office holding, he remained a defender of those rights and of the people, white and black, who struggled to sustain them long after the nation abandoned them. As governor of Mississippi during the revolution of 1875, he knew better than most the nature of the movement that destroyed Republican power in Mississippi. The failure of President Grant to confront that extralegal revolution demonstrated the weakness of will of the national Republican administration as it acquiesced in the nullification of the Reconstruction laws and constitutional amendments. The failure of Republicanism in Mississippi was also the failure of the nation, and Ames felt both keenly. He never returned to political life, nor to Mississippi. He returned to the army, however, to serve as brigadier general in the Spanish-American War, during which he commanded the Second Division of the Fifth Corps under General Shafter in 1898 at the invasion of Santiago de Cuba.

After the end of Reconstruction, Ames went back to the North, where he turned very successfully to business in a variety of enterprises and became a man of means. Ambitious for success, whether as a soldier, politician, or businessman, and indeed, as husband and father, Ames was what one might call "driven," but certainly not unusually so for one coming from his heritage, that of a reasonably prominent, well-off and well-educated New England family involved in public life and with a strong religious and revolutionary tradition.[2] None of this "determines" Ames, but it is of relevance in understanding him and his high expectations of himself.

By the end of the war, Ames had been brevetted major general, and he served in North Carolina until early September 1865, when he was appointed to command the District of Western South Carolina. He remained there until April 30, 1866. He was not at all sure when he came to Columbia that he would stay in the peacetime army, and had taken to studying law in his spare time. This period of service, however, was to make a deep impression on him as he struggled to instill some control over the way southern whites treated the ex-slaves. Nonetheless, it did not resolve his concern about his future.

Just two months after he took command of the district, he endorsed the Freedmen's Bureau commissioner's report about the prevalence of murders, attempted murders, and "brutal whipping" of freedmen by whites. The extent of such behavior was "alarming" and could "hardly be credited by one not living in this country." Ames wanted the "deplorable" situation of the freedmen known at headquarters.[3] In late November, he wrote to his parents lamenting bitterly the treatment of the blacks by the whites of the South. Ames despaired of ever convincing "the pious people" of South Carolina that it was a sin to kill a Negro but hoped to convince them that the law said it was a crime. He found it all pretty difficult.[4]

Four months later, in March 1866, Ames reported an improved state of affairs for much of his district. He does not claim credit for this, though it seems from the reports that he had acted energetically to keep matters in hand.[5] The freedmen were nearly all employed and housed on the plantations where they had been slaves and were working more industriously than even their supporters expected. The distrust felt by the freedmen late in the fall of 1865 as a result of employers sending crops to market before the shares were divided had given way to confidence that the system would work fairly in 1866. Indeed, Ames the New Englander had worried previously about the potential for government assistance to undermine work values. But now he was impressed, and noted that the freedmen benefited from the excess of demand for labor over its supply.

Nonetheless, the abuse of freedmen, especially of Negro mechanics by poor whites and white mechanics, continued. This puzzled Ames, who thought that the end of slavery might have been to the benefit of the poor whites as well as of the slaves. The problem was that these whites and many others could admit of no distinction between a "negro and [a] slave. Fact is," said Ames, "we call them freedmen but down here they are niggers" and their lives not taken seriously in that the "5th commandment was not applicable" to them in South Carolina. Ames recounted the interaction of white and black and the terms on which that traditionally took place: "After the old way of thinking, the faintest disrespect, on the part of the negro to a white person, is tortured into insolence, and the slightest show of resistance, even in self defense, is a [premeditated?] insurrection, for which simple death seems too mild a punishment." Such punishment might be delivered in a cooly calculated manner or in an absolute fury. Ames found it chilling that most of the people condoned this treatment and upheld the perpetrators.[6] Where there was fair treatment, Ames believed it to be the product of military supervision and self-interest, not of any change of heart. "Upon the slightest cause the volcano breaks forth."[7] Ames nonetheless expressed to his parents in March 1866 a preference for Johnson's approach overall to that of the Congress, though he worried that Johnson would "go too far in his reconstruction and too soon relieve the South from the debt its actions during the past four years has brought upon itself."[8]

In his final report before going to Europe, Ames confirmed the picture just given, reiterating the prevalence of disloyal sentiment and contempt for the Union uniform. Five of Ames's soldiers had been murdered, several wounded, and many shot at. No help whatsoever came from the white residents. With disgust Ames reported that an outlaw who ran for Sheriff in Anderson received 600 votes and the argument used to defeat him was that he would be executed by the Yankees if he was elected! To his superiors Ames reported that if he catalogued all the disloyal and lawless acts he had witnessed, they would share his "convictions" [Ames's term], forged by the events of every day of the last seven months that he had commanded the district. Hatred of northerners ran so deep that no northern man could live there if the troops were withdrawn.

Nor had the treatment of the freedmen improved. "The condition of the freedman is simply this, so long as he is subordinate after the manner of a slave and not of a freedman, and does as well[,] he is safe from violence; but when he attempts to depart from his old discipline and assert a single privilege[,] he meets opposition; and in localities is punished with death. This results from the fact that many, especially the ignorant can see in a negro only the slave." In referring to the "liberal policy" of the president, Ames commented that the strength of anti-Union feeling prevented even the "most liberal and enlightened men in the state" from breaking the traditions of John C. Calhoun and South Carolina.[9] Ames's experience here had convinced him that the path to reform would not be attained through democratic processes left to southern whites. He did not then conclude that Negro suffrage was the solution, but he became convinced that prejudice and anti-Union hatred were so entrenched that if northerners and freedmen were to be safe, the army must remain and moderates encouraged and sustained by the political and military authorities of the Union. A disciplined military force adequate to enforce order and respect for other people's rights in the South was therefore essential for reconstruction.

His contempt for southern "chivalry" and his condemnation of the barbarous behavior it engendered dates at least from this time. The dislike was mutual. "The people here do not like the Yankees and the Yankees do not like them."[10] The suspicion with which he viewed southern white protestations of concern for black rights lasted a lifetime and did much to bedevil his relations with southern white Republicans when he emerged as a leader of the Republican party in Mississippi during Reconstruction. But in 1866, Ames was still a long way from his later commitment to reform politics and to the political rights of the freedmen.

Ames had been pleased to be retained in the army and to be able to travel in Europe in 1866–1867 as an officer. Had he been returned to his regular army posting with the Fifth Artillery, which was sent to Dry Tortugas for four years, he would have resigned immediately. However, when his leave came through for the end of April 1866, he retained his attachment to the army, at least for the moment. His travels, he assured himself, were designed to improve him, to educate and uplift him—he studied the languages and the culture and the architecture—and increasingly he enjoyed himself as his language studies lagged. This year abroad was a period of great growth for Ames, as he shed some parochial attitudes and became more tolerant of and sensitive to the religion and society of Europe.

It was also a time of growth in his political sentiments. Indeed, his developing opinions were causing him some difficulty. His experience in the Carolinas had convinced him of the need for an army presence in the South to protect northerners and the freedmen and to sustain the civil rights of the freedmen, such as they were when Ames left South Carolina. That experience had not apparently led him at that stage to any deeper thinking about how to reconstruct the South successfully. He had reservations about Johnson's approach, but so too about that of Congress. Black suffrage he had not considered either a right or a need. He thought it unattainable anyway and saw no logic in pushing for it.[11]

Ames was perhaps beginning to change his ideas on Negro suffrage in the last quarter of 1866. A recent discussion in Paris with an "American" on "Negro suffrage" left him unsettled, as he had argued quite unconvincingly "the only true policy—which is that the negro ought not to be allowed to vote." He promised to write out the case in his diary, but he never did.[12] Around the same time, he had engaged in a "warm" discussion with an English gentleman over suffrage in England, in which Ames became exasperated by the man's opposition to the extension of suffrage in England and by the man's defense of a property-based franchise. Ames's American company in Europe in late 1866 and early 1867 was strongly Republican in sympathy, and by the beginning of 1867, when he received his commission as a lieutenant colonel in the regular army, he had become disgusted with President Johnson. On March 4, 1867, the day on which Congress called itself into special session after having passed the First Reconstruction Act over Johnson's veto, he wished he was there to know what was happening.[13]

It seems likely too that during this time his observations on the society of Europe and its undemocratic base were influencing his thoughts about the American situation. In France, Switzerland, Italy, Austria, Prussia, England, and Ireland, he commented on the similarities between the European nobility and the so-called chivalry of the South, with no liking for the pretensions of either. The dominance of the nobility he saw as a despotism based on the ignorance in which the lower orders in Europe were kept.[14] Ames thought that some of the society he observed might be rooted in the nature of different races, and in this regard he believed the English and their American cousins (the Anglo-Saxons) had a deeper drive for liberty than the French, whose undemocratic politics and society he excoriated.[15] Yet much of social differences, he thought, were rooted more in laws than in natures. In Londonderry, Ames was struck by the poverty, grime, and filth of Ireland—the houses he referred to as "the constantly occurring low, dirty hovel of the lower and dirtier peasantry. . . . The contrast between this Ireland and England is very marked. People ascribe it to the nature of the Irish. It may do so to a certain degree, but I have no doubt that had they such laws as to cause them to look forward to those things which are good in themselves or produce it; such influences as to arouse their ambition—general education etc etc they would very materially improve." In Ames's view, the situation of Negroes in America was very similar in essence to that of the Irish.[16]

The completeness with which the lives of the poor was disposed of in parts of Europe offended his values. After leaving Potsdam in late August 1866, he observed a colony of Russian peasants, a present of the czar of Russia to his brother and neighbor the king of Prussia. Their houses, dress, and way of life had been preserved as they were, and the village appeared prosperous. Yet the Yankee soldier and Republican who had helped destroy a slave empire and liberate its subjects "could but think all the time how unjust and tyrannical the governments which gave and received them, their wishes being, undoubtedly, never for a moment thought of. This is but one of the innumerable instances where this thought has occurred to me."[17]

Ames resolved his uncertainty about his future when he returned to the army in July 1867. His decision to return was influenced heavily by the limited number of viable options. What the army gave Ames after he returned to it was not only an avenue for his ambition but a purpose to that ambition. Ambition by itself seemed pointless unless linked to a worthy goal, and this took shape as he implemented congressional policy in 1867–1868, a policy with which he had developed a great deal of sympathy.[18] Among Ames and his comrades from the war the emotional link between the Emancipation Proclamation and the claims of black soldiers to citizenship became strong. Without awareness of the integrity of this association as it formed, one cannot understand the developing strength of their reactions against the unfolding policies and behavior of President Andrew Johnson. Central to these emotions—and Reconstruction was a time of high public emotion—was the spectacle of the executive increasingly at odds with Congress, the voice of the people, as Congress moved to protect the civil rights of the freedmen in the South and as the president had become identified increasingly with the leadership of the white South. For many of the men who had fought with Ames, Johnson's "white man's government" philosophy betrayed the pledges they believed implicit in the Emancipation Proclamation and due the black soldier for his sacrifices in the war. As their disappointment in the president they had initially supported grew, it changed to contempt.[19]

Three months after his return to military service as acting inspector general in Mississippi, Ames applied without result for a posting as acting commissioner for the Bureau of Freedmen, Refugees, and Abandoned Land. In the course of his service in Mississippi during 1867–1869, his acceptance of congressional Reconstruction became complete. He had always seen Congress as the true voice of the people, and his own inclinations and his own Republican ideological heritage combined in his "Mission," an ideal that drew from him a full commitment. He saw his mission as an extension of the principles of the Declaration of Independence, of the integrity of the Union war aims for which he and others had fought, and the implementation of the laws of the land then being embedded in the Constitution. By 1869 all these elements were linked in Ames's mind to the future of the freedmen.

Ames energetically exercised the powers of his position as provisional governor of Mississippi (June 15, 1868–March 17, 1869) and commander of the Fourth Military District (March 18, 1869–February 23, 1870) to implement congressional policy on Reconstruction. His tenure in these positions did much to strengthen the languishing Republican party, which had suffered defeat in the election of 1868, in part because of the effective use of violence and fraud on the part of the conservative opposition. His use of force to suppress lawlessness, his replacement of officials who had doubtful loyalties, and his supervision of voting registrations and elections, together with his known support for the policies of Reconstruction, played a significant part in the Republican victory of 1869, which brought the state back into the Union. His actions earned Ames the respect of many Republicans of both races. It was in recognition of his contribution that they elected him to the United States Senate in 1870.

The late 1860s was also the period in which he courted Blanche Butler, twelve years his junior and the daughter of Benjamin Butler, general and politician from Massachusetts, known throughout the South as "Beast" Butler or "Spoons" Butler, both appellations stemming from his sojourn as commander of occupied New Orleans. Blanche, as a well-informed and principled political observer, may have strengthened the direction of his thinking also. The attendance of General Ames and Miss Blanche Butler at the impeachment proceedings against President Johnson was noted by Washington newspapers. Their marriage, which began in 1870, was a warm and loving one, conventional in terms of its deference to patriarchy, fruitful in the biblical sense, with six children, three of whom became distinguished.

Ames served in the Senate until 1873, when he was elected governor of Mississippi in a bitter contest with James Lusk Alcorn, the leading southern white Republican of Mississippi and also a United States senator. The falling-out between these two and their supporters, triggered by Ames's support for federal intervention in Mississippi to suppress the Ku Klux Klan and inflamed by rivalry for control of the party, cost the Republican party dearly. Ames was inaugurated in January 1874, and his administration saw carpetbaggers and blacks assume much more visibility in government. Ames in January 1875 lamented to his father-in-law that the North did not understand the white South. The North wanted to believe that the South now loved the Union, but was deluded. Hatred of the Union still found enthusiastic expression in public affairs in Mississippi, especially when connected, as it usually was, with hostility to equal rights for all people. Southern whites "are not willing to admit the logical results of the last three amendments of the Con[stitution]. . . . The whole story of negro suffering and the injustice and outrage heaped upon them is horrible." The real state of affairs in the South is not told to the North, which believes white southerners when they "profess angelic virtues."[20]

There were signs, too, that Ames was wearying of the huge task confronting him. Having won control of a divided party and having carried the state in the 1873 election, a contest and victory that he relished, he found governing a frustrating experience. This frustration derived not only from the outright hostility of radical white supremacists but from shortcomings within the Republican camp. Just months after the Vicksburg riots had put the supremacists in power there, Ames acknowledged the inadequacy of the Republicans in Vicksburg and doubted that the legislature of the state would prove "equal to the emergency" it confronted. The Republicans had "a large majority in the Senate," but at a time when black rights were under direct challenge by all manner of means, six Republicans (three white and three black) were absent, thereby destroying the Republican majority. Ames found such behavior very trying. It confirmed his misgivings about the future of Reconstruction in Mississippi should the North not act and became one of the elements that led him later in 1875 into the famous bargain with the Democrats by which he agreed to disband the state militia (such as it was) and they agreed to an end to the terror and killing of black and white Republicans. The Republican governor saw the conflict between the Republicans (the Ames Republicans) and the Democrats in Mississippi as an extension of the old struggle between the "old confederate armies," now in the form of the white man's party, and the Union. The power of the United States government was urgently required in order to prevent Republican defeat.[21]

Ames was probably not far from the truth in seeing the radical white Democratic elements in such terms. The mass of southern whites, he believed, adopted essentially similar attitudes to those of white racists. How far these convictions influenced his conceptions of southern white Republicans is hard to say with any certainty, but it seems likely they had some effect. His conflict with the southern white element of the Republican party predated the 1873 election, in which Mississippi's leading southern white Republican and leading northern white Republican contended for the governorship. This conflict, a long time in the making, had split the party and was a vital ingredient among the factors that enabled the 1875 terror campaign to be put in place and to be successful. Efforts to resolve differences between Senator Ames and Governor Alcorn were made by Mississippi's first black senator, Hiram Revels, who wrote to Ames in late 1871 urging an end to the differences, which had spilled out of party forums and into the public arena. Revels said frankly that Ames was wrong to doubt the integrity of Governor Alcorn's Republicanism and vigorously defended Alcorn's record on equal rights and appointments. He pointedly denounced as a "gross misrepresentation" the charge that Alcorn intended to eliminate carpetbaggers, a conviction Ames had formed.[22] Revels's plea for Ames to work "in harmony" with Alcorn did not produce results. When Ames became governor in 1874, he removed Revels from the presidency of Alcorn University, the black university. Ames's experience, perspective, commitment, and ambition, the very things that brought him to such central involvement in Reconstruction in South Carolina and especially in Mississippi, underlay his differences with the scalawags of Mississippi. The clash of cultures, of traditions, and of values between two of the three major Republican groups in the region complicated and bedeviled Reconstruction across the South.

In Mississippi the carpetbagger-scalawag clash was reinforced by the strong personalities and ambitions of Alcorn and Ames. Both were leaders temperamentally, not followers. Alcorn's statement to his wife about his need to be first in things had some applicability to Ames. "My nature rebels at the idea of *following*; I wish to fall out with any party that says I must follow. I was not made for this. I had rather be *first* in *Coahoma* than stand second to any one. I recognize no master. I yield to no power save that which comes from Heaven. Oh! Miserable nature that I have! All my life my passion has burned like a [V]esuvius. Alas, I should ask that passion be made to sleep, but it will not."[23] The contest between these two men and their supporters, black and white, critically weakened the party at a time when the nation's commitment to Reconstruction was becoming strained.

Ames's political inexperience contributed significantly to the course of developments also. Politically experienced carpetbaggers were scarce in Republican circles in the South, and Mississippi was no exception. The factional politics of the army and the cliques and personal patronage system that operated within it had been Ames's only experience of mediating ambitions and influence, and he took these conceptions with him into politics. Perhaps as a result, he was apt to see things in personal rather than in party terms. Politics remained for Ames a vehicle for promoting one's cause and one's leadership rather than a mode of binding a range of viewpoints into something workable. Even when he attained the Republican leadership by routing Alcorn, he was buoyed that "true Republicanism" (that is, his outlook) had triumphed. The person of Ames then was important in the history of Reconstruction in Mississippi.

The matter of his residence illustrated the manner in which Ames's personal behavior and outlook affected events. He is listed on his marriage certificate in 1870 as a planter in Mississippi, a description that was perhaps more aspiration than reality. As a United States senator from Mississippi, Ames increased his vulnerability to attack as an outsider when he took quite some time to buy a house and was then hardly in Mississippi except on official business. While this may not constitute a serious offense, it betrayed an insensitivity by this most prominent of carpetbaggers to the controversial issue of local residence, with all that signified to the southern electorate.[24] Nonetheless, this insensitivity seems trivial alongside the spectacular lawlessness and violence of the Democratic campaign that eventually drove him from Mississippi.

The 1875 election campaign had restored the Democrats to power in Mississippi through one of the most effective exercises in terror seen anywhere. The Democrats then brought impeachment charges against Ames, and Ames waited only until they withdrew the charges before resigning on March 28, 1876. Ames left politics altogether after his resignation. He remained a close observer of the political scene, however, always on the alert for signs of the South rising again to control national politics, which is how he understood Cleveland's election in 1884. He served in the Spanish-American War as a brigadier general and went to Cuba with the Fifth Corps under General Shafter. Stationed in South Carolina for a period, he noted the change in sentiment toward the flag from Reconstruction days. Ames remained a Republican to the end, hoping for Hoover's success in the 1932 election. He died in 1933, the last of the Civil War generals.

Almost a quarter of a century after the overthrow of Republican government in Mississippi, Ames became engaged in correspondence with a number of people about Reconstruction. One was the young historian James Garner, then at work on a history of Reconstruction in Mississippi. Garner wrote to Ames for information and access to his papers, which Ames supplied readily, knowing only that Garner was a young college professor.[25] Ames, presenting himself as a "victim" of Reconstruction, took Garner at his word and hoped that he as a young man would, as Garner promised, "be free from the prejudices and animosities of other days, and that you will be able to understand the integrity of my purpose at all times; that you will examine the matter from every standpoint and set forth in charity, as well as justice, your findings without fear or favor."[26] Ames emphasized that the impeachment proceedings against him were "an unjustifiable wrong" and requested the chance to answer any charge Garner felt had substance.[27] Garner assured Ames again that he wanted to be as impartial as possible and that he was aware that much of the opposition to Ames had been simply prejudice against northern men. His viewpoint would be "that of neither a Northern man nor a Southern man, but that of an American, or perhaps I should say that of the *historian.*" In elaboration of the latter, he was "seeking after the honest truth."[28]

Ames must have been reassured when Garner notified him that his researches had demonstrated that there were no grounds for the impeachment action and that a number of his Democratic enemies admitted that the election of 1875 was carried unfairly. Indeed, "many are even willing to confess that they did wrong."[29] Garner had already told Ames of the large amount of credible testimony from Ames's political opponents in Reconstruction as to his "integrity" and good intentions for the state but raised their charge that Ames was an outsider with "bad advisers" and was out of touch with "the people," by which they and Garner meant white people.[30]

In response to Garner's inquiry, Ames explained that his motive in giving up his flourishing career in the military to go into politics was that "it seemed to me that I had a Mission with a large M. Because of my course as Military Governor, the colored men of the State had confidence in me and I was convinced that I could guide them successfully, keep men of doubtful integrity from control, and the more certainly accomplish what was every patriot's wish, the enfranchisement of the colored men and the pacification of the country." Ames conceded to Garner that from the perspective of 1900, his decision in 1870 to leave the military to go into politics "seems almost inexplicable" and his explanation "ludicrous," but to one with his "New England associations and education," the call to service was strong. Ames emphasized to Garner that he had acted as the agent of duly constituted authority. When Garner implied critically that Ames had made jurors of "colored" men, Ames responded that the nation's laws rather than Ames had made them "full-fledged citizens" and put them "on an equality with the whites, giving the right to vote, hold office, act as jurors and equal protection." He was bound to uphold those laws, and he did.[31]

Ames had to remove civil officers who would not uphold the laws of the land.

By 1900, when he explained himself to Garner, and with an eye to current developments in the South, Ames wished that historians would spend as much energy in studying Reconstruction as they did studying the Civil War. Ironically, Ames himself was engaged directly in rewriting the history of the Civil War through his writings on Fort Fisher, where he had directed the troops engaged in the assault only to find himself written out of the published accounts of the fall of the fort. Despite his counsel to Garner, he did not write a history of Reconstruction and declined requests to provide one.

Ames had, however, reflected much on the failure of Reconstruction. He had come to focus on the idea of race and its influence in American society, and had reached the conclusion that race feeling and identity was a more profound force in human affairs than religious consciousness. "A race conflict stirs more profoundly the depths of our natures than does religious conflicts. The best man is crucified with less regret in the first instance than in the second." The assertion of dominance or superiority by European races over others seemed to Ames a striking feature of the last few hundred years of interracial contact. More inhumanity and brutality had been committed in the name of race than in that of religion, at least by the European races who had over the preceding three hundred years either "subjugated or annihilated" what Ames called the "inferior races." And he saw no prospect of change, so pervasive was this determination, this "need" of whites to control the blacks.[32]

In the abandonment of Reconstruction and the refusal of Congress to take any action to protect blacks in the exercise of their voting rights in the South, Ames saw North and South united "on this race issue," united, that is, on white dominance and on the measures necessary to ensure it. His mission had not failed, as many charged, because of corruption; Mississippi had been in fact largely free of that, even though "the debts of South Carolina were made to do duty in Mississippi, where there were no debts." Reconstruction failed because southern whites believed "giving the negro the ballot" meant "political equality," which for whites in the South translated to "negro supremacy." And that prospect was considered to justify all manner of outrage and violence against the law of the land.[33]

Ames knew that his failure was also the failure of the Reconstruction acts and the Emancipation Proclamation to make "free and equal citizens" of the freedmen.[34] By the turn of the century, Ames had lost the confidence of the youthful crusaders of Reconstruction about the future of the Negro in America. Then as now, only "one fate" awaited anyone who challenged the subjugation of the blacks—to be "denounced and vilified in unmeasured terms" as the carpetbaggers and scalawags of Mississippi had been. These men, whose mission was so repugnant to their society and to current practices, were in fact "worthy sons of the fathers who founded this republic" and those who paid with their lives he called "noble martyrs to their political faith."[35] The offense of the northern Union men in Mississippi during Reconstruction had been to sustain the political equality of the Negro, which happened to be the law of the land. So powerful, however, was the determination of the "superior race" to dominate the "inferior race" that all standing in the way—whether individuals committed to equal rights or the laws of Congress proclaiming equal civil and political rights or presidential proclamations—were swept aside. The fact is now universally known that "at all times and places the inferior race must succumb to the superior race," a necessity before which even the power of the United States gave way.[36] It seemed from the perspective of the 1900s that personal and political differences among Republicans were far less significant in the outcome of things than he believed in 1873, when his concern was the triumph of "true Republicanism" over that of the scalawag Alcorn. Likewise, Ames was far more accommodating to Garner about the claims of various groups in the policy and patronage realms of the party than he was in the heat of the political battle. What had seemed critical issues as he struggled to shape the future along the lines of his vision for the South and to protect it from the corruption he feared from Republicans with other visions paled into insignificance as racial ideologies, and more specifically white supremacy, saturated current thinking and shaped events.

In coming to focus on the centrality of race and the inevitability of white domination to explain the failure of his political crusade, Ames identified factors outside his control. It was an analysis that might give rise to questions about how well he understood the task he was undertaking when he committed himself to making a reality in the South of the Civil Rights Act, the Reconstruction laws and the Fourteenth and Fifteenth Amendments. That he was unprepared to exercise the political leadership of the state, he readily acknowledged. As military governor, he had carried out instructions in the spirit of the Reconstruction laws, but to Garner he conceded, "As to the U.S. Senate: I am frank to confess that I was but poorly equipped for the position." He also conceded the magnitude of his undertaking: "To say that I did not comprehend the simplest elements of the problem to be solved, is to say that I was no wiser than the Nation's wise men who enacted the laws I had been executing." In resigning from the regular army to become United States senator for Mississippi, and thereby foregoing a career that would have taken him to the top of the military establishment by the time of the Spanish-American War, he acted "with little wisdom and much faith." In reply to the charge that the carpetbaggers and scalawags were "out of place or had mistaken ideas of their duty," Ames challenged the historians of his time to say "exactly what they [the carpetbaggers and scalawags] should have done—what unquestionably honest men would have done under the circumstances."[37] To his Reconstruction ally Judge Hill, a scalawag, he replied at the turn of the century, "I have thought much of those days and even now can not see how I could have conducted affairs of the state to secure the approval of the white people."[38] His critics and some of his Republican colleagues doubtless could have made some suggestions, but Ames sensed that his identity, his values and his goals were far more decisive than his tactics in producing the outcome.

Ames never doubted the rightness of his mission or the injustices done to the Reconstructionists, white and black. Nor did he ever concede that the depth of opposition to him and other Republicans in Mississippi was a reason not to do what was right and, indeed, what was the duty of the nation, to establish and protect the civil and political rights of the freedmen. He did come to an understanding of why he and his associates had failed, and he came to sense perhaps that the failure may have been inevitable, given the nature of the forces at work in the issue of race and caste. But unlike some other northerners—such as Governor Chamberlain of South Carolina, a New Yorker—Ames did not think it had been wrong to try. He was convinced that the failure to secure equal rights, civil and political, for the blacks was a tragedy that would continue to mock the ideals of the country and the dictates of its professed religion. That conviction marked him as out of step with the racial orthodoxies of his time. For that, he remained unrepentant.[39]

The power of race feeling had preoccupied Ames's reflections upon Reconstruction by the turn of the century. His understanding of its pervasiveness reflected the intellectual currents of the period. At the time that James Ford Rhodes was declaring slavery to be the curse of southern men, not their crime, and depicting the Civil War as a conflict of irreconcilable values, a perspective that offered understanding of the limits of human responsibility, the white protagonists of Reconstruction in Mississippi were coming to new understandings of their former adversaries. At the same time, Ames received informed comments that his actions were being viewed "in a much more favorable light now [1899] than when those events transpired," news of which pleased him. He acknowledged that he too now saw Reconstruction in a different light. He understood, as he had not in the 1860s and 1870s, that "two different races, especially if one be the Anglo-Saxon, can never live together on terms of equality." The bitterness he felt for years over the battles in Reconstruction had given way to sympathy for the sad plight of both races in the South, locked in a "most grievous" situation. Suppressing the rights of the blacks, however, was no solution. "There should be no servile class among a free people," declared the old Republican even as he sympathized with Hill that the relations of the races in the South was, in Ames's words, "a problem to tax [the] wisdom [of the South's wise men] to the utmost." "Progress," however, had to be made, "for the sake of the individual, the state and the nation."[40] To a white Mississippian in the 1920s, he advised reading Walter Hines Page on the condition of the South and declared, "Caste is the curse of the world. You have it in the South exaggerated by reason of race." Ames did not foresee any easing of the feelings involved for many years to come.[41]

As time passed, Ames understood more and more how remarkable had been the men who had joined to support equal rights in Reconstruction. Like others of the more radical Reconstructionists with whom Garner corresponded, Ames indicated the religious terms within which they had seen their mission. In May

1914, Henry W. Warren, a Yale graduate from Massachusetts who went to Mississippi after the war, published *Reminiscences of a Carpetbagger*, which Ames praised highly. Ames wrote to him, "I do not hesitate to say that for singleness of purpose (and high ideals according to their capacity) in man's and God's service[,] the republicans of Mississippi with few exceptions of the days you write have rarely been surpassed."[42] After the black Congressman John R. Lynch published *The Facts of Reconstruction* in 1914, Ames reaffirmed that he had never met more honest or idealistic men than those who served the Republican party in Mississippi during Reconstruction. "We were all young, each and every one believed he was doing God's service and that the final result of his labors would be the elevation of an unhappy class of the human race."[43]

To both Lynch and Warren, he gave the same explanation for failure. "Greed, the father of all slaves since time began [,] was too much for us." He saw exploitation as the companion of the caste and race system. The ex-slave was now directed by the Christian nation of America to find his "road to life and liberty and pursuit of happiness" as a serf. In his letter to Lynch, Ames returned to an enmity that had puzzled him as a young officer in South Carolina in 1865, the enmity of the poor white of the South for the blacks. Ames felt that progress for blacks would not begin until the poor white of the South recognized that "cheap serf labor degrades him. . . . But when will that time come who can say?"[44] The old blindness was currently at work with President Woodrow Wilson, described by Ames as "the leader of the men of Greed in the South who have made a serf of the black slave, whom we set free," trying to force the Spanish Mexican "to divide his land with the Indian peon." Ames thought Wilson ought to make the southern landowners divide the land with the "black peons" of the South before attending to inequities elsewhere.[45]

The conviction that Republicans in Reconstruction were doing God's work was an important source of strength to Ames and other northern Republicans as they sought to reconstruct the state and as they coped with the rejection of their mission by the South and then by the nation. It helped Ames to maintain his belief in the justice of the cause of black rights and his admiration for the white and black Republicans who had sought to secure and sustain those rights. That conviction may have contributed also to the priority he gave during Reconstruction to "true Republicanism" and the "purity" of the party over more pragmatic considerations, such as the accommodation of competing groups, differing ideologies, and personal enmities.

POSTSCRIPT

A postscript to Ames is not without relevance to understanding his significance and the meaning of his mission. In the early 1950s, the state legislature of Mississippi directed the Mississippi Department of History and Archives to complete the collection of portraits of Mississippi governors for the new Hall of Governors in the State Legislature. The request for a portrait duly went to the Ames family, who supplied a striking portrait of Ames—in the full dress of a Union general, replete with five war medals prominently displayed. The portrait was duly hung in mid-1952. In late January 1958, a few months after federal intervention began in Little Rock, Arkansas, and after the 1957 Civil Rights Act had been passed, news stories featured the portrait in the Jackson Sunday *Clarion-Ledger* and Jackson *Daily News*. Uproar followed. Only one of the stories indicated the painting was not a recent acquisition.

Henry M. ("Doc") Fraser of Jackson led the effort to have the portrait banished. Fraser had achieved prominence as an "unreconstructed Rebel" at the Democratic Convention in Philadelphia in 1948 after the passage of a Civil Rights plank of the party platform. He cut the Mississippi flag from the balcony railing and led the state delegates out of the convention.[46] Reportedly, in a letter to Secretary of State Heber Ladner, who was responsible for the administration of the building, Fraser said he was "shocked beyond adequate words" by the portrait of a carpetbag and earlier military governor hanging in the state legislature of Mississippi. "Are the portraits of Hitler, Mussolini, Joe Stalin and others of their ilk hanging in the capitol building in Washington?" he wanted to know. As if any portrait of Ames would not be offensive enough, "to add insult to injury, the portrait shows him in the uniform of a Union Yankee general with his chest adorned with medals won at the cost of lives of Southern soldier boys." Ironically, Ladner could not be reached for immediate comment as his office was closed like all other state offices in Mississippi in observance of Robert E. Lee's birthday.[47] Dr. Dunbar Rowland, admirer of Claude G. Bowers's *The Tragic Era* and former head of the Department of Archives and History and of the Mississippi Historical Society, was cited to reiterate the Redeemer catalogue of offenses charged to Republican rule in Mississippi.[48]

But the portrait stayed. Several factors worked to keep it there. Governor J. P. Coleman pointed out that the Hall of Governors was a historical record and not a Hall of Fame—the hanging of the portrait in no way endorsed what Ames had done or what he represented.[49] The president of the Mississippi Chapter of the United Daughters of the Confederacy adopted a similar line, explaining that "we of the UDC want to perpetuate historical facts" and since "we cannot dispute that Ames was a Governor of Mississippi," the portrait should stay. The Associated Press writer Douglas Starr pointed out in the Jackson *Daily News* that Ames in fact had claims to be regarded as a "state hero" in that he had deferred his resignation so as to prevent Lieutenant Governor A. K. Davis, a Negro, then accused of corruption, from becoming governor. And so the portrait of Ames stayed in the post-Brown South, though protests from organized groups such as the Jackson Civil War Round Table were made again in 1962. It seemed at last that Mississippi had accepted, however grudgingly, its carpetbag governor, though it had yet to accept his mission.[50]

NOTES

1. C. Vann Woodward, "Equality: The Deferred Commitment," in *The Burden of Southern History* (New York, 1960); 1st ed., pp. 69–87.

2. Adelbert's great grandfather was Oliver Hazard Perry, who fought the Barbary Pirates and later defeated the British on Lake Erie in the War of 1812. His great-great uncle Matthew Galbraith Perry commanded American ships sent out to suppress the slave trade from West Africa to the New World. Blanche Ames Ames, *Adelbert Ames 1835–1933: General, Senator, Governor* (Northestern, Mass., 1964), p. 4. The influence of these heroic models close to him as a source of strength and inspiration in later years ought not to be discounted. They also give an insight into his choice of career and ambition to get into West Point.

3. A. Ames, HQ, Military District Western South Carolina, Columbia, November 8, 1865, Endorsement on the report of Bvt. Brig. Genl. Ralph Ely, Act. Sub. Asst. Commissioner, BFR & A L, Columbia, November 7, 1865; National Archives Record Group (hereafter NA RG) 393, No. 4112.

4. Ames to his parents, November 24,1865, Sophia Smith Archives, Ames Family Papers (hereafter SS AFP), Series IV, Box 19A.

5. Cf. letter of Governor James L. Orr of South Carolina to Major General D. E. Sickles, Commander, District of South Carolina, April 30, 1866, commending Ames's initiative in establishing extra courts in the district to expedite the hearing of cases, NA RG 393, No. 4109, Box 11.

6. A. Ames, HW MD WSC, Columbia, March 9, 1866, to Lt. Col. Wm. M. Burger, AAG, Dept. of South Carolina, NA RG 393, No. 4112.

7. A. Ames, HQ MD WSC, Columbia, March 14, 1866 Report, NA RG 393, No. 4112.

8. A. Ames at Columbia to his parents, March 4, 1866, SS AFP, Series IV, Box 19A.

9. A. Ames, HQ MD WSC, Charleston, April 4, 1866, NA RG 393, No. 4112.

10. Ames to his parents, January 27, 1866, SS AFP, Series IV, Box 19A.

11. Adelbert Ames, unpublished Diary, Vol. 1, September 25, 1866, SS AFP, Series II, Box 3A.

12. Ames, Vol. 1, September 15, 1866 (both quotes).

13. Ames, Diary, Vol. 2, March 4, 1867.

14. Ames, Diary, Vol. 1, November 24, 1866.

15. Ibid., December 10, 1866.

16. Ames, Diary, Vol. 3, April 20, 1867.

17. Ames, Diary, Vol. 1, August 25, 1866.

18. The radical Republican sentiments of Ames's friends clearly anticipated his endorsement, as they attacked Johnson's ideas of a "white man's government" and expressed the contempt for Andrew Johnson that Ames and nearly all of his associates shared after the 1866 election campaign; H. C. Lockwood to Ames, June 11, 1868 (SS AFP, Series IV, Box 9, Folder 91) shows strong political commitment to the radical Republican cause, being very critical of Johnson and the "white man's government" attitude. P. P. Brown (formerly Col. 157 NY Vols. Inf.), St. Louis to Ames, January 26, 1870 (SS AFP, Series IV, Box 9, Folder 95) congratulated him on his election to the Senate and voiced the contempt for Andrew Johnson that seems to have been shared by nearly all Ames's associates in the war who wrote to him, whether or not they were with

him when the crisis developed between Johnson and the Congress. For Ames as for many Republicans, the process of commitment to civil and later political rights for blacks took shape in the context of (and largely in reaction against) events in the South rather than developing inexorably out of an inner dynamic in Republican thinking about freedom and citizenship.

19. Johnson had lobbied the War Department on Ames's behalf. President Andrew Johnson to the War Department, August 15, 1866, National Archives Microfilm M1 395/2.

20. Adelbert Ames, Executive Office, Jackson to General Benjamin Butler, January 10, 1985, SS AFP, Series IV, Box 20B.

21. Ibid.

22. H. R. Revels to Adelbert Ames, November 1871, SS AFP, Series IV, Box 15.

23. James Alcorn, U.S. Senate Chamber, to Amelia Alcorn, April 13, 1872, copy in Mississippi Department of Archives and History (hereafter referred to as MDAH), P. L. Rainwater Collection, Box 3, Folder 40.

24. Alcorn attacked Ames on this ground, among others, shortly before he declared his candidacy in the 1873 campaign; "The Friar's Point Delta," reprinted in *The Clarion*, August 14, 1873, MDAH Rainwater Collection, Box 3, Folder 40.

25. James W. Garner to General Adelbert Ames, August 13, 1899. Ames responded positively and promptly, and Garner assured Ames of his bona fides; Garner to Ames, September 5, 1899, and H. P. Judson, Dean of the Faculties of Arts, Literature, and Science, The University of Chicago, to General Adelbert Ames, September 19, 1899. All three letters are in SS AFP, Series IV, Box 19.

26. Ames to Garner, for "victim," n.d. (probably October 11, 1899), MDAH Garner Papers (copy dated October 11, 1899, in SS AFP, Series IV, Box 19); Garner to Ames, September 19, 1899, for Garner's objectivity, SS AFP, Series IV, Box 19; Ames to Garner, January 17, 1900, MDAH Garner Papers, for Ames's expectations of Garner.

27. Ames to Garner, n.d (probably October 11, 1899), MDAH Garner Papers.

28. Garner to Ames, September 19, October 13, 1899, SS AFP, Series IV, Box 19.

29. Garner to Ames, January 6, 1900; SS AFP, Series IV, Box 19.

30. Garner to Ames, December 4, 1899, SS AFP, Series IV, Box 19.

31. Ames to Garner, January 17, 1900, MDAH Garner Papers.

32. Ames to Mr. E. Benjamin Andrews, President of Brown University, May 24, 1895, draft of letter, MDAH Adelbert Ames Papers.

33. Ibid.

34. Ames to Garner, January 17, 1900, MDAH Garner Papers.

35. Ames to Mr. E. Benjamin Andrews, President of Brown University, February 29, March 11, 1896, MDAH Adelbert Ames Papers.

36. Ames to Garner, January 17, 1900, MDAH Garner Papers.

37. Ames to Mr. E. Benjamin Andrews, President of Brown University, May 24, 1895, draft of letter, MDAH Adelbert Ames Papers.

38. Ames to Judge R. A. Hill, December 21, 1899 (copy), MDAH Adelbert Ames Papers.

39. Ames to Mr. E. Benjamin Andrews, President of Brown University, May 24, 1895, draft of letter; Ames to Judge R. A. Hill, December 21, 1899 (copy); Ames to Andrews, February 29, 1896; Ames to R. H. DeKay of Pontotoc, Mississippi, October 22, 1923; all in MDAH Adelbert Ames Papers.

40. Ames to Judge R. A. Hill, December 21, 1899 (copy), MDAH Adelbert Ames Papers.

41. Ames to R. H. DeKay of Pontotoc, Mississippi, October 22, 1923, MDAH Adelbert Ames Papers.

42. Ames to Henry W. Warren, May 22, 1914, draft of letter, SS AFP, Series IV, Box 19.

43. Pencil draft of letter, Ames to John R. Lynch, n.d (between April 15 and May 14, 1914), SS AFP, Series IV, Box 19.

44. Ibid.; Ames to Warren, May 22, 1914, SS AFP, Series IV, Box 19. Lynch replied to Ames that it had been a "real pleasure . . . to place on permanent record my estimate of your character and worth as a man, a citizen, a soldier and a gentleman, and of the valuable services you rendered the State of Mississippi as Military and Civil Governor thereof, and as a United States Senator." John R. Lynch to Ames, May 14, 1914, SS AFP, Series IV, Box 19.

45. Ames to Warren, May 22 1914, SS AFP, Series IV, Box 19.

46. (Jackson) *Clarion-Ledger*, January 21, 1958.

47. *State Times*, January 20, 1958; (Jackson) *Daily News*, January 20, 1958.

48. (Jackson) *Clarion-Ledger*, January 19, 1958; (Jackson) *Daily News*, January 19, 1958. On Dunbar Rowland's admiration for the work of Bowers, see his praise for The Tragic Era given in an interview with a *Clarion-Ledger* reporter. Rowland inserted the typed account between two letters of September 16, 1929, in his correspondence. MDAH Record Group 31, Volume 19, Correspondence of Dunbar Rowland.

49. *State Times*, January 21, 1958. About this time, enough state money was found to move the statue of Jefferson Davis to a place of honor in front of the state legislature building.

50. Jackson *Daily News*, January 20, 25, 1958; November 20, 1962.

8

Frank Cushing and W. E. B. Du Bois: Religion, Social Science, and Traveling South in the Late Nineteenth Century

Sam Elworthy

There is an old and powerful narrative about the end of the nineteenth century that tells of how Americans lost God, church, and Henry Ward Beecher and found science. Paul A. Carter, James Turner, and other historians of religion have documented this "spiritual crisis" and found the "origins of unbelief" in Gilded-Age America.[1] Work on early social science by Thomas Haskell and Dorothy Ross has suggested how university professors, speaking a language of detached objective expertise, began to replace ministers of religion as molders of public opinion on questions of morality, mind, and social order.[2] This is the classic tale of modernization as Max Weber conceived it: bureaucratic rationality and science stealing the world from religion to forge a society of "specialists without spirit; sensualists without heart."[3]

The stories of the anthropologist Frank Hamilton Cushing and the historian, sociologist, and activist W. E. B. Du Bois traveling south in the late nineteenth century suggest a different understanding of the relationship between religious experience and social science. While both draped themselves with the authority of science, they also struggled to understand the continuing power of ritual, belief, and the irrational—spheres of human experience that social scientists had largely rationalized away in a wave of what William James called "medical materialism."[4] To extend the scope of anthropology and sociology, Frank Cushing and W. E. B. Du Bois appropriated religious vocabularies and ideas drawn from their research among Native Americans and African Americans. In the stories of these two social scientists, modernization appears not as the triumph of bureaucratic rationality, not as the hegemony of a secular North over a benighted, superstitious South, but rather as a nervous dialogue between North and South, between white and nonwhite, and between detached rationality and religious commitment.

In 1879, Frank Hamilton Cushing fled his desk job at the National Museum in Washington, D.C., and ventured into the land of the Zuñi in the American Southwest. When the rest of his party moved on, the anthropologist remained, alone and dependent on the local chief for food and shelter as he struggled to capture on paper the spiritual life of what he called "this most profoundly religious" people. One day, as Cushing sketched a sacred Zuñi dance, the ceremony took a strange new turn. Objecting to the intruder drawing their rites, the dancers approached with chants of "Kill him! Kill him!" Fortunately, Cushing had a sense of ritual. He stood slowly, pulled a knife, and placed it on the ground beside him. After a moment's hesitation, the Zuñi turned away and slaughtered a hapless dog. As Cushing later recounted the story to readers of *Century* magazine, this incident showered mana on the anthropologist, and he gradually entered the tribe's religious rituals, at first as a nervous observer and finally as a robed Zuñi priest.[5]

Three years later, Frank Cushing cut off his long hair, shed his Zuñi clothes, headband, and earrings, and journeyed back to Washington, D.C., for a ritual of a different sort. On April 22, 1882, flanked by six Zuñi chiefs, he stood before the National Academy of Sciences to reveal the results of his research in the Southwest. That evening, Cushing presented a detailed structural analysis of the Zuñi social and religious systems. Yet he fostered in the same moment an exotic sacred aura, promising to "proceed very simply, as would a Zuñi priest, could he address you, in a discussion of mythology and religion."[6] While Cushing aimed to bring scientific rigor to anthropology, friends stressed rather his "unconscious sympathy" for Zuñi culture and pictured him "in delirious sleep, delivering harangues in the Zuñi tongue."[7] Cushing was in many ways an iconoclastic figure. But his desire to draw upon the power of both sacred visions and secular rationality, to slip between his roles as Zuñi priest and Washington anthropologist, was characteristic of a broader impulse within early American anthropology.

Frank Cushing's encounter with the Zuñi in 1879 marked the beginnings of the sustained study of Native American society and culture by white Americans. Over the following twenty years, a motley group of former soldiers in the Indian wars, physical scientists, government bureaucrats, and other enthusiasts gathered around the Bureau of American Ethnology, the American Folk-Lore Society, and numerous local organizations to forge an American science of anthropology. Writing frequently for popular middle-class magazines and drawing crowds to public lectures, amateurs like Cushing catered to widespread eastern curiosity about a "primitive" people within the nation's borders, a curiosity that developed in tandem with the United States Army's removal of the threat of Native American violence.[8]

American Indian religious beliefs and rituals especially fascinated anthropologists and the public. In part, it was the attraction of the exotic.

Railroads taking tourists to the Pueblo Indian snake dance during the 1890s played up the apparently bizarre nature of "that unparalleled dramatic pagan ceremony."[9] But anthropologists also focused on the sacred because they sensed that, in stark contrast to the "modern doubt" and perfunctory Sunday Christianity of white Americans, Native Americans' religious sentiment enveloped the whole of their lives. The photographer and popular writer Edward S. Curtis echoed a common refrain when he wrote in *The North American Indian* (1907): "The Apache is inherently religious; his life is completely molded by his religious beliefs. From his morning prayer to the rising sun, through the hours, the days, the months—throughout life itself—every act has religious significance."[10]

American anthropologists sought the keys to this sacred world. They represented Native American religious experience as characterized by passionate group experience and the blurring of boundaries between body and mind, self and world. The Philadelphia physician and prolific ethnographer Daniel Garrison Brinton, for example, explained in his influential *Religions of Primitive Peoples* (1897) that the "vertiginous passion" excited by religious rituals "whirls those who yield to it out of themselves, beyond their senses, into some lofty, hyper-sensuous state, where reason totters and reality fades." Drawing on recent psychological research, Brinton argued that in these moments "the unplumbed abyss of the subconscious mind" erupted into consciousness to produce potent religious visions.[11] Religious enthusiasm formed part of a cosmology not yet broken apart into Cartesian dualisms. Anthropologists maintained that Native Americans, unable to grasp either the solid world of dead matter or pure abstractions like God, lived in an enchanted universe where stuff was alive with spirits. Washington Matthews, an anthropologist and friend of Cushing, was typical when he wrote that for Native Americans, "everything not made by human hands . . . possesses a spirit, or more properly a shade." These shades infused rocks and animals, as much as people, with vitality and supernatural power. Shades leapt between individuals and things in rituals and dreams, turning the world into a web of spiritual connection.[12]

Native Americans' sacred universe became, in the writings of anthropologists, a strange land of ecstatic feeling and wandering spirits, apparently far from the individualism, rationality, and materialism that evolutionary social science attributed to white America. Such portraits of Native American religious experience sat easily within a long tradition of descriptions of the Indian as radically "other." Some whites gazed over it all with obsessive revulsion. Frederick Morgan Davenport, in *Primitive Traits in Religious Revivals* (1905), described Native Americans during religious rituals as wallowing in "the slime of the subliminal, the lower mystical marshlands of the human spirit," a slime that modern men and women had thankfully left behind in their onward march toward "the sunlit hills of full rational consciousness."[13] Others, like George Wharton James, in *What the White Man May Learn from the Indian* (1908), drew on a tradition of "romantic racialism" to whisper in awed reverence of the inherent spirituality and otherworldliness of Native Americans.[14]

Nevertheless, both disgust and reverence left Native Americans in a distant universe.

Frederick Hoxie has argued recently that such portraits of American Indians pervaded white culture in the late nineteenth and early twentieth centuries. "The scientific discovery of the continent's indigenous traditions and beliefs," he writes, "provided an opportunity for [white Americans] to incorporate Indian people into a progressive conception of human history that ran from ancient backwardness to modern achievements." These evolutionary narratives, he continues, rendered Native Americans "irrelevant to contemporary concerns."[15] Among anthropologists, however, one can hear different voices.

As James Mooney traveled among western tribes joining the Ghost Dance during the 1890s, he began to unravel radical otherness. After months of searching for the Paiute messiah, Wovoka, founder and spiritual leader of the Ghost Dance movement, Mooney came across the unexpected. Wovoka was a Native American dressed in the clothes of a white man, he worked as a laborer for a local white farmer, and he was known in the area as Jack Wilson. Most followers of the Ghost Dance had been educated in white schools or worked in white communities. Mooney sensed that this outburst of religious enthusiasm was not a product of the backwardness of a "primitive" culture. Entering the sacred circle of dancers, he felt the real power of the dance's "hypnotic action." Back in Washington, James Mooney traced parallels between the Ghost Dance and white revivals stretching from Joan of Arc to contemporary sects like the Beekmanites.[16]

When Mooney's account of the Ghost Dance appeared in the Bureau of American Ethnology's annual report of 1896, readers understood that he was entangling Native American spirituality with white modernity in unsettling ways. John Wesley Powell, explorer of the Southwest and founding head of the Bureau of American Ethnology, warned in his introduction: "Caution should be exercised in comparing or contrasting religious movements among civilized peoples with such fantasies as that described in the memoir. . . . In mode of thought and action, red men and white men are separated by a chasm so broad and so deep that few representatives of either race are ever able clearly to see its further sides."[17] Through his comparative analysis, Mooney closed the apparent chasm between Indian "fantasy" and white "religion." Other readers saw different connections. Mooney's vivid description of white violence at Wounded Knee prompted Washington Matthews to comment in a review: "When we have finished this chapter, we cannot but feel that many centuries of Aryan civilization have laid but a thin varnish of respectability over a white-skinned savage, as wild as any savage on earth."[18]

Matthews's continuing racism is obvious. Still, James Mooney's understanding of the power of unconscious feelings and hypnotic group rituals in sacred Indian dances, in contemporary religious movements among whites, and in slayings by the United States Army, shows the uses of anthropological work to white Americans at the end of the nineteenth century for cultural critique.[19]

Accounts of Native Americans suddenly became relevant to white concerns. Mooney and Matthews inhabited a nation where violent crowds of workers mattered as much as polite, rational debate, where Christian Science and hypnosis were as pervasive as chemistry and medicine. Their work on Native Americans offered a means of suggesting that the magic of the unconscious and the power of the crowd might lurk in the center of "civilization" as much as in strange religious ceremonies in the West.

The first generation of American anthropologists drew upon their understanding of Native American religion in a similar manner as they struggled to define a methodology for their youthful discipline in the late nineteenth century. They faced a dilemma. On the one hand, they resented the prominence given to such English anthropologists as E. B. Tylor and James Frazer, who sat and speculated from comfortable libraries while Americans engaged in research among real, living Indians. On the other hand, most early students of Native American society were skeptical of anthropometry, which reduced all questions of culture to cutting and measuring brains and bodies. Cushing's generation sought to create some route between the idealism and distance of their English colleagues and the radical materialism and contact of scientists brandishing scalpels and rulers.[20]

During the final years of the nineteenth century, anthropologists like Frank Cushing and Alice C. Fletcher defined that middle route by developing a style of research later called "participant observation." In 1900, Fletcher, working independently of the Bureau of American Ethnology among the Omaha Indians, described how during the 1880s she and Cushing had abandoned the stance of detached objectivity and thrown themselves head-first into the lives of their subjects. Research became "going to live with the natives, accepting the natural conditions and merging ourselves, as far as possible, with the people."[21]

Clearly there were many different sources for this new science of participant observation, but when Fletcher struggled for words to describe the approach, she drew upon a vocabulary of Native American religion. Talking as much about her own methods as his, she argued that Cushing was led by an "unconscious sympathy into the environment" and used his "divining power" to engage with the world of Native Americans. She wrote: "To him everything was alive; nothing was dead or incapable of responding to his vital touch. Like these spring days, when every twig and bough and buried root is sending forth in unmeasured profusion tokens of the life hidden within it, so, in the atmosphere of his mind, the crude ceremony, the archaic thought, the mnemonic symbol, each and all gave forth to him the secret meaning which through them was struggling for expression."[22] Here was the enchanted sacred world of Native Americans in a new idiom. Other writers attributed the same sacred powers to Cushing, writing that his incarnations as scientist and Indian priest proved that he was really a "Zuñi familiar," a spirit at home in different worlds.[23]

The religious allusions were not merely loose words, rhetoric that the historian can pass over. Feeling the force of the broader "revolt against dualism" in late–nineteenth–century thought, Fletcher, Cushing, and other anthropologists were frustrated with detached rationality and empiricism as scientific methods.[24] They sought to show the power and possibilities of losing one's own identity for a time in another society, of cultivating unconscious, emotional, sympathetic connections with a people and with a world alive with meanings. Notions of the Native American sacred world as a realm of social emotion, loss of identity, and enchantment provided a powerful imaginative vocabulary to challenge dominant ways of doing science.

Native Americans provided a mirror for a generation of anthropologists to articulate their frustration with the white Victorian world of men like John Wesley Powell, where detached rationality, individualism, and materialism defined the limits of experience. Mooney, Matthews, Cushing, and Fletcher were not completely at home in Powell's white "civilization," nor did they fully immerse themselves in the world of Native Americans. Instead, they tried to make a world out of journeys back and forth between Washington and the West, between commitments to science and a feeling for the power of religion, between white selves and Indian others.

In 1885, W. E. Burghardt Du Bois embarked upon a similar journey. He traveled south from Great Barrington, Massachusetts, to study at Fisk University in Nashville, Tennessee. He later wrote: "I . . . was being sent to a far land among strangers who were regarded as (and in truth were) 'mine own people.'" Brought up in the whiteness and restraint of New England, Du Bois sought to understand those strangers and immerse himself in southern black culture by working summers as a teacher amidst "the hard, ugly drudgery of country life" in east Tennessee. Like Frank Cushing, Du Bois found the heart of this world in sacred rituals. Wandering from the schoolhouse each Sunday, he entered a church resounding with "wail and groan and outcry, and a scene of human passion as I had never conceived before." Moved to tears by the spirituals and awestruck by the "pythian madness" of the revival service, Du Bois entered into a lasting romance with southern black "folk" culture and African-American religious expression.[25]

W. E. B. Du Bois soon headed back north to Harvard and on to Berlin. He discarded organized religion as a personal faith and pictured himself as a "cold and scientific investigator with microscope and probe," dissecting black society and American racism.[26] In *The Souls of Black Folk* (1903) and *Darkwater* (1920), however, Du Bois continued to cultivate a more mystical identity. Drawing on biblical language and stories of the black "folk," he put prayers and spirituals on the same page as empirical research. The result was a strange alchemy of religious exhortation and detached science. Contemporaries felt the religious associations of both works. Black Americans talked of *The Souls of Black Folk* as a bible, of Du Bois as a messiah, and youths like J. Saunders Redding mumbled in church the "dark, passionate words" of Du Bois's "A Litany at Atlanta" as a personal prayer.[27]

W. E. B. Du Bois was not Frank Cushing. Du Bois was black, Cushing was white; Du Bois was an activist, Cushing a collector and dreamer. Nevertheless, there are real parallels. Both were interested in the slipperiness of racial identity, both found the detached empiricism that dominated anthropology and sociology unsatisfying, and both drew upon religious language to articulate new modes of social thought. Placing Du Bois's story alongside Cushing's illuminates how traveling south set up a creative tension between social scientific and religious impulses in the work of at least two early American social scientists.

When Du Bois began to cultivate a romance with southern black religion, he was entering a field extensively tilled during the years after the Civil War by white folklorists. From the 1870s, white southerners formed numerous folklore societies and filled the pages of the *American Anthropologist* and the *Journal of American Folk-Lore* with accounts of the "superstitions" and "primitive" religion of black neighbors. African Americans unsettled white folklorists and anthropologists in a way that Native Americans did not. Anthropologists had cultivated an exotic allure around Native Americans, who themselves remained distant and silent. While Cushing might parade Zuñi chiefs before the National Academy of Sciences, in the end it was he alone who interpreted the tribe's sacred rituals. Studying African Americans was different. Samuel J. Barrows, a clergyman and reformer, commented in a discussion of African-American religion before the Brooklyn Ethical Association in 1892: "The Indian is no longer a menace to our civilization. We have continually pushed him outside of it. But a great strip of dark Africa has been woven into the tissue of our republic."[28] Not only were African Americans obviously implicated in modern American society, but they could also talk back in discussions of their own souls. If Native Americans offered whites a mirror for reflecting on their own anxieties, black Americans were scratching and twisting the glass in disconcerting ways.

White folklorists and anthropologists eased their fears by neglecting research in favor of stylized portraits of African-American religion and "superstition" cribbed from the nostalgic plantation fiction of Joel Chandler Harris, Thomas Nelson Page, Mary Alicia Owen, and George Washington Cable. The New Englander Thomas Wentworth Higginson prefigured the anthropological approach in 1867 when he, as commander of an African-American regiment during the Civil War, recalled his encounter with black religion:

> Often in the starlit evening I have returned from some lonely ride by the river . . . and, entering the camp, have silently approached some glimmering fire, round which the dusky figures moved in the rhythmical barbaric dance the Negroes call a "shout," chanting, often harshly, but always in the most perfect time, some monotonous refrain. Writing down in the darkness, as best I could . . . the words of the song, I have afterward carried it to my tent, like some captured bird or insect.[29]

Higginson's narrative illustrates the almost universal form of late-nineteenth- and early-twentieth-century studies of African-American Christianity and voodoo. Like Higginson, reporters crept up on dark and misty nights to peer through the undergrowth at writhing black bodies. Higginson imagined himself as Walter Scott venturing through the Scottish heather. Others depicted similarly romantic quests into a secret world that they might capture and reveal to a voyeuristic public.[30]

A deep sense of both rapture and revulsion filled white accounts. Southern racists as well as New Englanders frequently recalled the romantic racialism of *Uncle Tom's Cabin* to evoke innocent, emotional, Christ-like African Americans singing the spirituals, which Higginson and others collected. On the other hand, the same writers argued that African Americans' credulity as well as their emotionalism and superstition prevented them from cultivating modern Christian character. While Higginson's black Americans were deeply spiritual, they were also "barbaric."[31]

In white accounts, the emotional power and the barbarism of African-American folk religion were remnants of the past, irrelevant to modern life and about to be swept away. John Hawkins, a white South Carolinian, for example, explained in the *Journal of American Folk-lore* in 1896 how the "ancient lore" told to him as a child by his "Maum' Sue" was fast disappearing: "The younger generation, with their school books, churches, and newspapers regard it only as a sort of harmless lunacy in their elders, and not what it really is,—the surviving fragments of earnest theories formulated in primitive times to explain the mystery of existence."[32] In contrast to the inventive and challenging studies of Native American spirituality, white writers coped with anxieties about black Americans in the present by telling themselves over and over romantic stories of a passing folk.

African-American intellectual leaders grappled uneasily with the wealth of spirituality thrust upon them by white stereotypes. The case of black students at the Hampton Institute at the turn of the century illustrates their dilemma. Writing in the institute's newspaper, the *Southern Workman*, in 1887, the white chaplain and vice principal, Hollis Burke Frissell, articulated one side of Hampton's attitude toward African-American religion. Hampton, he declared, was dedicated to ending rural black Christianity's "disgraceful orgies" and inculcating the "military discipline" and "moral earnestness" of true Christian character into its students.[33] Yet white trustees and teachers also cultivated the sacred aura of the folk among black youths. Upon hearing that students were refusing to sing spirituals because they found them demeaning, the Philadelphia merchant and philanthropist Robert C. Ogden, chair of the board of trustees, urged black pupils to take pride in "the depths of religious feeling" expressed in these "simple" slave songs.[34]

Alice Mabel Bacon, a white teacher at Hampton, formed the Hampton Folk-Lore Society in 1893 to foster among black graduates some sympathy for a rural "folk" culture that they appeared to despise.[35] Attended by blacks and whites, the society's work nevertheless played straight into the white appropriation of black spirituality. Members listened to tales by white speakers of the "gay times . . . on the plantation in the days befo' de wah!" When the Hampton society presented its work on African-American song to the 1894 meeting of the American Folk-Lore Society, four white teachers sang the "rude words" and "wild strains" in "the true plantation style."[36] Hampton offered black students a crude choice between white ideals of disciplined individualism and a black folk heritage made nostalgic and ridiculous by white appropriation. As Eric Sundquist has pointed out, it was a dilemma that has plagued African-American intellectuals from Charles W. Chesnutt to James Weldon Johnson, Zora Neale Hurston, and W. E. B. Du Bois.[37]

In a Berlin apartment on the evening of his twenty-fifth birthday, Du Bois dedicated himself to the life of a scholar. In a candlelit ritual of Greek wine, oil, song, and prayer, he declared: "Be the Truth what it may I shall seek it on the pure assumption that it is worth seeking, and Heaven nor Hell, God nor Devil, shall turn me from my purpose till I die." In his dedication to "Truth," Du Bois joined the powers of modern science to a sense of moral calling inherited from his Congregationalist youth.[38] He contrasted his own moral and scientific approach to life with the attitude of fiery religion exemplified in the black church. "I think if the latter was tried and wills relaxed," he wrote in his notebook during one of William James's lectures at Harvard, "the world would go to the devil."[39] Both *The Philadelphia Negro* (1899) and the series of Atlanta University publications on African Americans testified to Du Bois's faith in scientific empiricism. His 1903 study of *The Negro Church*, which culminated in an inquisition into the presumed ignorance and immorality of black preachers, indicated Du Bois's unease with enthusiastic Christianity.[40] Yet the exotic and ritualistic birthday celebration hinted that even at the moment when Du Bois constructed a secular self, he was playing with religious forms and meanings.

In Germany at the same time, Du Bois was working on a first novel called "A Fellow at Harvard." This obviously autobiographical tale narrated the life of John Johnson, a black youth who went to Fisk, Harvard, and Berlin, took up radical politics, and died insane. In the first chapter Du Bois departed from his own life story and refashioned sacred roots for both his fictional hero and himself. John Johnson originates not in New England, but among the black "folk" on a southern plantation. Opening amidst the "passionate frenzy" of a religious revival, the novel describes how John takes up the legacy of his grandfather, a blacksmith, preacher, and healer during slavery who had disappeared after smashing his overseer's head open with a hammer. At midnight, deep in the woods, chanting mystical African words, John finds a box of old bones and two hundred dollars in a rusty anvil, an inheritance left by the old blacksmith preacher for his grandson to fight the devil. Young John assumes the mantle: "He had a holy mission from his own flesh and blood, nay perhaps from a prophet of the high God, a mission to lead the people he loved into the promised land." Money in hand, John sets off for Fisk.[41] The conclusion is rather anticlimactic. Somehow Du Bois has to manage a transition from the high drama and mystery of folk origins into his own bourgeois, scientific life of money and education. The novel never got any further, yet it illustrates a fascination with black "folk" religion that ran alongside scientific commitment in Du Bois's novels and works of social protest from the 1890s through the 1930s.

Critics have often criticized Du Bois's King James English, melodramatic religious tales, and lines from the spirituals as gooey refuse from a romantic unconscious that the tough, secular social scientist could just not quite repress. To get beyond that dualistic assessment, one has to appreciate the uses religious ideas and religious rhetoric might have in the late nineteenth and early twentieth century for a social scientist who wanted to deal with emotion and with political commitment. Du Bois appreciated that the staunch objectivity of *The Philadelphia Negro*, "devoid of human sympathy, and careless of human ideals," avoided real moral questions and encouraged more white voyeurism, as "car window sociologists" set off into the South "gleefully" to catalog black barbarism.[42] In *The Souls of Black Folk*, Du Bois stepped out of the car. Like Cushing and Fletcher, the scientist from New England became "bone of the bone and flesh of the flesh" with the African-American folk whom he studied. Both within and outside the veil, "hot and indignant" political advocate as well as detached sociologist, Du Bois fashioned himself as a social scientist who gained magical vision, a "second sight," on America from his experience as a member of an oppressed race.[43]

To signify his immersion in the black folk and establish his experiential authority to a white audience, the light-skinned northerner depended upon appropriating the power of the African-American sacred world. An anonymous review of *The Souls of Black Folk* in *The Nation* indicates the extent to which Du Bois placed himself within the long tradition of white romantic depictions of black spirituality:

> The Negrophobist will remind us that Mr. Du Bois is not so black as he has painted himself, and will credit to the white blood in his veins the power and beauty of his book. But the fact is that the features of Mr. Du Bois's mind are Negro features to a degree that those of his face are not. They are the sensibility, the tenderness, the "avenues to God hid from men of Northern brain" which Emerson divined in the black people. The bar of music from one "Sorrow Song" or another which stands at the head of each chapter is a hint (unintended) that what follows is that strain writ large, that Mr. Du Bois's thought and expression are highly characteristic of his people, are cultivated varieties of those emotional and imaginative qualities which are the prevailing traits of the uncultivated Negro mind. The book will come as a surprise to some persons who have heard Mr. Du Bois speak upon his people's character and destiny, and, finding him coldly intellectual, have not been at all prepared for the emotion and the passion throbbing here in every chapter, almost every page.[44]

Du Bois appropriated the sacred powers of tenderness, emotion, and imagination that whites had ascribed to African Americans in order to sanctify something more than "coldly intellectual" science. He developed instead a passionate analysis of race issues from "within the veil." But even while he invoked white stereotypes, Du Bois questioned their nostalgic quality by writing as a modern black scholar, a social scientist, in the present. Like Cushing, Du Bois drew the sacred and the folk into modern society to refashion both himself and social science.

During the twentieth century, it has been easy to tell tales in which African-American and Native-American "folk" beliefs and rituals are passing away. Standing at some backward southern station, they wait on the rolling wheels of modernization and secularization to come screeching through. Whether framed as eulogies for the purity of a lost sacred world or as paeans to progress, historians as much as anyone have accepted that modernity means the crushing of the sacred and the "folk." An analysis of the uses of the religion of American Indians and African Americans in the social scientific work of Frank Cushing and W. E. B. Du Bois suggests a more nuanced understanding. In their visions of the sacred world, they imagined a modernist America made out of journeys between science and the sacred, between whiteness and nonwhiteness, and between modernity and the "folk" or the "primitive." Theirs are not isolated tales. In fact, they seem archetypal modern American narratives: the heroic anthropologist venturing into the exotic for spiritual renewal; the deracinated black intellectual finding roots in the rural South.[45] As we venture into an age in which ethnic diversity and postmodern fragmentation cast doubt over the old stories of Western progress and scientific rationality, those stories are worth telling.

NOTES

1. Paul A. Carter, *The Spiritual Crisis of the Gilded Age* (De Kalb, Ill., 1971); James Turner, *Without God, without Creed: The Origins of Unbelief in America* (Baltimore, 1985).

2. Thomas L. Haskell, *The Emergence of Professional Social Science: The American Social Science Association and the Nineteenth-Century Crisis of Authority* (Urbana, Ill., 1977); Dorothy Ross, *The Origins of American Social Science* (New York, 1991).

3. Max Weber, *The Protestant Ethic and the Spirit of Capitalism*, (New York, 1958), p. 182.

4. William James, *The Varieties of Religious Experience, the Works of William James* (Cambridge, Mass., 1985), p. 20.

5. Cushing describes his encounter in "My Adventures in Zuñi," *Century* 25 (December 1882), pp. 191–207; Ibid., 25 (February 1883), pp. 500–511; and in Jesse Green, ed., *Cushing at Zuñi: The Correspondence and Journals of Frank Hamilton Cushing, 1879–1884* (Alberquerque, N.M., 1990), pp. 218–19. See also Sylvester Baxter, "An Aboriginal Pilgrimage," *Century* 24 (1882), pp. 526–36. For Cushing's sense of Native Americans' religious nature, see Curtis Hinsley, "Ethnographic Charisma and Scientific Routine: Cushing and Fewkes in the American Southwest, 1879–1893," in

George W. Stocking, ed., *Observers Observed: Essays on Ethnographic Fieldwork, History of Anthropology*, vol. 1 (Madison, 1983), p. 57.

6. F. H. Cushing, "The Zuñi Social, Mythic, and Religious Systems," *Popular Science Monthly* 21 (1882), pp. 186–92.

7. Washington Matthews, "Remarks on Frank Cushing," *American Anthropologist*, n.s. 2 (1900), p. 187; Matthews, "Review of Frank Hamilton Cushing, *Zuñi Folk Tales*," *American Anthropologist*, n.s. 4 (1902), p. 144; Alice C. Fletcher, "Remarks on Frank Cushing," *American Anthropologist* n.s. 2 (1900), pp. 769–71.

8. On the first generation of anthropologists and folklorists, see Curtis Hinsley, *Savages and Scientists: The Smithsonian Institution and the Development of American Anthropology, 1846–1910* (Washington, D.C., 1981); Simon Bronner, *American Folklore Studies: An Intellectual History* (Lawrence, Kans., 1986); George Stocking, *Race, Culture, and Evolution: Essays in the History of Anthropology* (Chicago, 1982).

9. Walter Hough, *The Moki Snake Dance: A Popular Account of that Unparalleled Dramatic Pagan Ceremony of the Pueblo Indians of Tusayan, Arizona, with Incidental Mention of Their Life and Customs* (Passenger Department, Santa Fe Route, 1898), p. 17.

10. Edward S. Curtis quoted in G. B. Gordon, review of Curtis, *The North American Indian, American Anthropologist*, n.s. 10 (1908), p. 437. On "modern doubt" and late–nineteenth-century fascination with intense religious experience, see T. J. Jackson Lears, *No Place of Grace: Antimodernism and the Transformation of American Culture, 1880–1920* (New York, 1981).

11. Daniel Garrison Brinton, *Religions of Primitive Peoples, American Lectures on the History of Religions, Second Series* (New York, 1897), pp. 178, 185.

12. Matthews quoted from a synthesis of the American "enchantment" argument, A. B. Ellis, "The Indwelling Spirits of Men," *Popular Science Monthly* 36 (1890), p. 800. The summary of anthropological arguments comes out of discussions in periodicals and monographs on Native American religion from 1880 to 1915.

13. Frederick Morgan Davenport, *Primitive Traits in Religious Revivals: A Study in Mental and Social Evolution* (New York, 1968; first published 1905), p. 279. Two studies of anthropological approaches to Native American religion stress, wrongly I think, only the theme of revulsion: Charles Reagan Wilson, "Shamans and Charlatans: The Popularization of Native American Religion in Magazines," *The Indian Historian* 12 (1979), pp. 6–13; Ake Hultkrantz, *The Study of American Indian Religion*, ed. Christopher Vecsey (New York, 1983).

14. George Wharton James, *What the White Man May Learn from the Indian* (Chicago, 1908). On "romantic racialism," see George M. Fredrickson, *The Black Image in the White Mind: The Debate on Afro-American Character and Destiny, 1817–1914* (New York, 1971), and Robert F. Berkhofer, *The White Man's Indian: Images of the American Indian from Columbus to the Present* (New York, 1978).

15. Frederick E. Hoxie, "Exploring a Cultural Borderland: Native American Journeys of Discovery in the Early-Twentieth Century," *Journal of American History* 79 (1992), p. 972.

16. James Mooney, *The Ghost Dance Religion and Wounded Knee* (New York, 1973.; first published 1896), p. 928; L. G. Moses, *The Indian Man: A Biography of James Mooney* (Urbana, Ill., 1984), pp. 52–96.

17. John Wesley Powell's introduction quoted in Moses, *The Indian Man*, pp. 91–92.

18. Hinsley, *Savages and Scientists*, p. 218; Washington Matthews, "Review of James Mooney, *The Ghost Dance Religion and Wounded Knee*," *Journal of American Folk-Lore 10* (1897), p. 248.

19. See George E. Marcus and Michael M. J. Fischer, *Anthropology as Cultural Critique: An Experimental Moment in the Human Sciences* (Chicago, 1986), on this intellectual tradition.

20. The jibes at the English and distrust of materialism fill the *American Anthropologist* and the *Journal of American Folk-Lore*. See, for example, W. W. Newell, "Notes on Books Received," *Journal of American Folk-Lore* 5 (1892), pp. 170–72, and Swan M. Burnett, "The Modern Apotheosis of Nature," *American Anthropologist* 5 (1892), pp. 251–55.

21. Fletcher,"'Remarks on Frank Hamilton Cushing," p. 367, and see also Fletcher "Leaves from my Omaha Notebook: Courtship and Marriages," *Journal of American Folk-Lore* 2 (1889), pp. 219–26. There are also issues of gender involved here, as Fletcher sought to fashion a feminine mode of science.

22. Fletcher, "Remarks on Frank Hamilton Cushing," pp. 367–70.

23. Washington Matthews, "Review of Frank Hamilton Cushing, *Zuñi Folk Tales*," in *American Anthropologist*, n.s. 4 (1902), p. 144.

24. For a general discussion of the broader "revolt against dualism," see especially Arthur O. Lovejoy, *The Revolt against Dualism: An Enquiry Concerning the Existence of Ideas* (La Salle, Ill., 1955).

25. Du Bois repeated the narrative frequently. See W. E. Burghardt Du Bois, *The Souls of Black Folk: Essays and Sketches* (Chicago, 1903), pp. 60–68, 189–91; W. E. B. Du Bois, *Darkwater: Voices from within the Veil*, (New York, 1920, 1969), pp. 5–23; W. E. B. Du Bois, *Dusk of Dawn: An Essay Toward an Autobiography* (New York, 1940), pp. 13, 19, 21–27; Du Bois, *The Autobiography of W. E. B. Du Bois: A Soliloquy on Viewing My Life from the Last Decade of Its First Century* (International Publishers, 1968), pp. 117, 119–20. Quotations from *Darkwater*, p. 13; *Autobiography*, pp. 117, 120. For an analysis of *The Souls of Black Folk* as a cultural immersion ritual, see Robert B. Stepto, "The Quest of the Weary Traveler: W. E. B. Du Bois's *The Souls of Black Folk*," in William L. Andrews, ed., *Critical Essays on W. E. B. Du Bois* (Boston, 1985), pp. 139–73. Three works are central on Du Bois: David Levering Lewis, *W. E. B. Du Bois: Biography of a Race, 1868–1919* (New York, 1993); Arnold Rampersad, *The Art and Imagination of W. E. B. Du Bois* (Cambridge, Mass., 1976); and especially the imaginative William Jeremiah Moses, *Black Messiahs and Uncle Toms: Social and Literary Manipulations of a Religious Myth* (University Park., Pa., 1982).

26. Du Bois presents himself as a scientist most clearly in *Dusk of Dawn*, quotation from p. 21, but see also pp. 26, 50–51.

27. Du Bois, "A Litany at Atlanta," in W. E. B. Du Bois, *Darkwater*, pp. 25–28. The sanctification of souls and Du Bois is evident in William H. Ferris, "*The Souls of Black Folk*: The Book and Its Era," in Andrews, ed., *Critical Essays*, p. 127; J. Saunders Redding, "Portrait . . . W. E. Burghardt Du Bois," in Andrews, ed., *Critical Essays*, pp. 23–24.

28. Samuel J. Barrows, *The Evolution of the Afric-American, Man and the State: Studies in Applied Sociology* (New York, 1892), p. 318. Mrs. Waller R. Bullock, founder of the Baltimore Folk-Lore Society, developed the same image in "The Collection of Maryland Folk-Lore," *Journal of American Folk-Lore* 11 (1898), pp. 7–8.

29. Thomas Wentworth Higginson, "Negro Spirituals," *Atlantic Monthly* 19 (1867), p. 685.

30. The literature on black Christianity and voodoo during the late nineteenth and early twentieth century is enormous, but one can get a sample from Bruce Jackson, ed., *The Negro and His Folklore in Nineteenth-Century Periodicals* (Austin, 1967), and find some useful assessments in Alan Dundes, ed., *Mother Wit from the Laughing Barrel: Readings in the Interpretation of Afro-American Folklore* (Englewood Cliffs, N.J., 1973). For archetypal quest narratives, see Marvin Dana, "Voodoo: Its Effect on the Negro Race," *Metropolitan Magazine* (New York) 27 (1908), pp. 529–38, and John Bennett, "A Revival Sermon at Little St. Johns," *Atlantic Monthly* 98 (1906), pp. 256–68.

31. Higginson, "Negro Spirituals," p. 685.

32. John Hawkins, "An Old Mauma's Folk-Lore," *Journal of American Folk-Lore* 11 (1896), p. 131.

33. H. B. Frissell, "Report of Moral and Religious Work," *Southern Workman* 16 (1887), p. 73.

34. Robert C. Ogden quoted in "A Sunday Evening Church Service at Hampton Institute," *Southern Workman* 24 (1895), p. 79.

35. Alice Mabel Bacon, "Work and Methods of the Hampton Folk-Lore Society," *Journal of American Folk-Lore* 11 (1898), pp. 17–21, and see also Bacon, "Proposal for Folklore Research at Hampton, Virginia," *Journal of American Folk-Lore* (1893), pp. 305–9.

36. On the "gay times," see Frank D. Banks (who was one of the singers from Hampton before the American Folk-Lore Society), "Plantation Courtship," *Journal of American Folk-Lore* 7 (1894), p. 147. The presentation at the American Folk-Lore Society is recounted in "Folk-Lore and Ethnology," *Southern Workman* 24 (1895), pp. 30–32.

37. Eric J. Sundquist, *To Wake the Nations: Race in the Making of American Literature* (Cambridge, Mass., 1993).

38. Du Bois, *Autobiography*, p. 170.

39. W. E. B. Du Bois, "Philosophy IV Notebook, William James Lectures and Notes, 1888–90," in Papers of W. E. B. Du Bois, University of Massachusetts Microfilm, Reel 87.

40. W. E. B. Du Bois, ed., *The Negro Church* (Atlanta, 1903).

41. Du Bois, "A Fellow at Harvard," Papers of W. E. B. Du Bois, Reel 87, p. 87; See also another unpublished novel centered around African-American religion, "Bethesda A.M.E.," on the same reel. Du Bois's use of religion is discussed in Rampersad, *Art and Imagination*, especially pp. 5–6, 36, 76–77, 105, and Moses, *Black Messiahs*, especially pp. 18–22, 67–69, 113–15, 142–74.

42. Du Bois, *Dusk of Dawn*, p. 62; Du Bois, *Darkwater*, p. 21.

43. Du Bois, *Souls of Black Folk*, pp. viii, 2, 9, 154.

44. Anonymous, "Review of *The Souls of Black Folk*," from *The Nation*, June 11, 1903, in Andrews, ed., *Critical Essays*, p. 31.

45. On anthropologists, see James Clifford, *The Predicament of Culture: Twentieth-Century Ethnography, Literature, and Art* (Cambridge, Mass., 1988), and on African American-intellectuals, Nathan Irvin Huggins, *Harlem Renaissance* (New York, 1971).

9

Race, Gender, and Modernism: The Case of Lillian Smith

Bruce Clayton

Do many people today still remember and read Lillian Smith? Many feminists do; so do some southern liberals and professors searching for a usable past or that elusive thing called the southern mind. In 1944, her novel *Strange Fruit* was a much talked about best-seller. It made some folks squirm; it was controversial, some said obscene; for a brief while the federal post office agreed. The novel is a melancholy tale of illicit interracial love, a tragedy that ends with a lynching. Boston banned it. Atlanta, still basking in the warm, romantic glow of Margaret Mitchell and *Gone with the Wind* (the book and the film), sold the book but snubbed the author. Five years later the north Georgia writer, who hurled her thunderbolts from atop Old Screamer Mountain where she ran a girl's camp, struck again with *Killers of the Dream*. It was an autobiographical kamikaze work that slammed racial segregation at every turn and warned darkly that Dixie's unholy trinity of white supremacy, worship of (white) women, and fervid religion corrupted the soul and emasculated the dream of decency and freedom.

Lillian Smith (1897–1966) was a brave, lonely voice crying out against racism and Jim Crow, and other forms of oppression, from as early as the 1930s. That was decades before the majority of white "liberals" (most of whom preferred to be called "moderates") could bear to think of a South without segregation. When the civil rights movement shifted into social activism in 1955 in Montgomery, Alabama, Smith embraced the crusade. The historic Supreme Court ruling of 1954 was "every child's Magna Charta," she announced in the *New York Times*, in a letter the Atlanta *Constitution* apparently refused to publish.[1] She then went straight to her writing desk to produce *Now Is the Time* (1955). This passionate tract pleaded with the white South to do the right thing.

If these and most of her other published writings (before her death from cancer in 1966) did not match the power of her first two books, it was not for lack of intensity or feeling.

But how well do we know this Cassandra in Dixie? Her one major biographer, Anne C. Loveland, concentrated on the public person—what she did, her books, their reception, her reputation.[2] But the private individual, the woman within, the person who once confided to a friend that she was an enigma, even to herself, has proved elusive. "To tell you the truth," she once wrote late in life, "I have so many selves that I wonder how I'd do an autobiography," and then added mysteriously: "I have touched the fringes of hell again and again and almost once or twice barely touch[ed] the edge of heaven."[3]

Whatever did "Miss Lil," as she was known to neighbors and several generations of campers and their parents, mean? And what prompted someone so gracious, so decorous, so properly dressed and conventionally coiffured—she certainly didn't look like a wild woman—to write those fierce books? And never marry? And live up on that mountain with her longtime companion and fellow writer, Paula Snelling?

Answers lurk in her published works and letters, a revealing number of which have been published recently. Smith was a prodigious, old-fashioned correspondent, and had it not been for two fires—one set by vandals in 1955, the other set some time earlier by Smith and Snelling—Smith's manuscripts and unpublished works would be an even greater trove, and her life much more amply documented. Even so, Lillian Smith's surviving letters, taken in conjunction with her published writings, provide substantial insight into her mind and psyche.

She was the soul of idealism. An invigorating optimism controlled her heart and guided her mind even as she battled cancer from the mid 1950s on. Her love of the South, when combined with her abiding conviction that ordinary southerners wanted to be humane, even toward their black neighbors, allowed her to look bravely at the South's scars and speak candidly. She yearned to do good, to be a voice of reason, to lead. She believed passionately that writers could meld social uplift and imagination and produce art. In that she was very much a child of her era, the 1930s, but closer to John Steinbeck than to William Faulkner. If the daunting goal of wrenching art from outraged morality proved unreachable and diminished her literary stature, her letters sound a fresh, authentic voice, a personal immediacy, and point to depths of jangled emotions. *Killers of the Dream* is ostensibly her life story, but it should be read as a coming-of-age parable, a psychological profile of life in a sexually repressive, segregated, biracial society. The book, some articles, and some fragmentary autobiographical manuscripts constitute the sources for her life before her writing career began in 1936, when she and Snelling founded the quarterly *Pseudopodia*.[4] That quirky title was quickly changed to *North Georgia Review* and, in 1942, to *South Today*. Loveland gave less than twenty pages to Smith's formative years—including her birth in Jaspei, Florida, in 1897; the family's move to Clayton, Georgia, in 1912; Smith's meager formal education; two stints at Baltimore's Peabody Conservatory of Music (1917–1918, 1919–1922); three years of teaching at a mission school in China; and her reluctant return in 1925 to help her ailing parents run Laurel Falls Camp. She purchased the facilities from her father in 1928 and assumed complete control of the camp. Royalties from *Strange Fruit* plus a generous publisher's advance to write another novel allowed her to discontinue the quarterly in 1946 and the camp three years later.

Lillian Smith was possessed by seriousness, dedicated to her writing and civil rights—which were often the same thing—and candid in her opinions, whether she was talking to a friend or Martin Luther King, Jr. Yet she was always, as are so many creative people, in the grip of her feelings. With money, she was generous almost to a fault. She could also be a warm, supportive friend. But even with friends, she was prickly and overly sensitive; she resented the slightest criticism or failure to "understand" or value her work. In her comments on other writers, however, particularly those whom she considered competitors, she was critical to the point of nastiness. In everything, she was opinionated, sometimes paranoid—though she was justified in the 1940s and 1950s in thinking that Atlanta's Ralph McGill and other white males like Hodding Carter loathed her and much that she stood for or represented in her personal life. She was extremely jealous of her reputation—what writer isn't?—but her outbursts about her critics frequently betrayed a fragile, easily bruised ego. To her, life was real, life was earnest.

Fleeting but revealing hints about her secret sexual life with Snelling appear in her letters. But mainly white-hot anger about racism singes all of her pages and competes with her tough love of the South and her stern desire to add understanding to judgment. She felt compelled to grab and shake white southerners and show them the error of their ways, to document the destructiveness of racism. This was obviously the case in *Strange Fruit.* Yet she bristled when anyone concentrated on the obvious, overriding theme of race. Race, racial prejudice, "the Negro problem," as whites said—these were incidentals; her novel was about the human condition. She groused about being pigeonholed or labeled that little southern lady who was "for" Negroes. She was for the human race, for all people. To the end of her days, she resented the judgment that *Strange Fruit* was a racial novel. She never understood why liberals applauded it mainly as a good deed.

Yet in 1942, two years before the book was published, she told Walter White of the NAACP that "my theme is basically concerned with the effect upon not only lives but minds and emotions which the concept of race in the South has. It is an indictment of the church in the South and I imagine the thesis is fairly apparent that the author doesn't think it is possible for a white person to be a Christian in the South; and hard for Negroes to be."[5]

A decade later, upon finishing *Now Is the Time*, she replied to Lawrence S. Kubie, a prominent New York psychoanalyst who prized her novel, that while she had not originally intended to "solve the 'color problem,'" many of the appreciative reviews made her weep for joy. "I did not even realize myself the urgency of the color problem until I was two-thirds through the book. My own book converted me to the importance, the urgency and, indeed, the universality of this 'problem.'" Even so, she maintained staunchly to the end, her novel was a "fantasy," with every character in it "myself or a mirror in which I looked at myself."[6]

She thought that at the time and in retrospect, or wanted to think that as she sorted out her experiences to discover what she had "really" intended. (It should be remembered that Smith had a temperamental artist's penchant for dramatizing herself as misunderstood or, worse, persecuted.) As the years went by and her anger about her literary reputation continued to fade, she was even more adamant that she was deliberately misunderstood and therefore "low rated."[7]

In 1961, a Hollywood agent wrote to her concerning the possibility of selling the film rights to *Strange Fruit*. Innocently unaware of her hurt feelings and fury, he made the mistake of suggesting that she should expect only a modest fee. She needed two fulsome missives to get him properly rebuked. She was not about to give her book away. "I know that *Strange Fruit* is an American classic and will in literary history and social history be considered so. Just now, it is being pushed aside, covered with silence, because it struck so deeply into white culture, laying bare so many of our self-destructive values and intellectual habits." She and her book—and her destiny—she said crossly, should be compared to Herman Melville and *Moby Dick*.[8]

Her second letter dripped with vitriol. The agent had obviously been listening to those white men who were still attacking her. She passed over in silence the stinging complaint from some blacks that her novel was highly racist.[9] (Nonnie Anderson, the young black woman at the center of the drama, is a bright college graduate, yet she works uncomplainingly as a domestic and does nothing with her life but wait, as though in a swoon, for Tracy Deen, her shallow white lover from across the tracks. Just what Nonnie, or anyone, would have seen in this marshmallow of a man is never explained, and the novel suffers badly as a result.)

Smith railed against the "tremendous anger against me felt by many white men not because of racial ideology but because I told their sex secrets—and secrets that are not too bright and honorable to look at." When the right offer came, she said, then she would allow a film version. "In my own opinion, some day I rather think *Strange Fruit* and *Killers of the Dream* plus my other writings give me the Nobel prize. I am patient; I know my worth; I know my historical value to this country; and I just don't have to sign [anyone's] contract."[10]

Smith's hurt feelings and dogged belief in the worth of her books is understandable. (Nietzsche says somewhere that artists simply cannot have too much ego, cannot believe too much in themselves: the world bulges with critics who live only to hurt and destroy.) But even Smith's fondest admirers must wonder what was in her mind when she wrote that if filmed, the book "should, under no circumstances, be a 'race' play. It should avoid this stereotype like poison."[11] She made the astounding suggestion that the role of Nonnie should be played by a prominent white American actress, or an Asian or European, perhaps the Italian star Sophia Loren. The "role is too hurting for any American Negro to do well."[12] Since virtually every major scene and line of dialogue in the novel depends upon the races of the two star-crossed lovers, Smith's suggestion (besides bordering on an unconscious and unintended racism) is mystifying to anyone not privy to her notion that the book was a "fantasy" based on her life.

When she finished *Strange Fruit* in the early 1940s, Smith resolved to be done with thinking about race. She would put a clamp on "Martha," the rational, critical half of her personality. From now on "Mary," the artistic, imaginative storyteller struggling to find a voice in Smith's writing, would be given free rein. Martha was rules and conscience, the superego working overtime; Mary was play and abandon, the libido in action. Smith was quite explicitly Freudian in her perception of her duality.[13] She embodied what Nietzsche saw as an ancient conflict in Western art: the struggle between the Apollonian regard for reason and right conduct and the Dionysian desire to play, to dance, in a frenzy of joy.

Critics assumed *Strange Fruit* had been written by Martha, stern voice of duty and right conduct. But she would show her critics by unleashing Mary to return and finish "Julia," a novella begun in the 1930s. "Julia," she told her publisher upon accepting a large advance in 1947, "is about a woman made so empty because her men filled her so completely with their dreams that she had no room to grow. In the big sense, it is a study of the role of Madonna worship in Western culture."[14] Now as Mary, Smith would concentrate not on race but on women (we would say gender) and their struggles to break free.

But old domineering Martha reasserted control. "Julia" went back into the drawer, and Martha wrote *Killers of the Dream*, placing race and its debilitating effects on gender and sex at the center of the southern experience. It was a book she felt driven to write. As she would later explain to Carson McCullers (and probably herself), she wrote not to give answers but to find them, and discover what she truly believed. But the task proved difficult. "Ghosts" crowded into her mind. It was "the hardest of all books for me to write," she remembered, because "it stirred deep and dangerous memories."[15]

She came to terms with her religious, right-thinking father (whom she deeply admired). But she could not confront her mother directly, portraying her merely as an obedient wife and conventionally nice person. Smith was never close to her mother (who died in 1938) and needed years to accept her lack of real affection for her. But in *Killers of the Dream*, Smith vented her repressed hostilities in a devastatingly critical chapter on "The Women," castigating them for, among other things, imposing their social timidity and sexual repression on their children.

Later, in correspondence with the psychiatrist Kubie, she dealt as frankly as possible with her feelings: "In *Killers of the Dream* I explored the depths with some thoroughness, I think. I realized the symbolic significance of darkness, body openings, etc. I also stressed the interrelationship of the body image and Puritanism. I stressed the effect of our bi-racial childhood, our colored and white mothers, or proximity to the black breast of our nurse, the black hand that bathed us, etc. I stressed the ambivalence in white southern men and women who had a nurse in childhood."[16]

Killers of the Dream made clear her conviction that racial prejudice, even when held by benign people like her parents, was intricately, and destructively, intertwined with assumptions about sex. In this she was hardly alone in her generation; W. J. Cash's imaginative speculations about the white South's attachment to an unhealthy, self-deceiving "gyneoltary" come to mind.[17] But Smith saw far more deeply than Cash or any of her contemporaries into what this meant for women.

Largely self-taught, she was as well prepared intellectually and as emancipated emotionally as any other white critic of her time to probe racism. Yet once again, as she put the finishing touches on *Killers of the Dream*, she cried out from the depths: "I hope to God I am through with race when I finish this book. I feel that I have had a thorough breakdown myself and I hope it purges me of certain guilts, and so on, forever!" Maybe she needed, as William James would say, a "moral holiday" from seriousness. She knew she had to laugh or cry at her slavish devotion to Martha and the dark humor of her predicament. She reported to her editor that when she told her secretary—"southern, smalltown, sweet and sensitive, and often whitefaced after a day's work on this thing"—that her next project would be a cookbook, "she beamed and whispered, 'Oh, yes, please.'"[18]

But there would be no cookbook in her future. A woman of cascading compassion, she knew that it was one thing to be "against" racism because of what it did to whites—traditionally, the unifying assumption of moderates and liberals—and quite another to care about, or even give any thought to what blacks endured.[19] Like W. J. Cash and very few other white southerners, she knew that the white South did not have a clue about what blacks thought or felt.[20] But unlike Cash and virtually every white moderate or liberal, she made it her business to try to find out. Starting in the 1930s and continuing on down through the 1950s, she convened interracial gatherings, usually of black and white women, at her mountaintop home. For several summers, she and Snelling traveled extensively through the South, listening and learning from the black community. Such trips filled her with despair about whites, but she was buoyed by the courage of blacks to endure.

After addressing a black audience in 1944, she cried out to a close friend that blacks "are a people almost without hope, and desperately searching for 'a Messiah.' Even a white one!" People like herself had to speak out. "Somehow white people must be shown what is happening to the minds and emotions of the Negroes. We have 13 million people on our hands who are heartsore and almost hopeless and desperate."[21]

Not surprisingly, she declined an invitation that year to join the Southern Regional Council, a moderate organization not yet ready to abandon Jim Crow. "We simply cannot turn away and refuse to look at what segregation is doing to the personality and character of every child, every grown up, white and colored, in the South today," she replied. "Segregation is spiritual lynching. The lynched and the lynchers are our own people, our own selves."[22]

Her anger at racism was such that she refused to support American involvement in World War II. Fascism was despicable, but joining the war effort would only divert attention from racism at home. Still, she understood, she told her friend Eleanor Roosevelt in 1942, why blacks where willing to serve. "There is something heartbreakingly valiant about the young of the Negro race, so eager to prove to white America their willingness to die for a country which has given them only the scraps from the white folks' democracy." But she knew there was "resentment" too, "a quiet, strong resentment, running like a deep stream through their minds and hearts; something I think few white Americans arc aware of, or want to face."[23]

For the most part, her white neighbors accepted Miss Lil—a fact she loved to point to as proof that the ordinary white southerner would be fine if demagogues would just shut up. Occasionally someone made a nasty remark. In 1947 a rumor spread that she had entertained "hundreds" of black women at a recent conference and had even been seen kissing some of them. But her neighbors, she reported proudly to a friend, rose up and said it wasn't so. One "of the old female gossips" knew it couldn't be true because Lil did not have room for "hundreds" of guests. And as for kissing, why, "'Lil doesn't kiss anybody except an occasional child." Another "poor old sister who was determined to do her part in my defense," Smith chuckled, said "'I bet it was Jews she kissed anyway; Jews and "darkies" (her word) look a lot alike in the twilight. I bet it was that.'"[24]

Usually, though, she could not contain her anger, privately or publicly. There was nothing funny—or forgivable—about the "timidity of our liberals" to condemn segregation or the demagogues exploiting Jim Crow, she said in a long letter in the *New York Times* on April 4, 1948. In January, President Truman had condemned segregation in his State of the Union address. In February, he sent Congress a civil rights package with teeth in it. Segregationist diehards like Senator Strom Thurmond of South Carolina, sensing that this president meant business, began to plot the Dixiecrat revolt.[25]

Why were the South's liberals so timid, Smith wondered aloud in her *New York Times* blast, which further convinced many white southerners that she was a loose cannon: "It is hard to understand such timidity at a time like this, unless we remember that Georgia, U.S.A., still has a lot in common with Georgia, U.S.S.R. Totalitarianism is an old thing to us down home." In 1959, after the bombing of an Atlanta synagogue, Smith allowed herself to hope that perhaps the outrage had awakened "Atlanta's best people" who for too long "had been moral zeroes."[26]

But Lillian Smith's mind went much deeper than anger. Her genius and greatness of soul was her abiding sensitivity, her empathy, her heartfelt willingness to try to put herself in the other's shoes. For her, the long-oppressed black southerner was the white South's inescapable "other." Doubtless, as a woman who was frequently dismissed as "odd," she saw something of herself in those whose "difference" in pigmentation prohibited them from voicing their true thoughts or living out their hidden feelings.

"It must be subtly frustrating to an intelligent Negro to be told by his white friends, by those white Americans who honestly believe in and cherish democracy," she wrote during World War II, "that although the Negro should be given democracy he hasn't the right to protest his lack of it."[27] In 1946, when Eugene Talmadge conducted a racist campaign in his quest for the governorship, Smith publicly charged him with germ warfare, with "scattering bacteria" over the state, infecting everyone with sickness. She thought of the harm racism inflicted on the South's children. "White children swelling with arrogance over having a white skin; colored children shamed to the bone over being 'colored.' White children overhearing 'nigger' jokes . . . colored children overhearing bitter reactions from their folks."[28]

How did blacks endure it, she cried out. In the 1950s, as she battled cancer, she took strength from the oppressed souls of black folk. "Always, when it begins to feel too hard, I remember the Negroes: all the Negroes who have lived in insecurity in the South and North; all who have taken snubs and humiliations day after day, sometimes for a lifetime." In this instance, Smith was responding to a plea from a northern educator seeking funds that would enable Alabama activists Clifford and Virginia Durr to send their child to a private school in the North and escape the local hardships of being the daughter of white pariahs. Smith tried to think of northern friends who might contribute. But she couldn't stop fretting about black children trapped in segregated, dilapidated schools. "It cannot be any harder for Virginia's child than it is for thousands and hundreds of thousands of Negro children. *We must see it in perspective* [emphasis added]; and we whites must be willing to endure, willing to suffer a bit."[29]

No wonder waves of turbulent emotions crashed over Smith in 1961 when she read John Howard Griffin's poignant book, *Black Like Me*. Griffin, a conscience-stricken white Texan, had secreted himself away, shaved his head and had his skin dyed brown. On meeting him unexpectedly, even old friends failed to recognize him and assumed he was a black man. He then toured the South for six weeks, experiencing the humiliations African Americans felt every moment. His heart-wrenching account of his sojourn in *Black Like Me* shocked a good part of the nation. When Smith started the book, she was mesmerized. "I felt a knife was turning in my heart and mind. I sat here, afterward, feeling we white southerners do not deserve even mercy; we do not deserve life; we are soft and rotten to the core, we put sugar in rotted wounds and think we are doing something highly healing and civilized, and bow down to our own futility."[30]

Smith's outpouring of feelings reveals more than her volcanic compassion or even her identification with the oppressed other. Griffin made her realize all the more the modernist insight that human intelligence is blinkered, bounded by time and space, and by abstractions. She sensed, once again, that the quest for certitude was "absurd," part and parcel of the futile human desire to "prove" everything and to substitute some abstraction, like "the Negro," for thinking and feeling. Life was in flux, nothing was permanent; human beings were "intricate and complex"—and unfinished, that was the awful beauty of life. To accept all that and "the uncertainty principle which Heisenberg writes about so elegantly" was the hallmark of the modernist mind and what it meant to "belong to the 20th century."[31]

None of this did Smith find depressing. She thought others, too, should find it liberating; maybe then they could begin to understand how humans should hurl abstractions aside and simply be and accept each other. "I wish I never had to hear the words *race relations* again; or *segregation* or *integration*, or *rights*. I long to be free to be human—and I have never been, and I know it." [32]

That dream and the intellectual foundations of her mind lead to the answer to one big question surrounding Smith. What accounts for her racial emancipation? Loveland found the answer in Smith's early experiences outside the South—in Baltimore and New York and, particularly, in China, where she saw, at an impressionable age, great social injustices, racism, and inequalities of wealth. Morton Sosna argued that "evangelistic religion" lies at the heart of her liberalism and the need to issue jeremiads—how else explain that she "fought segregation with the fervor of a fundamentalist preacher attacking sin."[33] Both Loveland and Sosna are partly right.

Smith frequently credited Gandhi with enlarging her sympathies. And there are references to "God" in her correspondence, but they are vague and fugitive. She approached life with a reverence in her heart for religious feeling and a roaming mysticism in her mind—particularly in her later years. But she was never conventionally religious, and there is little evidence that Methodism did much more than impart a moralistic tone to her public voice. Her comment to Martin Luther King, Jr., soon after the success of the Montgomery bus boycott in 1956 suggests Smith's objective, rational—not subjective or deeply felt—view of religion: "I, myself, being a Deep South white, reared in a religious home and the Methodist church[,] realize the deep ties of common songs, common prayer, common symbols that bind our two races together on a religio-mystical level, even as another brutally mythic idea, the concept of White Supremacy, tears our two people apart."[34]

Like many secular intellectuals of the 1950s who had discarded their religious upbringing, Smith read Paul Tillich and hastened to assure him that she agreed "that religion is the dimension of depth in all our spiritual functions."[35] In this period also, when she was undergoing treatment for cancer that went in and out of remission, she read widely and with considerable feeling in the works of modernist writers like Miguel de Unamuno, Pierre Teilhard de Chardin, Rainer Maria Rilke, and other mystical theologians and poets who found some spirituality and deeper meaning amidst the flux and uncertainty of modern life. But she came to most of these late modernists near the end of her life, long after her racial emancipation had begun.

Her intellectual base, built when she was young and refortified throughout her life, was Sigmund Freud. Smith "read all of Freud," says Loveland, and Fred Hobson has argued correctly that Freud's imprint can be detected on every page of *Killers of the Dream.*[36] Smith did not agree completely with Freud, she hastened to inform psychiatrist-historian Robert Coles in 1961, but "'his books were a raft that I hopped on and escaped from the whirlpools of life.'" Freudianism "'helped me to come to grips with many of my false guilt feelings, and with my Puritanic upbringing; it also helped to loosen this awesome bond to my family which made me feel I must always be the 'Martha' in every situation, although I longed to get away from family.'"[37]

Reading Teilhard de Chardin's *The Phenomenon of Man*, Smith found renewed personal hope and a shield against despair brought on by her illness. She also discovered, particularly in Teilhard de Chardin's reconciliation of science and faith, a way to see evolution as an antidote to life's manifest irrationality and, in the language of modernism's last gasp, "absurdity."[38] Like Henri Bergson of Freud's generation, Smith found her answer in a chastened version of what the modernist Bergson had called "creative evolution." "If you will read the last chapter of the revised (1962) edition of *Killers of the Dream*," she explained to a friend, "you will see what I mean by man evolving into something far more complex, intense, *thinking*[,] than he has been before. He is[,] in a very real sense, and utterly unlike the rest of the material world, participating in his own evolution by the tensions set up by his own discoveries and thoughts."[39]

But how well did modernism serve Smith in her private life? She credited Freudianism with helping her resolve or cope with many of her guilt feelings. But what about her sexual life—her need to accept herself, her erotic feelings, her sexual desires, and her long-standing love of Paula Snelling?

The two women met in 1921, the year Snelling came to work in the athletic department of Laurel Falls Camp. But it was not until 1925, when Smith returned from China, that the two women got to know each other well. Smith was on the rebound following two failed love affairs with older men —attachments with obvious Freudian overtones, given Smith's complicated relationships with her parents. Revealingly, she rejected both older men because they were apparently more interested in sex than in the "sharing of real interests."[40]

In the fall of 1927, while studying psychology and education for a semester at Columbia University's Teachers' College, Smith shared an apartment with another young female camp counselor. Whatever their relationship, it ended "drably," Smith remembered. By the time Smith's father died in 1930, she and Snelling were close friends, perhaps already lovers. Smith had named Snelling assistant director of the camp as soon as she purchased it, and the two began a permanent relationship.

That they became intimate is obvious from the few letters that escaped the fires. After reading Wilhelm Reich's *Function of the Orgasm* in 1946, Smith wrote playfully that Reich at times "let his enthusiasm for orgasms run away with him. Still, I'm all for orgasms—and shall continue to argue that you should be!"[41] Snelling feared that Smith's failure to write often indicated that she had stopped loving her. Not at all, Smith replied gently. She had long ago discovered that if she wrote to Snelling, "I won't write books. I am afraid of not having enough libido for both. And remember[,] when I am wholly in love I can't write a line! So there!" Smith closed saying, "I'd love to feel your lips on mine . . . and I can imagine other feelings too[.]"[42] Smith mentioned her avid reading of Freud's *Leonardo da Vinci* and expounded on the id and the superego, and the imperative need she felt not to indulge in love letters and thus squander her "fantasy life," the very point Freud makes in *Three Essays on the Theory of Sexuality.*

The letters that escaped the flames offer clues to Smith's tangled feelings about her sexuality—and suggest what a snare modernism could be. In a letter writen in 1952 from New York City, Smith's wording suggests that the burning was quite recent. "It did you good to go through the old letters, didn't it. The picture of you [writing the early letters?] swung me back through the years. You were so darned cute and attractive. You are 'sweeter,' 'finer' now but had something then that was so *young* and—nice, that bi-sexual charm which no one dares admit is seductive—except in real life."[43]

Then Smith lays bare her continued guilt. "I am sorry my letters are burned, that is my ambivalence. My shame about something different and completely good. It has been that shame that has destroyed the keen edge of a pattern of love that was creative and good. Blurring it, dulling it."[44] She uses the word shame twice. Her ambivalence and shame had not only blunted her love for Snelling but dulled her deepest emotion that was "creative and good." The inference here is inescapable: Smith's inability to shake free of the taboos of lesbianism had also limited her seriously as a writer. One wonders whether she ever allowed herself to believe fully and to acknowledge that the sexual orientation that rendered her an outsider had given her a special sensitivity to the South's great excluded, segregated race.

Yet in spite of her own complex feelings, Smith urged Snelling to write a candid book. "Perhaps you want to go to your grave with your 'secrets' but I don't think so. It is not in your family tradition to express. But you are different." Was Smith actually urging her friend, someone she loved deeply, to let the world know who and what they were, and had been, up there on their closeted mountain? Unless she knew full well that Snelling would never do it, Smith appears to be genuinely willing for Snelling to break the silence.

"However esoteric or strange or special," Smith wrote passionately, "*you should put down your feelings about you and me and life* [emphasis added]. What it has meant to you. What this relationship has meant. *It* might be *the* masterpiece, [and greater than] my poor little attempts to tell the world how to be good."[45]

What Snelling thought of this is unknown, but Smith could not publicly, or as a writer, knock down the doors of her prison of sexual inhibitions. Her heart (her libido) felt one thing about her erotic personal life, but her head (that old superego) "knew" something else. Freud's language is more than suggestive here; she had absorbed his categories and assumptions. Having read "all of Freud," she indeed knew, as her references to squandering her "fantasy life" indicated, his *Three Essays on the Theory of Sexuality*. She had, quite obviously, accepted Freud's theory that homosexuality was the result of an adult having never fully worked through and transcended an earlier stage of sexual orientation, specifically narcissism, in which libidinal energy is directed back toward one's own body.

Her willingness to follow Freud attests to her intellectual rigor and the grip the taboos of her youth and culture had on her. But accept Freud she did, however painful she found it, however much guilt and shame it burned into her psyche. Her own term, "ambivalence," tells the tale, yet it permitted her to live two lives, one private, one public—and to live actively, to write and to commit herself to the defining social issue of our time, the civil rights movement.

Whatever strains and stresses she felt about sexuality, however, she disguised or distorted in her books. Both *Strange Fruit* and *One Hour* (1959) make only fleeting, noncritical references to lesbianism. But in *Killers of the Dream*, in the bitter chapter on "The Women," Smith obliquely but harshly described sexually disgruntled daughters who turned against their mothers: "The protesters turned toward the cities, gathering together, a grim little number, cropping their hair short, walking in heavy awkward strides, and acquiring, as do subjected people who protest their chains, the more unpleasant qualities of the enemy." But they did not fully understand themselves. "Not daring in the secret places of their minds to confess *what they really wanted* [emphasis added], they demanded to be treated 'exactly like men.'" They were part of a larger uprising of women in "Western culture, a kind of *fibroid growth of sick cells* [emphasis added] multiplying aggressiveness in an attempt to cure." Needless to say, "there was no comfortable place for such women in the South, though a few lived in every town."[46]

When she shifted her attention to the effect of traditional southern mothers on their sons, Smith specifically, using Freudian language, made a slurring reference to homosexuality. No one would "dare" to "censure" the mothers, Smith wrote. "But we know that these women, forced by their culture and their heartbreak, did a through job of closing the path to mature genitality for many of their sons and daughters, and an equally good job of leaving little cleared detours that led downhill to homosexual and infantile green pastures, and on to alcoholism, neuroses, divorce, to race-hate and brutality, and to a tight inflexible mind that could not question itself."[47]

Lillian Smith wrote that in 1949. Did she ever regret her words? In 1961 she brought out an expanded version of *Killers of the Dream* and made no changes in a sentence that slandered homosexuality by listing it with such sins as "race-hate and brutality," two of her lifelong objects of criticism.

Ugly rumors spread about her relationship with Snelling. "Odd" and "queer" were bandied about behind her back. She knew what people said. Their words cut to the bone. It was one thing for an uncouth, bullying politician like Eugene Talmadge to scatologically dismiss *Strange Fruit* as a "literary corncob."[48] It was another to feel the butcher knife of verbal abuse Hodding Carter wielded when he called her a "sex obsessed old maid."[49] Still, she soldiered bravely on, an embattled racial liberal. "Well—this is my South," Lillian Smith wrote pensively to Paul Tillich in 1960, "the South I was born in and still love." There was "cruelty and blindness" yet warmth and resiliency in Dixie's people. But sometimes she despaired for the white race. She confessed that "I say this only to a few; I rarely say it at all; but sometimes as I write, talk, work[,] trying, like a Cassandra, to warn my people, I feel the words breaking to pieces against my own face."[50]

But was she a Cassandra in Dixie? On the racial issue, yes. She told the truth. But what is one to make, finally, of the conflict between her private life and her public pronouncements about sexuality? Maybe she tried to speak candidly. She insisted, not once but several times, that *Strange Fruit* was a "fantasy," and every character in it was herself—"or a mirror in which I looked at myself."

Suppose, for a moment, that is true. Make that leap of the imagination. Lillian Smith certainly earned the right to be heard as sympathetically as possible. If she was every character, or every other one was "a mirror" of herself, then she could well have thought that in a "fantasy" she was both a white male and a black female. The novel is about forbidden relationships, crossing lines, breaking rules, being different, rejecting prescribed roles, transcending categories—and all those racial "abstractions" Smith abhorred. If in her mind the novel was not about race, then it must have been about some other forbidden "strange fruit."

That nobody got it, and that no one decoded the novel, is not the issue. Nor was her unwillingness or inability to spell out any such fantastic interpretation. Anyway, what artist wants to have to tell the audience what the play or poem "means"? Nor is it of any special importance, at this late date, to say that if everybody missed the point, she obviously lacked the artistry to create a work that would reveal not just a "meaning," but layers of meaning. That she did not succeed does not mean that she did not try. Cassandras, after all, are cursed by the gods to fail.

NOTES

This chapter is a revised and extended version of a paper that originally appeared in the *Georgia Historical Quarterly* 78 (1994), pp. 92–114.

1. *New York Times*, June 6, 1954.

2. Anne C. Loveland, *Lillian Smith: A Southerner Confronting the South, a Biography* (Baton Rouge, 1986); see also Morton Sosna, *In Search of the Silent South* (New York, 1977), pp. 172–97; Fred Hobson, *Tell about the South: The Southern Rage to Explain* (Baton Rouge, 1983), pp. 307–22; Leslie W. Dunbar, "A Southerner Confronting the South," *Virginia Quarterly Review* 64 (Spring 1987), pp. 202–14; Jo Ann Robinson, "Lillian Smith: Reflections on Race and Sex," *Southern Exposure* 4 (Winter 1977), pp. 43–48; Redding S. Sugg, "Lillian Smith and the Condition of Woman," *South Atlantic Quarterly* 71 (Spring 1972), pp. 155–64; Margaret Rose Gladney, "A Chain Reaction of Dreams: Lillian Smith and Laurel Falls Camp," *Journal of American Culture* 5 (Fall 1982), pp. 50–55; "Lillian Smith's Hope for Southern Women," *Southern Studies* 22 (Fall 1983), pp. 274–84; "Lillian Smith: A Southerner Confronting the South," *Southern Changes* (March 1987), pp. 13–14.

3. Lillian Smith to Wilma Dykeman, October 30, 1965, Lillian Smith Papers, Hargrett Rare Book and Manuscript Libraries, University of Georgia; reprinted in *How Am I to Be Heard? Letters of Lillian Smith*, edited with an introduction by Margaret Rose Gladney (Chapel Hill, 1993), p. 333. Since most of the letters cited in this chapter are included in Gladney's collection, my citations to all reprinted letters will be to Gladney's fine anthology.

4. Lillian Smith, *Killers of the Dream* (New York, 1949; rev. and enlarged ed. 1978); "The Old Days in Jasper: A Reminiscence," *Virginia Quarterly Review* 58 (Autumn 1982), pp. 677–82.

5. Lillian Smith to Walter White, February 14, 1942, Gladney, *Letters*, p. 55.

6. Lillian Smith to Lawrence S. Kubie, June 2, 1955, Gladney, Letters, p. 167.

7. Lillian Smith to Jerry Bick, September 9, 1961, Gladney, *Letters*, pp. 278–79.

8. Ibid., Gladney, *Letters*, p. 278.

9. Loveland, *Lillian Smith*, pp. 68–69.

10. Lillian Smith to Jerry Bick, October 27, 1961, Gladney, Letters, pp. 287–88.

11. Lillian Smith to Jerry Bick, September 9, 1961, Gladney, *Letters*, p. 278.

12. Lillian Smith to Jerry Bick, September 9, 1961, Gladney, Letters, p. 280.

13. Loveland, *Lillian Smith*, pp. 18–21, 26, 113, 244, 258.

14. Lillian Smith to Lambert Davis, March 21, 1947, Gladney, *Letters*, p. 116.

15. Quoted in Gladney, *Letters*, p. 115.

16. Lillian Smith to Lawrence S. Kubie, June 2, 1955, Gladney, *Letters*, p. 167.

17. W. J. Cash, *The Mind of the South* (1941; repr. New York, 1969), pp. 87, 89; Bruce Clayton, *W. J. Cash: A Life* (Baton Rouge, 1991), pp. 208–11.

18. Lillian Smith to George Brockway, [June, 1949], Gladney, *Letters*, pp. 125–26.

19. Bruce Clayton, *The Savage Ideal: Intolerance and Intellectual Leadership in the South, 1890–1914* (Baltimore, 1972), pp. 185–216.

20. For a discussion of race in the life and thought of Cash, see Bruce Clayton, "The Proto-Dorian Convention: W. J. Cash and the Race Question," in *Race, Class, and Politics in Southern History*, ed. Jeffrey J. Crow, Paul D. Escott, and Charles L. Flynn, Jr. (Baton Rouge, 1989), pp. 260–88.

21. Lillian Smith to Glenn Rainey, [January 1944], Gladney, *Letters*, p. 79. For an excellent recreation of Lillian Smith's world, her determination, and her generation's confrontation with the race question, see John Egerton, *Speak Now against the Day* (New York, 1994), pp. 260–63, 288–90, 312–16.

22. Lillian Smith to Guy B. Johnson, June 12, 1944, Gladney, *Letters*, 87; Egerton, *Speak Now against the Day*, p. 356.

23. Lillian Smith to Eleanor Roosevelt, April 7, 1942, Gladney, *Letters*, p. 58.

24. Lillian Smith to Edwin R. Embree, February 5, 1948, Gladney, *Letters*, pp. 117–18.

25. The best recent discussion of these years is Egerton, *Speak Now against the Day*, pp. 467, 471–95. See also Nadine Cohodas, *Strom Thurmond and the Politics of Southern Change* (New York, 1993), pp. 126–53.

26. Lillian Smith to Lawrence S. Kubie, June 29, 1959, Gladney, *Letters*, p. 227.

27. Lillian Smith letter to the editor, *PM Magazine*, January 16, 1943, Gladney, *Letters*, p. 66.

28. Lillian Smith, Address to the Board, "Committee for Georgia," June 3, 1946. Gladney, *Letters*, pp. 103–4.

29. Lillian Smith to Carmelita Hinton, June 18, 1955, Gladney, *Letters*, p. 173.

30. Lillian Smith to Margaret Long, December 3, 1961, Gladney, *Letters*, p. 292.

31. Ibid., pp. 292–93.

32. Ibid.

33. Loveland, *Lillian Smith*, pp. 11–21; Sosna, *In Search of the Silent South*, p. 197.

34. Lillian Smith to Martin Luther King, Jr., March 10, 1956, Gladney, *Letters*, p. 193.

35. Lillian Smith to Paul Tillich, November 17, 1959, Gladney, *Letters*, p. 232.

36. Hobson, *Tell about the South*, pp. 315–17.

37. Lillian Smith to Robert Coles, September 18, 1961, quoted in Loveland, *Lillian Smith*, pp. 18–19.

38. Lillian Smith to Jane Stembridge, November 21, 1960, Gladney, *Letters*, p. 260.

39. Lillian Smith to Phyllis L. Meras, October 2, 1964, Gladney, *Letters*, p. 310.

40. Lillian Smith, Autobiographical Manuscript, quoted in Gladney, *Letters*, p. 5.

41. Lillian Smith to Paula Snelling, January 30, 1946, Gladney, *Letters*, p. 98.

42. Lillian Smith to Paula Snelling, [February 6, 1946], Gladney, *Letters*, pp. 100–1.

43. Lillian Smith to Paula Snelling, [June 19, 1952], Gladney, *Letters*, p. 136.

44. Ibid.

45. Ibid., p. 137.

46. Smith, *Killers of the Dream*, pp. 140–41.

47. Ibid., p. 153.

48. Quoted in Sosna, *In Search of the Silent South*, p. 191.

49. Lillian Smith to Chloe Fox, February 1956, Gladney, *Letters*, p. 191.

50. Lillian Smith to Paul Tillich, December 1960, Gladney, *Letters*, p. 263.

III

LABOR IN THE NEW SOUTH

10

Aspects of Modernization in the Loray Mill Strike of 1929

John Salmond

In 1929, a wave of strikes swept through the textile mills of the southern piedmont. Mostly short in duration, usually unorganized, always defeated, at times by a combination of management and state power, this unrest nevertheless profoundly shook the southern textile industry. Of the strikes the one with which people remain most familiar was that at the Loray Mill, in Gastonia, North Carolina, which began on April 1, 1929. Certainly not the most successful of these several outbreaks, nor even the most violent, the unfolding events of the Gastonia strike—the shooting of the town's police chief in a clash with the strikers; the wave of violence that followed his death; the trials of the alleged perpetrators, all members of the Communist-controlled National Textile Workers Union (NTWU); the martyrdom of the strike's balladeer Ella May Wiggins; the conviction of the Communist leaders and their subsequent flight into the vastness of the Soviet Union; and, finally, the half-dozen "proletarian" novels based on the Gastonia story—have all served to make it a tale well known in outline to historians of the twentieth-century South. They have given it a special resonance, down the years, that the events of themselves may not deserve. Moreover, despite Liston Pope's marvellous study *Millhands and Preachers*, published in 1942, the details of what occurred in Gastonia that year remain shadowy.[1]

Jacqueline Hall, in her analysis of the deeper meanings of another of the 1929 strikes, that in the Glanztoff mill in Elizabethton, Tennessee, and with her coauthors in *Like a Family*, has provided a model for unraveling the Gastonia story, emphasizing as she does the Elizabethton strike's connections with "modernity," or "modern values." By "modern values" I mean those associated with the social and economic processes of industrial development and the change, as Dan Singal has described it, from a personal and localistic world to "one increasingly urbanized, beaureaucratic and hurried"—a world becoming freed from Victorian constraints, increasingly secular, a world in which greater "selfhood" could be realized. It is Hall's model that I intend to follow in this chapter. In Elizabethton, women activists predominated, and as Hall writes, "The activists of Elizabethton belonged to a venerable tradition of 'disorderly women,' women who, in times of political upheaval, embody tensions that are half conscious or only dimly understood. Beneath the surface of a conflict that pitted workers and farmers against a new middle class in the town lay an inner world of fantasy, gender ideology and sexual style." In developing her argument, Hall talks convincingly about the "gender based symbolism" of the women's protest style, discussing the inner meaning of their dress patterns, their language, and their gestures, as well as emphasizing the erotic undercurrent of much of it. The young women of Elizabethton, she wrote, "combined flirtation with fierceness on the picket line." Their story was not only firmly part of the female protest tradition, it was also part of their particular quest for the liberating trappings of modernity. As the authors of *Like a Family* write percipiently, "Young people who had led the protests of the 1920s had come of age in a society very different from the one their parents had known. Their identities had been formed in the mill village; they had cast their fate with the mills." Yet, at the same time they were becoming part of a national, even global, culture, a world of radio, Ford cars, and fast-changing value systems, "the popular culture of their generation's changing times."[2]

Gastonia's young people, no less than those elsewhere, were caught up in this process of change. Within a day or two of the strike's beginning, a correspondent remarked favorably on the youthfulness and enthusiasm of many of the strikers. "How happy they are, the young folks, to be taking part in the strike," he exclaimed. "They are thrilled; the young girls laugh; some have on overalls; they flirt." Not every observer, however, was similarly enthusiastic about the involvement of the young in the strike. Later in the year, testifying for the prosecution in the trial of those alleged to have murdered the police chief, Mrs. Walter Grigg admitted that what she disliked most about the strike was the way the young people seemed to lose all restraint as a result of it. They were always making noise, she complained, "hugging and kissing" all the time, once "right before my sister and what company we had one night." She thought it was "downright disgusting."[3]

In particular, it was the presence of substantial numbers of young women among the strikers, how they dressed and how they acted, that most exercised some observers. Cora Harris, writing in the *Charlotte Observer*, first drew attention to this phenomenon. "If Gastonia has never realised that militant women were within its bounds," she noted, not altogether approvingly, "it certainly knows so now." Commenting on the previous day's mass meeting of strikers, she stated that most of those present had been women "dressed in their gay Easter frocks and a few with spring coats. I was particularly attracted," she admitted, "by the popularity of silk stockings." The women listened attentively to the speaker, Ellen Dawson, who urged them to take the lead in spreading the strike, "for there are sixty per cent women in the textile industry today." When she had finished, "a well dressed and rather fiery young woman jumped up to the platform and screamed 'yes, they put me in jail and I'm proud of it. I never did nothing to go to jail for. They said it was for disorderly conduct. Well, I thank God I can stand up for my rights and I'll go again and shed blood if it will help this 'ere Union.'" Her audience went wild. "A profound applause and a big reception for the daring young women followed," recorded the less than impressed Harris.[4]

The same day, Mary Pressley, writing in the *Charlotte News*, also commented on the female strikers' dress and behavior. "To the younger girls of the mill village," she asserted, "the strike is a thrilling affair. It gives them a chance to ramble about at their leisure, chatting with their friends, and hoping for more excitement. Many of them are wearing knickers or overalls, not at all disconcerted by the contrast of these utilitarian garments with long collars or other feminine adornments."[5]

It was left to two correspondents for the *Gastonia Gazette* to apprehend the unease such behavior brought. "It isn't decent for a respectable lady to go on the streets," one woman wrote. "I have seen young girls, I mean strikers, going up and down the street with old overalls on and men's caps, with the bills turned behind, cursing us, calling the cops all kind of dirty things." A Loray employee complained that what disgusted him was "women mixing in this strike. A really to goodness woman would not loiter around, and fight and curse like men. In all strikes I think, the women ought to go home and leave the men to settle it."[6] With unconventional styles of dress, unseemly, even "unwomanly" behavior, the strike in the Loray Mill was clearly having an unsettling effect on the behavior and attitudes of some of Gastonia's young women. What Hall found in Elizabethton—distinctiveness in language, in dress, in gesture—was also present over the mountains.

What of the erotic undercurrent to the protest style of these young women? It, too, can be identified among the youthful strikers of Gastonia. Certainly the general secretary of the National Textile Workers Union (NTWU), Albert Weisbord, recognized its presence, and moved to turn it to the Union's advantage. In his first speech to the strikers, he told the young women that they had a particular task to undertake, and that was to use their sexuality to unsettle the young National Guardsmen presently protecting the Loray Mill. "You girls and women, go in a body to these soldiers," he exhorted. "They are not hard-boiled gunmen," but rather young, vulnerable, local boys. He told the girls to flirt with them, to ask them, "Do you mean to shoot us down and stab us and our children [?]. Urge them to create trouble in their ranks," so they would no longer obey their officers. The girls had the sexual power to do this, he asserted. They would see "these boys throwing down their guns and uniforms" in the face of such an approach. More than one observer, too, commented on the sexual energy that George Pershing, one of the party officials sent to assist the strike's leader, Fred Beal, seemed to excite among Gastonia's girl strikers. The handsome and well-connected Pershing, according to Cora Harris, had a real "Chesterfield manner," and moved about the town surrounded by a cluster of young women. Even Vera Buch, who arrived in Gastonia on April 5 to be Beal's deputy and who was utterly contemptuous of Pershing, admitted the power of his sexual appeal. Many of the young women were quite besotted with him, she said, and were heartbroken when, after only a few weeks, he wangled his return to New York.[7] Young women remained loyal to the NTWU, even after the cause was hopelessly lost. At the trial of those accused of shooting Chief Aderholt, there they were in the courtroom, "flappers," said Cora Harris, "in their brief skirts, colorful blouses and chokers, bracelets and hats at jaunty angles"—"modern girls," Gastonia-style.[8]

Yet to overemphasize the role of young women in the Gastonia strike and to look for the prime reasons for their involvement as being in the realm of the psychosexual would be to neglect the centrality of the economic and class concerns that bound all the strikers together. Cora Harris, in her disapproving way, got it right when, after noting the youthfulness of so many of the female strikers and after having remarked on their silken hose, she also commented that there were "some pathetic old women in the crowd," or at the very least, women old before their time, "whose backs were bent with life's heavy burdens." She had even met one of them, Mrs. John Faulbright, a mill worker for nine years and head of the hastily formed strike relief committee who, "with a babe in her arms and two on the floor," told her in "an infuriated manner" what it was like to raise a family on a combined weekly wage of $18.50, less charges for accommodation and utilities deducted by the mill. She had spent the previous night in the city jail, Mrs. Faulbright said, and had been given egg and beef sandwiches for her supper. It was "the best meal" she had had for six months. Mrs. Faulbright was mad at the mill and its management, and "I says a plenty when I gets mad."[9]

Mary Pressley made essentially the same point. The young girls may have found the strike's first days "thrilling" and liberating, but the older women were much more serious. The unrest of 1929, after all, was caused mainly by the introduction of a range of cost-cutting, labor-saving devices known collectively as "the stretch-out." Everyone suffered as a result of these, but women operatives most of all. Some lost their jobs to male workers as a consequence, as they were physically unable to meet the increased demands placed on them. Others found themselves transferred to piecework, their pay packets drastically reduced. Such women demanded shorter hours and higher wages, an end to the demeaning cost-cutting devices—especially the "hank-clock" and the stretch-out—and better living conditions for themselves, their husbands, and, especially, their children. They would not give in lightly, Pressley thought, even if it meant going to jail, and they believed in the union, for, as Bertha Hendrix recalled, "it was the first time I'd ever thought things could be better."[10]

These women did go to jail, much more frequently, in fact, than their men, for they did most of the picketing, a dangerous occupation indeed, in the lawless situation that came to prevail in Gaston County. They were beaten, they were abused, turned out of their homes by mill management, often deserted by their husbands, and eventually forced to live in tents provided by the Communists, which they turned into a community. They were there, too, in the courtroom, when all was lost. There were older women, said Harris, "with deep lined faces," often sitting with their flapper daughters or, like Mrs. Eva Heffner, throwing her arms around her seventeen-year-old son, one of the defendants; "'God bless you my boy,'" she cried as she "kissed him tenderly." Outside the court, she told waiting reporters how proud she was of him. For these older women, the NTWU had promised a better future, and they stuck with it accordingly.[11]

Perhaps in the person of Ella May Wiggins, remembered as the strike's balladeer and revered as its martyr, we have someone who exemplified both the changing values highlighted by some of the strikers and the deep, class-based issues that motivated others. Ella May—for she used her maiden name once her feckless husband, John Wiggins, had left her in 1926—did not work at the Loray Mill, but at the American Mill in nearby Bessemer City, where the NTWU was also active. When the union came, she threw herself enthusiastically into the activities, becoming not just the strike balladeer, but an effective local organizer and a rousing speaker at strike rallies, drawing on her own experience of having lost four children to the cumulative effects of poverty and trying to raise the remaining five on a weekly wage of $9. Ella May was a woman of sufficient independence to have publicly taken a lover after Wiggins left her, to have had a child by him, and to have her lover recorded on the birth certificate as the father. Moreover, employers had singled her out, long before the strike began, as someone likely to cause trouble. She was a "hard-boiled type of woman," they thought, "who loved a quarrel and a fight, and her home had been the scene of many disorders." Yet when she spoke and when she sang for the union, it was her children she emphasized, those she had lost and those for whom she dreamed of a better future, once the class battle was won. When in a widely publicized confrontation on Capitol Hill she took on North Carolina's junior senator, Lee Overman, about conditions in the mills, it was his remark about children that set her off. "How can I send my children to school when I can't make enough to clothe them decently," she demanded of him. "When I go to the mill at night I have to lock them up at night by their lone selves. I can't have anyone to look after them. Last winter when two of them were sick with the flu I had to leave them at home in bed when I went to work. I can't get enough good clothes to send them to Sunday School." "Lock them up at night by their lone selves"—what bitterness is embodied in that simple statement.[12]

Finally, what of a group of people largely lost to history, with the exception of Fred Beal? That is, the strike's leadership, the NTWU and party officials who came South in 1929 to help bring on the revolution, who ended up being tried for murder in Charlotte's courts. They, too, were young. David Clark, the spokesperson for mill management, initially believed that was one reason for not taking the strike too seriously. "It has been started by two boys and a girl," he wrote dismissively in the *Southern Textile Bulletin*. The majority of those who came were women, and they were modern. There was Vera Buch herself. Born in Connecticut of a mother who could trace her New England ancestry back to 1635, Vera grew up in New York City. She had been valedictorian of Hunter High School and was a graduate in French from Hunter College with a distinguished academic record. She had also been a Communist since 1920, had been active in the great textile strike in Passaic, New Jersey, in 1926, and later did party work in the Pennsylvania coalfields and the automobile plants of Detroit. She was also the unmarried lover of Albert Weisbord.

There was Amy Schechter, born in England, daughter of Solomon Schechter, formerly a Cambridge don, then president of New York's Jewish Theological Seminary. A graduate of Barnard, she had grown up in comparative luxury, in large houses with spacious gardens, and had lived a large part of her adult life in the United Kingdom. Now, when not on the road for the party, she lived in a tiny Chicago apartment, which she and her sailor husband shared with Earl Browder, of whom, according to Mary Heaton Vorse, she was a "feverish admirer." There was Juliet Stuart Poyntz, another daughter of privilege. Born in Nebraska, with a degree in history from Columbia, she had studied at both Oxford and the London School of Economics, and had taught at Barnard and Columbia. A dedicated Communist, she was shortly to be directed to end her open party involvement in favor of secret work, and it is probable that she was eventually murdered by the KGB. There was Sophie Melvin, who worked with the children. Only nineteen at the time she arrived in Gastonia, born in Ukraine of Jewish parentage, survivor of a long and perilous journey from her village to the United States, Melvin's toughness was masked by her "cherubic, pretty face." She had come to full party work the hard way, through the Pioneers, the Young Communist League, and the Passaic strike, and already had had her share of unconventional life experiences, including hitch-hiking from New York to Gastonia.[13]

There was scarcely a Victorian value left in any of these women. Moreover, how different their lives had been from those of the southerners with whom they came to work. Yet much more than Beal, Pershing, and the other male leaders, they gave the strike its backbone, they were its day-to-day leaders, they were at the head of the picket parades—unlike Beal, who refused to picket—they were beaten up, and they went to jail. Moreover, they lived with the strikers in the mill village—again unlike Beal, who did not live in Gastonia at all, but at a secret address in Charlotte. These women eventually formed a real bond with the southerners with whom they worked, a closeness evident to the most casual observer when Buch, Melvin, and Schechter were first brought in to the Gastonia courthouse to stand trial for Aderholt's murder. The mill women in the crowd, young and old, clustered around them eagerly. "There was a great deal of waving, bowing, smiling and greeting between them and their friends," noted

Harriet Herring. Vera Buch, touched by this reception, remarked that they "nearly ate us up at their joy at seeing us." Obviously the spirit of dedication, the way these women had really made themselves part of the strike community, goes a long way toward explaining the warmth of this particular welcome, but could it also have arisen, at least partly, from the modern values they represented, values that the mill women were beginning to share?[14]

In the one song that has come down to us, across the years, from the Gastonia strike, "Mill Mother's Lament," Ella May talks of the deprivation of her own life, of that of her children, and of all the women of the mills.

Now it grieves the heart of a mother
You everyone must know
But we cannot buy for our children
Our wages are too low.

I wish I could have heard her sing that, in her deep, resonant voice, accompanying herself on her guitar, her audience, serious in demeanor, nodding appreciatively. But I wish, too, I could have been present when Amy Schechter, as she loved to do, sang her songs to the mill women, the bawdy, Cockney ballads of her English years. "Oh girls, oh girls take warning," she would warble, as all around her cracked up, "and never let it be. Never let a sailor go higher than your knee." For that, too, is a song of the Gastonia strike.[15]

NOTES

1. Narrative accounts of the Gastonia strike can be found in Liston Pope, *MillHands and Preachers* (New Haven, 1942), and Tom Tippett, *When Southern Labor Stirs* (New York, 1931). Fred Beal, the strike's leader, published his version of events in *Proletarian Journey, New England, Gastonia, Moscow* (New York, 1937); Vera Buch, Beal's second in command, published hers in Vera Buch Weisbord, *A Radical Life*, (Bloomington, 1976).

2. Jacqueline Dowd Hall, "Disorderly Women: Gender and Labor Military in the Appalachian South," *Journal of American History* 73, (September 1986), p. 377; Jacqueline Dowd Hall, James Leloudis, Robert Korstad, Mary Murphy, Lu Ann Jones, and Christopher B. Daly, *Like a Family: The Making of a Cotton Mill World* (Chapel Hill, 1987), p. 222; Daniel J. Singal, *The War Within: From Victorianism to Modernism in the South, 1919–1945* (Chapel Hill, 1982), p. xii.

3. *Daily Worker*, April 19, 1929; *News and Observer*, (Raleigh, NC) September 6, 1929.

4. *Charlotte Observer*, April 5, 1929.

5. *Gastonia Daily Gazette*, April 6, 1929, reprint from the *Charlotte News*.

6. *Gastonia Daily Gazette*, April 18, 25, 1929.

7. *Charlotte Observer*, April 4, 5, 6, 1929; *Daily Worker*, April 5, 11, 1929; *News and Observer*, April 8, 1929; Buch, *A Radical Life*, pp. 185, 195–97, 205. Pershing was

a nephew of Edgar J. Pershing, then chairman of the Indiana Republican State Committee, and was a distant relative of the famous military commander "Black-Jack" Pershing.

8. *Charlotte Observer*, July 28, 1929.

9. *Charlotte Observer*, April 5, 1929.

10. *Charlotte Observer*, April 5, 1929 (quote); *Gastonia Daily Gazette* April 6, 1929 (reprint from *Charlotte News*); Bertha Hendrix, "I Was in the Gastonia Strike," in Marc S. Miller, ed., *Working Lives, the Southern Exposure History of Labor in the South* (New York, 1980), pp. 169–71; Hall et al., *Like a Family*, pp. 226–29.

11. *Southern Textile Bulletin*, April 10, 1930. Harriet Herring to Beulah Amidon, August 20, 1929, Harriet Herring Papers, Southern Historical Collection, Wilson Library, University of North Carolina at Chapel Hill, Box 1, Folder 11; *Gastonia Daily Gazette*, July 29, 1929; *Charlotte Observer*, July 28, 29, 30, 31, 1929; Vera Buch to Mary Vorse, August 1929, Mary Heaton Vorse Papers, Walter P. Reuther Archive for Labor History, Wayne State University, Box 155.

12. *Southern Textile Bulletin*, April 10, 1930; *Charlotte Observer*, May 11, 1929; *Baltimore Morning Sun*, May 11, 1929. For Ella May's life, see Jo Lynn Haessly, "Mill Mother's Lament, Ella May, Working Women's Militancy and the Gaston County Strikes of 1929" (M.A. thesis in history, University of North Carolina at Chapel Hill, 1987).

13. *Charlotte Observer*, April 6, June 16, 1929; *Southern Textile Bulletin*, April 11, 1929; Buch, *A Radical Life*, pp. 228, 31 (quotes); see also, pp. xvii, 113, 181–82, 212; and "Recollections of Loray," Vera Buch Weisbord Papers, Chicago Historical Society, Box 4, Folder 3; Dee Garrison and Mary Heaton Vorse, *The Life of an American Insurgent* (Philadelphia, 1989), pp. 216–18; author's interview with Sophie Melvin Gerson, Conway, New Hampshire, July 8, 1993.

14. Harriet Herring to Beulah Amidon, August 20, 1929, Herring Papers, Box 1, Folder 11; Vera Buch to Mary Vorse, August 1, 1929, Vorse Papers, Box 155; Buch, "Recollections of Loray," Buch Papers, Box 4, Folder 3; Buch, *A Radical Life*, p. 194.

15. Beal, *Proletarian Journey*, pp. 153–59; "Mill Mother's Lament" can be found in Margaret Larkin, "Ella May's Songs," *Nation* 129, October 9, 1929, pp. 382–83. Amy Schechter's song can be found in Buch, *A Radical Life*, p. 231.

11

Coming into the Real World: Southern Textile Workers and the TWUA, 1945–1951

Timothy J. Minchin

In 1950, southern textile workers, unlike workers in most other mass production industries, had been unable to unionize successfully in the two preceding decades. Indeed, by 1955 less than 20 percent of the South's textile workers had been brought under union contract.[1] Moreover, this failure was clearly related to the fact that the majority of the industry was located in the South, for textile unions in the 1930s and 1940s had gained considerable strength in the North. The weakness of textile unionism in the South has meant that observers have continually sought to develop theses to explain why the South's textile workers have failed to join unions. Studies by both contemporaries and modern historians have emphasized the anti-union hostility and corporate dominance of the South's small textile communities and have argued that this produced a worker culture pervaded by feelings of powerlessness and fear.

As early as 1928, Lois MacDonald found terrible working conditions in the mill villages that she studied; however, she also found the workers unable to challenge the company and protest against these conditions: "No connection was made between the (supposedly) good policies of the company and these conditions."[2] MacDonald was part of a group of sociologists, economists, and other observers who found in the piedmont of the late 1920s and early 1930s an ideal location for social observation. The writings produced by this group, which also included Tom Tippett, Frank Tannenbaum, Marjorie Potwin, and Jennings J. Rhyne, have become acknowledged classics that have influenced historians considerably.[3] While the conclusions drawn by these different writers varied, most linked the apathy they found among the workers to their physical weakness and poor working and living conditions. Frank Tannenbaum, for example, described them as "long, emaciated figures, wan and sleepy-looking and without any vividness or interest."[4]

As conditions improved in the 1940s and 1950s, observers and academics turned to psychology to explain southern textile workers' lack of activism. Thus, in 1960 Solomon Barkin, research director for the Textile Workers Union of America (TWUA), wrote concerning "the Southern textile worker": "His profile is distinctive . . . he is generally without knowledge of, or confidence in, the ability of collective action to effect any significant change. Fearful of the outside world, he has continued to accept the social and economic pressures within his own closed community."[5] John Kenneth Morland, in a 1958 study, described the workers in "Kent" as passive and docile, since they believed that they lacked the ability to bring about an improvement in conditions—"there is little the individual can do."[6]

While the last decade has seen a wide variety of increasingly sophisticated scholarship on southern textile workers, the influence of these past writings can still be felt. For example, Barbara Griffith, in her 1988 study of the CIO's Southern Organizing Drive of 1946–1953, concluded that the main problem was worker fear, born of the fact that they "lived under the most debasing kind of police tyranny." Another major study within the last decade claimed that "the mills often exerted complete control over the communities. Local merchants and professional people were happy to accept the economic and social philosophies of the companies that operated the mills."[7]

It is important to test, however, the extent to which this failure to unionize the South was due to these factors, which can be determined by an examination of the experiences of the main textile union, the TWUA, in its attempts to organize the South in a specific time period, the years between 1946 and 1951. During this period, the TWUA participated in the CIO's Operation Dixie, a concentrated and well-financed attempt to organize Southern textile workers. First, however, it is important to consider the role that community support and worker culture played in the process of unionization in more general terms.

If unionization did indeed depend upon these factors, it is logical to assume that northern workers who did unionize received a much greater degree of community support and possessed more awareness of the power of collective action. While it is clear that southern textile communities were, and remain, a very hostile environment in which to organize unions, this was not necessarily decisive: many unions were born among workers previously termed "docile" and against the most violent anti-union sentiment. Indeed, the observations made about southern textile workers were often similar to those made of other industrial workers, especially prior to the New Deal. The United Mine Workers, for example, made repeated attempts to organize in such areas as West Virginia and the midwestern metal-mining fields, often blaming the miners themselves for the union's failure. As one organizer wrote, "We have often wondered what kind of animals they have digging coal in West Virginia. Their ignorance must be more dense, their prejudice more bitter, and their blindness more intense than that of any other body of miners we have ever heard tell." Malcolm Ross, a staff member of the National Labor Relations Board in the mid-1930s, wrote that the miners of the tri-state region of Oklahoma, Kansas, and Missouri were an "unfailing reservoir" of "hungry hillbillies" who retained a "passion for independence and were likely to resent unionization."[8]

These remarks caution us against overestimating the strength of organized labor before the New Deal and point to common problems faced in trying to organize American industrial workers. The 1920s were marked by an influx into industry of women and green hands who, according to Mark Perlman, "saw in the factory an opportunity to get good wages providing they did as he was told." With this labor force, as with southern textile workers, strikes tended to be sporadic and violent but produced few lasting institutional gains.[9] Defeat continued to be a prospect that hung over virtually all attempts to organize industrial workers even in the New Deal years. Thus, a steelworker described the rank and file movement of steelworkers in 1934 as "a terrific publicity show," because if workers were forced to strike, "we were almost certain to lose."[10] In attempting to build unions during the New Deal, northern workers also had to battle against a legacy of defeat—yet they frequently succeeded. Such defeats in textiles have been held up as one of the principle obstacles of unionization. Barbara Griffith, for example, has argued that unionization was held back by an oral tradition of defeat. In Flint, Michigan, during the 1937 sit-down strike, Sidney Fine points out how many strikers were haunted by the 1930 strike at Fisher Body Plant #1, when men had "fled like a bunch of scared rabbits because we did not want to get run down by horses." In steel, workers had to battle against memories of the bitter 1919 strike and the climate of cynicism left in its wake.[11]

The relationship between community support and unionization is also an ambivalent one. In the Flint sit-down strike, the majority of the community was hostile to the strike. In fact, Flint shared many features with southern textile communities, including a local power structure and economy dominated by the company. The opposition to the strikers culminated in the formation of the Flint Alliance by leading business and professional people, who were determined to break the strike. This pattern of avid community opposition was repeated at the sit-down strike of rubber workers in Akron, Ohio, where former mayor C. Nelson Sparks led the formation of a powerful Law and Order League to try to break the strike. Throughout the strike, a large number of workers also remained opposed and repeatedly called on local authorities to protect their interest in working. As Daniel Nelson has noted regarding the Akron strike, "A vote at any time during February 1936 probably would have given the non-strikers an overwhelming victory."[12]

It is also clear that as American industrial communities went, southern textile communities were far from being the most hostile in which to organize unions. Many mining communities were characterized by a far greater degree of repression than ever existed in the majority of mill villages. Typical rules, for example, banned more than three miners from meeting at night. Baldwin-Felts company guards kept track of miners' every move. As one West Virginia miner remembered, "They rode horses and wouldn't let anyone they didn't like walk on the railroad tracks. Worse though, you couldn't go into the office and tell about mistakes or complain about the store. They would just kick you off the porch."[13]

The assumption that workers in these communities received less community support is, however, a flawed one. Company domination could have the effect of alienating the middle class. If there was one battle in the 1930s that symbolized class warfare, it was the lengthy attempt to unionize "bloody" Harlan County, Kentucky, where coal operators ruled supreme over workers. Yet in Harlan County, significant sections of the community supported the miners. There were pro-union politicians such as Sheriff Clinton Hall and the mayor of the town of Evarts. The attempts of the radical National Miners' Union to organize Harlan County were also heavily supported by local Holiness preachers.[14]

The similarities between southern textile workers and other industrial workers should not be overdrawn, especially as many northern industrial workers were able to overcome the barriers that faced them and unionize. There were crucial differences between North and South, including the ability of northern workers to secure a degree of protection from local politicians that could make a crucial difference in strike situations. To secure control of local political machinery was very difficult for southern workers both because of low political participation and, frequently, the total lack of any local political machinery. On the other hand, at the beginning of the New Deal, there was little to indicate that auto workers would end up with a much higher rate of unionization than southern textile workers. Contemporary observers regarded all industrial workers as a difficult proposition.

Some even expressed more optimism about southern textile workers than about other groups. This optimism was rooted in the strikes that swept through the South between 1929 and 1931, and in the fact that union charters were issued to dozens of southern mills in the early 1930s. These developments were seen by southern liberals as the beginnings of change in the textile industry. Southern economist Benjamin Ratchford wrote in 1932, "Unionization must come eventually to the Southern textile industry." Tom Tippett wrote that unions would have "no problem" in organizing southern textile workers. When the New Deal came, lasting institutional gains continued to be a problem in many industries. According to Sidney Fine, as late as fall 1935, only 5 percent of the auto industry was signed up—mostly outside of the key state of Michigan.[15]

Nevertheless, it has become common to approach the problem from the other end, with assumptions about different degrees of militancy built in. Moreover, the key development in the birth of industrial unionism—the sit-down strike—was deliberately conceived as a means whereby workers could protest and protect themselves from community hostility and attempts to bring "scabs" into the plant. Its success was based on the fact that it was able to put considerable economic pressure on companies who wanted to run, rather than on widespread worker or community support. General Motors, for example, had invested heavily in new technology prior to the Flint strike and was receiving large orders for its models. The strike reduced production from 15,000 cars a week to 150; it also led to the signing of a contract. In the southern textile industry, unionism's success would also depend to a large extent on the ability to force recognition of unionism through strategic economic power.[16]

Although the TWUA was involved in southern organizing in the 1937–1939 period through the Textile Workers Organizing Committee (TWOC), the major work of this drive was actually concentrated in the North. Southern efforts were curtailed by a severe economic recession that hit the industry in 1938 and by the death of the drive's leading southern organizer, A. Steve Nance. In the postwar period, the TWUA took part in the CIO's specifically southern drive, which also occurred at a time of economic growth. Solomon Barkin wrote that the period 1945–1951 was "the most critical for it was during these years that the union's efforts were most futile in the South, and it never recovered from the stagnancy which set in during that period." It is therefore vital to explore the reasons for this failure.[17]

The most important campaign for the TWUA in this drive was the attempt to organize the Cannon Mills chain, which employed 41,000 workers in and around Kannapolis, North Carolina. Assistant Director George Baldanzi, for example, described the Cannon campaign as "the most important and the most significant in the South." Kannapolis was an unincorporated company town dominated by the mill's owner, Charles Cannon. If ever there was an example of paternalism and fear holding back union organization, this seemed to be it. TWUA's own publication claimed that Cannon's "vast power" was responsible for the failure of its organizing efforts in the late 1940s.[18] However, according to the written reports and oral testimony of those involved in the Cannon drive, the main problem was not this but rather another issue that dogged many campaigns at this time. The union found that the tremendous wage increases that it had won during the war had been universally applied by unorganized companies, making it very difficult to sign up workers because they believed that conditions would continue to improve without taking the considerable risk of joining a union. Joel Leighton, who was in charge of the Cannon campaign for over six months, remembered that when he returned from the war, wages had increased 100 percent in only three years. The workers "now had cars, they bought their own homes, and they had not even had to strike or organize, or do anything. Uncle Sam took care of them. They told us, '[W]hat do we need a union for, we've never had it so good.'"[19]

Once the war ended, moreover, wages continued to rise frequently. Nonunion mills, driven partly by a labor shortage, followed any wage increases that were won in organized mills—all done to prevent unionization. As Don McKee, an organizer in Rock Hill, South Carolina, recalled, "It worked very well." When McKee tried to sell a union wage increase to unorganized workers, he found that they had already received it. Most questioned why they needed to pay union dues to receive the same they were already getting, and some even thanked McKee for the union's efforts in raising their wages while refusing to sign union cards.[20] In addition, unorganized mills also matched any fringe benefits the union was able to negotiate. So effective was this tactic of matching union pay and benefits that Solomon Barkin called it the "great play" by the industry.[21]

To a large extent, the TWUA found itself a victim of its own success in raising textile wages. TWUA's president, Emil Rieve, successfully used federal machinery during the war to win a series of wage increases. Wages for southern textile workers more than doubled between 1941 and July 1947. The effect of these increases, along with the inability of the TWUA to establish a union pay scale that was above the level of the unorganized plants, dogged the union in many campaigns. Dean Culver, who directed the Kannapolis campaign in its early stages, wrote repeatedly that the biggest problem was that Cannon "will meet union standards almost as soon as they are established in this industry." This meant that there were no "short range popular issues" on which to base a campaign. Culver wrote with increasing frustration that a "new approach" was needed both at Cannon and in other textile campaigns. Culver argued that the union needed to secure an "Industrial Master Agreement" which would "secure anything like economic justice for the workers in the Textile Industry when one compares the textile wage with the wages generally existing in the organized steel industry, the auto industry, the electrical industry." Culver concluded that the TWUA must elevate the organized textile worker over the unorganized. It was impossible to organize workers "without being able to promise them, in terms that they can understand, this kind of economic justice."[22]

Those involved in the Cannon campaign also emphasized that rather than community isolation being a problem, the opposite was the case. Culver wrote that "the actual physical insulation from outside influence and contacts is considerably less than in the average mill village. The workers can and do read. They own radios and many automobiles. They have travelled and visited around considerably."[23] These social changes illustrated the extent that the postwar textile mill village had been transformed by the impact of disposable income. Joel Leighton, who organized before the war, went into service, and then returned to organizing afterward, remembered these profound changes. Conditions before the war had been "socially primitive," with many houses having no indoor plumbing or underpinning. With vastly improved wages, many changes took place. Indoor plumbing was installed in most houses. Workers were able to afford some of the things they had considered luxuries before. Because of their improved living standards, they were also less likely to be called "lintheads" when they went to town to shop, whereas before "they had looked a little ragged." Many workers also took immense pride in the fact that for the first time they had some money to support the churches that large numbers of them attended.[24] The changes that were taking place were well summed up by one textile worker, Ernest Cole, in Rockingham, North Carolina, who remembered that after the war textile workers were "coming into the real world."[25]

Not surprisingly, many who had lived through the long hours and very low pay of the industry before the war were cautious about endangering their relative prosperity. It was very difficult for the union to overcome the feeling that because of the vast improvement that had taken place, a union was unnecessary. As one Cannon worker explained, "I know that when there is a time for better pay, Cannon is always ready to start better pay first and always tries to give better living conditions when possible. I make more money now in nine and a half hours than I made in 120 hours when I first came here. So you can see why I like to work here and don't want a union of any kind."[26]

The importance of this social change did not mean that the power and dominance of Cannon Mills over Kannapolis was not a problem. Culver, for example, complained of "a general pattern of rationalization built around the prestige of Charles Cannon." However, as organizer Ruth Gettinger pointed out, the popularity of Cannon was an issue in part because the union lacked other, particularly economic, sources of appeal. "The workload is up to standards set in many union contracts. The only issue we have is freedom from Cannon domination, and Cannon is very popular."[27]

Although a variety of other factors had a negative impact on the TWUA's drive, the willingness of companies to give wage increases and match union conditions was a constant theme. Along with Kannapolis, another crucial location for the union was Gaston County, North Carolina. From Bloom Mill in Gastonia, however, organizer Jim Prestwood wrote that "the interest in Bloom is bad at present. It seems that the ten cent raise the company put into effect has served its purpose." Nearby, from Gambrill Mill in Bessemer City, came the report, "Plant has raised wages and committee cannot get started signing cards."[28] The story was the same elsewhere. Workers at an American Thread Company plant in Tennessee told organizer Carl Holt that "unions would not help them because they have practically the same benefits" as workers at the company's unionized mill of Dalton, Georgia.[29] Tennessee CIO director Paul Christopher reported from Standard Knitting Mills in Knoxville that a union campaign was faltering because "this company matches all benefits TWUA-CIO Local #513 members have at Brookside Mills in Knoxville." The crucial drive at the Avondale Mills chain in Alabama never got off the ground because, as Edmund J. Ryan reported, mill owner Donald Comer "is still paying 17 percent above our wage scale so that we are unable to advance or get much interest."[30]

Despite the central importance of this problem, the role that other factors played in defeating the TWUA's attempts should not be overlooked. Operation Dixie also failed because of effective opposition by companies who frequently were able to rely upon the support of community and law enforcement agencies. In campaigns in Georgia and Alabama, in particular, companies met union drives often simply by firing large numbers of union leaders and openly flouting the National Labor Relations Board (NLRB). Alabama director Edmund Ryan reported that at the National Mattress Company in Jasper, Alabama, when the union signed up the majority of workers, "the company promptly fired all our active people."[31] In other campaigns, the TWUA was beaten out by effective collusion between the company, local business, and law enforcement officials. At the Russell Mills of Alexander City, Alabama, for example, collusion between the city police and the company in arrangements to beat up organizers and deprive workers of their civil liberties was so effective that it brought investigation by both the NLRB and the FBI.[32] The important campaign in the Bibb Manufacturing Company chain of Macon and Porterdale, Georgia, was defeated by circulation of the viciously anti-union newspaper, *The Trumpet*, to all eight thousand workers. As Barbara Griffith's valuable study has shown, in many campaigns organizers had to battle against collective memories of previous failed strikes, a problem especially acute in the campaign at the Firestone (formerly Loray) mill in Gastonia.[33] Moreover, it could also be said that the workers' failure to see the need for unionization when conditions were good and inability to realize the vulnerability of the gains that they had made indicated a lack of union tradition or union culture such as might have been found in some northern centers.

Nevertheless, the impact of wage increases and the matching of union conditions needs to be emphasized because of its centrality to the failure of Operation Dixie. Other problems in the campaign, moreover, were also a product of the war. Operation Dixie began with great optimism, typical of the mood of the early postwar years. Labor leaders and liberals were confident that the South could be organized. This confidence was based on the success that many unions, and especially the TWUA, had experienced with the aid of government protection during the war. TWUA, for example, had more southern workers under contract in 1945 than at any other time.[34] At the 1946 TWUA convention, secretary-treasurer William Pollock reported triumphantly that "it has been in the last four years a simple matter to organize plants and get them under contract." He added, "I don't think there can be much wrong with a union with a record like that."[35] This confidence fed into Operation Dixie, where the emphasis was very much on winning elections, and winning them as fast as possible. Director Van A. Bittner felt that this could best be achieved through the assignment of aggressive northern staff to speed up organizing. He wrote South Carolina director Franz Daniel that what the drive needed was "energetic boys from the North." This approach, however, caused the TWUA to lose repeated elections because it was unprepared for last-minute employer opposition or because it overestimated its degree of support. A common problem was highlighted by a frustrated Baldanzi when he wrote, "many times we have been carried away by the false notion that even though people don't sign cards they will vote for the union. . . . [I]t has been proved time and time again that when a worker will vote for the union he will be willing to sign a card."[36] In other cases TWUA misjudged the effect of wage increases and the changed social conditions caused by the war upon organizing prospects. Georgia director

Charles Gilman wrote of the string of lost elections in his state: "The thing that seems to be the trouble in the textile industry is that we are going into elections before the people are really organized." This was due, he continued, to the fact that the workforce "have been treated so good, so they claim, by the companies in the past several years, and too, their wage rates are exceedingly high."[37]

TWUA also found that without the protection that had been provided by the National War Labor Board, winning an election was a very different matter from actually gaining a contract and establishing a secure local union. Often, elections were won, but companies refused to bargain or forced strikes. By May 1947, there were thirty-seven southern mills where elections had been won but no contract reached. TWUA's house organ, *Textile Labor*, wrote, "Winning elections isn't enough," and added that election victories were becoming "a potential financial drain until a contract is signed."[38]

The structure of the textile industry also became crucial in defeating union campaigns. In the postwar period, chain ownership was becoming increasingly common in the southern textile industry.[39] In addition, the industry continued to go through operating cycles, especially after 1948 when the postwar boom in the industry evaporated. These two factors gave management an enormous advantage over the union in a strike, preventing the union from exerting the kind of economic pressure that ensured the success of the sit-down strikes in the North. A good example of this occurred at Hart Mill in Tarboro, North Carolina, which was one of a chain of mills controlled by Ely & Walker of St. Louis, Missouri. In 1949, the company forced a strike during a slump in the market. The mill showed little interest in solving the dispute, as attested by manager Marcus Carter: he "expressed himself as being indifferent as to whether or not the union struck, as he could sell all the cotton he had in the warehouse and make more money than by operating the mill with it."[40] After six long months, the Tarboro local abandoned the strike, leading to the disbanding of a local that TWUA had successfully organized in the immediate postwar period. In other strikes, TWUA found itself battling against chain companies who could switch production from the struck plant to other, unorganized plants. Thus, in a losing strike at Highland Park Manufacturing Company in Rock Hill, South Carolina, TWUA representative Charles Puckett noted that the company owned sixteen plants in North and South Carolina: "The company can use its plants in North Carolina to produce while it fights the union at Rock Hill. . . . [T]he union has been unable to organize any of their mills in North Carolina, and for this reason the company has the advantage."[41]

TWUA suffered because, unlike industries where there was a significant degree of concentration and the union was able to put itself in a position of strategic power, the textile industry was too scattered and too competitive for a union to be able to do the same. Instead, TWUA found itself financially ill equipped to fight against chain companies with numerous and geographically dispersed plants, companies who often made a conscious decision to victimize union plants specifically. Since the companies were in such a position of strength, these strikes tended to be long, causing enormous financial and relief problems for TWUA. The relief problems were especially acute, as many workers had just bought refrigerators, cars, and other consumer items on credit with their improved wages, and therefore faced extreme financial pressure when they went on strike. Baldanzi summed up this problem for the union when he told an Executive Council meeting in 1951, "It is safe to say that because of the evolution of living standards brought about by the union, we are faced with terrific relief problems. These people are not going to see their cars go and their refrigerators go—they'll go to work first."[42] TWUA's problems were also the result of its policy of only providing food relief, a policy that was very unpopular at the local level. In a 1949–1950 strike at Clifton Manufacturing Company in Clifton, South Carolina, local strikers threatened that the union would be "torn up" unless some of their bills for their installment plans were paid.[43] In a strike at Safie Manufacturing Company in Rockingham, North Carolina in 1947, union representative R. C. Thomas wrote that the success of the strike depended on TWUA being able to take care of some of the strikers' financial responsibilities as the strike went into its fourth month. Overall, these strikes placed an enormous financial burden on TWUA. In 1948, the Executive Council Report to the TWUA convention stated that the union was in serious financial straits because it had spent over half a million dollars in strike support in the previous two years.[44]

Such was the position of strategic power that companies had in many of these strikes, that issues of worker or community support were often unimportant. TWUA representative Charles Puckett, for example, marveled at the militancy of strikers at Hamrick Mill in Gaffney, South Carolina, after they had been on strike for over sixteen months: "It is remarkable to see a group of workers remain on strike for so long with so few breaking rank and returning to work."[45] In Tarboro, too, the strike was well supported by the workers, and the company was never able to get more than a part of one shift operating. The union there received considerable support from the community, along with public criticism of the company's intransigence by Governor Kerr Scott. Local union official Mae Dawson recalled that "the whole town was involved . . . , on the common we had a big cook-out, and a lot of the different preachers, we asked them to speak. . . . Mr. Milton Brown [a local merchant] furnished all the drinks." However, both the Tarboro and Gaffney strikes were called off by the national union after it became obvious that the companies had no interest in reaching a settlement.[46]

The problem that dogged TWUA throughout Operation Dixie—its inability to establish a clear wage gap between organized and unorganized plants—led the union into a general strike in the South in 1951, which set back the union's remaining hopes of organizing the region. TWUA tried to win a large wage increase and a variety of fringe benefits that would have placed unionized southern textile workers on par with northern unionized workers, as Dean Culver had called for in Kannapolis. However, southern manufacturers resisted the union's demands, and the strike crumbled. The reasons for the strike's failure were diverse, including a political fight among TWUA's top leadership. The strike collapsed at the crucial Dan River Mills in Danville, Virginia, because of determination by local management to operate. According to Emanuel Boggs, Danville TWUA representative, workers, many of them union members, went back to work because "when people are accustomed to a higher standard of living they are reluctant to lose what they have partly paid for."[47] He added that the cutting off of credit had placed considerable economic pressure on the strikers and that management had realized that the most effective way to break the strike was not simply by open opposition and intimidation, but by pressuring credit agencies. *Southern Textile News*, an employer publication, wrote that the strike had failed because of workers' "anxieties about the mill-owned houses they are buying on the instalment plan but with payments they cannot meet, and this is true of thousands buying cars out of weekly earnings and who, if they were to lose their cars, would have no transportation each day to and from their mill job." Thus the breakdown of the traditional mill village worked to the union's disadvantage.[48]

The loss of the strike was felt as episodic by most in TWUA. The union was so weakened that manufacturers stopped giving pay raises to prevent unionization. The southern textile industry actually gave no more wage increases until October of 1956. With the loss of the strike, TWUA also seemed to lose its early postwar belief that it could unionize the South. As Solomon Barkin recalled,

> It was the last great gasp of being a big factor in the South, it was after that we began to say "now what the hell is wrong," self-criticism became the subject of the day. . . . It was the watermark because after that we never dreamed of the South as something we could take over, like Sherman marching through Georgia. We had to become piecemeal about it, couldn't conceive of it as a unified operation.[49]

An analysis of the experiences of TWUA in the immediate postwar years illustrates, therefore, that specific social and economic changes originating in World War II guided a large part of the union's fortunes in its attempts to organize the South. The war caused textile wages to rise dramatically, which altered the organizing climate considerably, making strikes harder to sustain as well as producing a sense of confidence in organizing among union officials, which proved misguided. In addition, the general structural nature of the textile industry, along with specific changes that occurred within the industry after the 1940s, limited the possibilities for organization. Many of the union's problems resulted from employer opposition; yet the effectiveness of this opposition was conditioned by chronologically specific factors, such as the spread of credit financing. The historiography that has illustrated the distinctive cultural problems facing southern textile workers, included the legacy of defeat and the problems of penetrating small southern communities where employers wielded considerable power, is both crucial and valuable, for it has highlighted continual problems facing textile unions in different time periods. What is clear, however, is that this framework needs to be qualified by the fact that specific factors operated at different times and in different locations. The crucial organizing drives of the immediate post-war years failed because of the social changes caused by World War II rather than an unchanging worker culture.

NOTES

1. F. Ray Marshall, *Labor in the South* (Cambridge, Mass., 1967), p. 261.

2. Lois MacDonald, *Southern Mill Hills: A Study of Social and Economic Forces in Certain Textile Mill Villages* (New York, 1928), p. 53.

3. Tom Tippett, *When Southern Labor Stirs* (New York, 1931); Frank Tannenbaum, *Darker Phases of the South* (New York, 1924); Marjorie Potwin, *Cotton Mill People of the Piedmont: A Study of Social Change* (New York, 1927); Jennings J. Rhyne, *Some Southern Cotton Mill Workers and Their Villages* (Chapel Hill, 1930). Other works from the same period include Harriet L. Herring, *Welfare Work in the Mill Villages, the Story of Extra-Mill Activities in North Carolina* (Chapel Hill, 1929); Broadus Mitchell and George Sinclair Mitchell, *The Industrial Revolution in the South* (Baltimore, 1930); and Paul Blanshard, *Labor in Southern Cotton Mills* (New York, 1927).

4. Tannenbaum, *Darker Phases of the South*, p. 70.

5. Solomon Barkin, "The Personality Profile of Southern Textile Workers," *Labor Law Journal* 11 (June 1960), pp. 2–3.

6. John Kenneth Morland, *Millways of Kent* (Chapel Hill, 1958), p. 51.

7. Barbara Griffith, *The Crisis of American Labor: Operation Dixie and the Defeat of the CIO* (Philadelphia, 1988), p. 60. Hodges, *New Deal Labor Policy*, p. 38. Examples of the most recent of this new scholarship include Douglas Flamming, *Creating the Modern South: Millhands and Managers in Dalton, Georgia, 1884–1984* (Chapel Hill, 1992), and Gary M. Fink, *The Fulton Bag and Cotton Mills Strike of 1914–1915: Espionage, Labor Conflict, and New South Industrial Relations* (Ithaca, N.Y., 1993).

8. Quoted in David Alan Corbin, *Life, Work and Rebellion in the Coalfields: The Southern West Virginia Miners, 1880–1922* (Urbana, 1981), p. 25. Malcolm Ross is quoted in George G. Suggs, Jr., *Union Busting in the Tri-State: The Oklahoma, Kansas and Missouri Metal Workers' Strike of 1935* (Norman, Okla., 1986), p. 13.

9. Mark Perlman, "Labor in Eclipse," in John Braeman, *Change and Continuity in Twentieth-Century America: The Twenties* (Columbus, Ohio, 1968), pp. 119–20.

10. Robert R. R. Brooks, *As Steel Goes: Unionism in a Basic Industry* (New Haven, 1940), p. 60.

11. Griffith, *The Crisis of American Labor*, pp. 59–60; Sidney Fine, *Sit-Down: The General Motors Strike of 1936–1937* (Ann Arbor, Mich., 1969), p. 66.

12. Fine, *Sit-Down*, p. 108; Daniel Nelson, "The Great Goodyear Strike of 1936," *Ohio History* 92 (1983), p. 14.

13. Corbin, *Life, Work and Rebellion*, p. 51.

14. John W. Hevener, *Which Side Are You On? The Harlan County Coal Miners, 1931–39* (Urbana, Ill., 1978), pp. 179–80.

15. Benjamen Ratchford is quoted in H. M. Douty, "Labor Unrest in North Carolina, 1932," *Social Forces* 11 (1933), p. 579; Tippett, *When Southern Labor Stirs*, p. 270; Fine, *Sit-Down*, pp. 82, 89.

16. Anthony J. Badger, *The New Deal: The Depression Years, 1933–40* (New York, 1989), p. 129.

17. Donald R. Stabile, *Activist Unionism: The Institutional Economics of Solomon Barkin* (New York, 1993), p. 18. Solomon Barkin, personal letter to author, November 27, 1993.

18. George Baldanzi to Van A. Bittner, June 19, 1946; North Carolina Organizing Committee Papers (Operation Dixie Archives), Perkins Library Special Collections, Duke University, Box 53. Collection hereafter cited as ODA; *Textile Labor*, July 10, 1954.

19. Joel Leighton, interview with Timothy Minchin, January 5–6, 1994, Boston, Mass.

20. Don McKee, interview with Timothy Minchin, November 26, 1993, Maplewood, N. J.; Solomon Barkin, interview with Timothy Minchin, January 7, 1994, Amherst, Mass.

21. Solomon Barkin, interview with Timothy Minchin, January 7, 1994, Amherst, Mass.

22. *Kannapolis Independent*, October 2, 1947. Dean Culver, organizing reports, July 9, 1946, and September 12, 1946, ODA, Box 85.

23. Dean Culver, organizing report, July 9, 1946, ODA, Box 85.

24. Leighton interview.

25. Ernest Cole, interview with Timothy Minchin, March 4, 1994, Rockingham, N.C.

26. *Kannapolis Independent*, October 2, 1946.

27. Dean Culver, organizing report, September 12, 1946, ODA, Box 85; Ruth Gettinger to Allan L. Swim, July 17, 1946, ODA, Box 86.

28. Jim Prestwood to George Baldanzi, July 21, 1946, ODA, Box 76.

29. Carl Holt to Paul Christopher, August 26, 1950, ODA, Box 148.

30. Paul Christopher to Van A. Bittner, March 16, 1948, ODA, Box 129; Edmund J. Ryan to Emil Rieve, October 25, 1946, ODA, Box 53.

31. Ibid.

32. TWUA vs. Russell Mfg. Co., 1949, 82 NLRB 1081 ff.

33. Barbara S. Griffith, *The Crisis of American Labor: Operation Dixie and the Defeat of the CIO* (Philadelphia, 1988), pp. 59–60. Jim Prestwood to George Baldanzi, July 23, 1946, ODA, Box 76.

34. Hodges, *New Deal Labor Policy*, p. 193.

35. Quoted in Paul David Richards, "The History of the Textile Workers Union of America, CIO, in the South, 1937 to 1945" (Ph.D. diss., University of Wisconsin, 1978), p. 207.

36. Van A. Bittner to Franz Daniel, July 2, 1946, ODA, Box 102; George Baldanzi to Paul Christopher, October 7, 1949, ODA, Box 127.

37. Charles Gilman to Paul Christopher, July 3, 1947, ODA, Box 191.

38. *Textile Labor*, May 3, 1947.

39. See Solomon Barkin, "The Regional Significance of the Integration Movement in the Southern Textile Industry," *Southern Economic Journal* 15 (1949), pp. 395–410, for more information on these changes.

40. NLRB vs. Hart Cotton Mills, 1950, 91 NLRB 739.

41. Charles Puckett to Emil Rieve, 19 May 1947, Textile Workers Union of America Papers, State Historical Society of Wisconsin, Madison, Wisc., Series 2A, Box 4. (Hereafter cited as TWUA Papers.)

42. Minutes, policy meeting of May 5, 1951, TWUA Papers, Series 1A, Box 20.

43. Charles Auslander to James J. Kelly, July 24, 1950, South Carolina State Director's Papers, Perkins Library Special Collections, Duke University, Box 318.

44. R. C. Thomas to R. R. Lawrence, July 23, 1947, ODA, Box 83; TWUA Executive Council Report, 1948.

45. Charles Puckett to Emil Rieve, November 13, 1946, TWUA Papers, Series 2A, Box 4.

46. NLRB vs. Hart Cotton Mills, 1950, 91 NLRB 749; Mae Dawson, interview with Timothy Minchin, March 3, 1994, Tarboro, N.C. The closeness of a Southern textile community could be a positive advantage in sustaining collective action. See Jacquelyn Dowd Hall, James Leloudis, Robert Korstad, Mary Murphy, Lu Ann Jones, Christopher B. Daly, *Like a Family: The Making of a Southern Cotton Mill World* (Chapel Hill, 1987).

47. Boggs is quoted in Minutes, Executive Council meeting, April 20, 1951, TWUA Papers, Series 1A, Box 20.

48. *Southern Textile News*, April 14, 1951.

49. Solomon Barkin, interview with Jim Cavanaugh, TWUA Oral History Project, tapes at the State Historical Society of Wisconsin, Madison.

Bibliographical Essay

The literature on southern history is immense, so vast that no bibliography could be comprehensive. The works selected here are relevant as background reading or extensions of the essays included in this book.

The best single volume history of the South is William J. Cooper, Jr., and Thomas E. Terrill, *The American South: A History* (New York, 1991). John B. Boles, *The South through Time: A History of an American Region* (Englewood Cliffs, N.J., 1995) is briefer but informative. These should be supplemented with Wesley Frank Craven, *The Southern Colonies in the Seventeenth Century, 1607–1689* (Baton Rouge, 1949); Charles S. Sydnor, *The Development of Southern Sectionalism, 1819–1848* (Baton Rouge, 1948); C. Vann Woodward, *Origins of the New South, 1877–1913* (Baton Rouge, 1951); George B. Tindall, *The Emergence of the New South, 1914–1945* (Baton Rouge, 1967); and Numan V. Bartley, *A New South, 1945–1980* (Baton Rouge, 1995). For a balanced synthesis of the period since the Civil War, see Dewey W. Grantham, *The South in Modern America: A Region at Odds* (New York, 1994). Two general histories serve as concise introductions to the recent South: Charles P. Roland, *The Improbable Era: The South since World War II* (Lexington, Ky., 1975), and David Goldfield, *Promised Land: The South since 1945* (Arlington Heights, Ill., 1987). However sweeping and controversial, no one should ignore W. J. Cash's masterpiece, *The Mind of the South* (New York, 1941). Serious students should also consult the excellent essays in John B. Boles and Evelyn Thomas Nolen, eds., *Interpreting Southern History: Historiographical Essays in Honor of Sanford W. Higgenbotham* (Baton Rouge, 1987). Virtually every facet of southern culture receives imaginative consideration in Charles R. Wilson and William Ferris, eds., *Encyclopedia of Southern History* (Chapel Hill, 1989).

For the colonial South the following are indispensable: Carl Bridenbaugh, *Myths and Realities: Societies of the Colonial South* (Baton Rouge, 1952); Edmund S. Morgan, *American Slavery—American Freedom: The Ordeal of Colonial Virginia* (New York,

1975); Gerald W. Mullin, *Flight and Rebellion: Slave Resistance in Eighteenth-Century Virginia* (New York, 1972); Richard Beale Davis, *Intellectual Life in the Colonial South, 1585–1763*, 3 vols. (Knoxville, 1978), an encyclopedic work; Rhys Isaac, *The Transformation of Virginia, 1740–1790* (Chapel Hill, 1982), a seminal work in ethnographical history; Peter H. Wood, *Black Majority: Negroes in Colonial South Carolina from 1670 through the Stono Rebellion* (New York, 1974); and Winthrop D. Jordan, *White over Black: American Attitudes toward the Negro, 1550–1812* (Chapel Hill, 1968), a treasure of information and ideas.

The literature on the Old South alone is immense. Here is a sampling of the best on slavery: Kenneth M. Stampp, *The Peculiar Institution: Slavery in the Antebellum South* (New York, 1956); John W. Blassingame, *The Slave Community: Plantation Life in the Antebellum South* (New York, 1972); Eugene D. Genovese, *Roll, Jordan, Roll: The World the Slaves Made* (New York, 1974); Herbert G. Gutman, *The Black Family in Slavery and Freedom, 1750–1925* (New York, 1976); Lawrence W. Levine, *Black Culture and Black Consciousness: Afro-American Folk Thought from Slavery to Freedom* (New York, 1977), a highly illuminating study of slave culture; John B. Boles, *Black Southerners, 1619–1869* (Lexington, Ky., 1983); Charles Joyner, *Down by the Riverside: A South Carolina Slave Community* (Urbana, Ill., 1984); Deborah Gray White, *Ar'n't I a Woman: Female Slaves in the Plantation South* (New York, 1985), the best book on this subject; and Peter Kolchin, *American Slavery, 1619–1877* (New York, 1993).

For the culture and attitudes of the white South, see Bertram Wyatt-Brown, *Southern Honor: Ethics and Behavior in the Old South* (New York, 1982); James Oakes, *The Ruling Race: A History of American Slaveholders* (New York, 1982); Edward L. Ayers, *Vengeance and Justice: Crime and Punishment in the 19th-Century American South* (New York, 1984); and the imaginative study by Orville Vernon Burton, *In My Father's House Are Many Mansions: Family and Community in Edgefield, South Carolina* (Chapel Hill, 1985). The intricate relationship between slavery and women, white and black, receives contrasting interpretations in Catherine Clinton, *The Plantation Mistress: Woman's World in the Old South* (New York, 1982), and Elizabeth Fox-Genovese, *Inside the Plantation Household: Black and White Women of the Old South* (Chapel Hill, 1988).

The continuing scourge of racism in the nineteenth century and the first half of the twentieth, much of it engendered by slavery, and the brutal violence directed toward black (and sometimes white) southerners is addressed in Ayers, *Vengeance and Justice*; Cash, *Mind of the South*; Wyatt-Brown, *Southern Honor*, and many others. For added perspective, see John Hope Franklin, *Reconstruction after the Civil War* (Chicago, 1961); Kenneth M. Stampp, *The Era of Reconstruction, 1865–1877* (New York, 1965); and the monumental study by Eric Foner, *Reconstruction: America's Unfinished Revolution, 1863–1877* (New York, 1988). The starting point for any discussion of lynching is the pioneering work by Arthur F. Raper, *The Tragedy of Lynching* (Chapel Hill, 1933). More recent, specialized studies suggest a growing scholarly sophistication: W. Fitzhugh Brundage, *Lynching in the New South: Georgia and Virginia, 1880–1930* (Urbana, Ill., 1993), and Steward Tolnay and E. M. Beck, *A Festival of Violence: An Analysis of Southern Lynchings, 1882–1930* (Urbana, Ill., 1995). The best study of the antilynching movement is Jacquelyn Dowd Hall, *Revolt against Chivalry: Jessie Daniel Ames and the Women's Campaign against Lynching* (New York, 1979).

To understand the ways racism became institutionalized, the best accounts remain C. Vann Woodward, *The Strange Career of Jim Crow*, 3rd rev. ed. (New York, 1974), and the relevant chapters in Woodward, *Origins of the New South*, and Edward L. Ayers,

The Promise of the New South: Life after Reconstruction (New York, 1992). Joel Williamson, *The Crucible of Race: Black-White Relations in the American South Since Emancipation* (New York, 1984), is eccentric but provocative. The essays in C. Vann Woodward, *The Burden of Southern History* 3rd ed. (New York, 1993), are brilliant. John Dittmer, *Black Georgia in the Progressive Era, 1900–1920* (Urbana, Ill., 1977), and Neil R. McMillen, *Dark Journey: Black Mississippians in the Age of Jim Crow* (Urbana, Ill., 1989), are model studies. Much can be learned about race, violence, and southern culture in general from James C. Cobb's majestic *The Most Southern Place on Earth: The Mississippi Delta and the Roots of Regional Identity* (New York, 1992).

Southern social thought and literary history continue to give birth to important works. In *The Promise of the New South*, Ayers adeptly integrates cultural and intellectual topics, as does Tindall, *The Emergence of the New South*. Both Daniel Joseph Singal, *The War Within: From Victorian to Modernist Thought in the South, 1919–1945* (Chapel Hill, 1982), and Richard H. King, *A Southern Renaissance: The Cultural Awakening of the American South, 1930–1955* (New York, 1980), probe deeply into the southern mind. For individual writers, see: Bruce Clayton, *The Savage Ideal: Intolerance and Intellectual Leadership in the South, 1890–1914* (Baltimore, 1972); Morton Sosna, *In Search of the Silent South: Southern Liberals and the Race Issue* (New York, 1977); Michael O'Brien, *The Idea of the American South, 1920–1941* (Baltimore, 1979); Anne Goodwyn Jones, *Tomorrow Is Another Day: The Woman Writer in the South, 1859–1936* (Baton Rouge, 1981); Fred Hobson, *Tell about the South: The Southern Rage to Explain* (Baton Rouge, 1983), a work of great breadth and erudition; Darden Asbury Pyron's definitive *Southern Daughter: The Life of Margaret Mitchell* (New York, 1991); Joel Williamson, *William Faulkner and Southern History* (New York, 1993), the one book on Faulkner historians ought to read; Bertram Wyatt-Brown, *The House of Percy: Honor, Imagination and Melancholy in a Southern Family* (New York, 1994); and Bruce Clayton, *W. J. Cash: A Life* (Baton Rouge, 1991); see also, James C. Cobb, "Does *Mind* No Longer Matter? The South, the Nation, and *The Mind of the South*, 1941–1991," *Journal of Southern History* 57 (November 1991), 681–718. John Egerton, *Speak Now against the Day: The Generation before the Civil Rights Movement* (New York, 1994), is passionate and stunningly comprehensive.

Women's history has built upon Anne Firor Scott's early work, *The Southern Lady: From Pedestal to Politics, 1830–1930* (Chicago, 1970). In addition to Clinton, *Plantation Mistress*, Fox-Genovese, *Inside the Plantation Household*, and Hall, *Revolt against Chivalry*, see Jacqueline Jones's thorough *Labor of Love, Labor of Sorrow: Black Women, Work, and the Family from Slavery to the Present* (New York, 1985); Marjorie Spruill Wheeler, *New Women of the New South: The Leaders of the Woman Suffrage Movement in the Southern States* (New York, 1993); and John A. Salmond, *Miss Lucy of the CIO: The Life and Times of Lucy Randolph Mason, 1882–1959* (Athens, Ga., 1988).

The South's road to industrial progress has been skilfully mapped in specific chapters in Woodward, *Origins of the New South*, Tindall, *The Emergence of the New South*, Ayers, *The Promise of the New South*, and with considerable sophistication by James C. Cobb in *The Selling of the South: The Southern Crusade for Industrial Development, 1936–1980* (Baton Rouge, 1982), and Cobb, *Industrialization and Southern Society, 1877–1984* (Lexington, Ky., 1984). The standard work on labor remains F. Ray Marshall, *Labor in the South* (Cambridge, 1967), but for specific places and events, see Liston Pope's informative sociological analysis, *Millhands and Preachers: A Study of Gastonia*

(New Haven, 1942); David Carlton, *Mill and Town in South Carolina, 1880–1920* (Baton Rouge, 1982); James A. Hodges, *New Deal Labor Policy and the Southern Textile Industry, 1933–1941* (Knoxville, 1986); Salmond, *Miss Lucy of the CIO*; Barbara Griffith, *The Crisis of American Labor: Operation Dixie and the Defeat of the CIO* (Philadelphia, 1988); the highly perceptive, influential work by Jacquelyn Dowd Hall, James Leloudis, Robert Korstad, Mary Murphy, Lu Ann Jones, Christopher B. Daly, *Like a Family: The Making of a Southern Cotton Mill World* (Chapel Hill, 1987); and Douglas Flamming, *Creating the Modern South: Millhands and Managers in Dalton, Georgia, 1884–1984* (Chapel Hill, 1992).

Although the civil rights movement in the South has yet to receive definitive treatment, the following add immeasurably to anyone's understanding: Richard Kluger, *Simple Justice: The History of Brown v. Board of Education and Black America's Struggle for Equality*, 2 vols. (New York, 1975); Harvard Sitkoff, *The Struggle for Black Equality, 1954–1980* (New York, 1981); William H. Chafe, *Civilities and Civil Rights: Greensboro, North Carolina, and the Black Struggle for Freedom* (New York, 1980); John A. Salmond, *A Southern Rebel: The Life and Times of Aubrey Willis Williams, 1890–1965* (Chapel Hill, 1983); Taylor Branch, *Parting the Waters: America in the King Years, 1954–1963* (New York, 1988); David R. Goldfield, *Black, White, and Southern: Race Relations and Southern Culture, 1940 to the Present* (Baton Rouge, 1990); John Dittmer, *Local People: The Struggle for Civil Rights in Mississippi* (Urbana, Ill., 1994). For perspective, see Egerton, *Speak Now against the Day*.

Index

About the Editors and Contributors

TREVOR BURNARD teaches history at the University of Canterbury, Christchurch, New Zealand. His research interests are in the history of the early Chesapeake and on white society in early Jamaica, and he has published articles on both topics.

BRUCE CLAYTON is the Harry A. Logan, Sr., Professor of History at Allegheny College, Meadville, Pennsylvania, and the author of *W. J. Cash: A Life.*

WARREN A. ELLEM teaches history at La Trobe University, Melbourne, Australia, and has published articles on Reconstruction in Mississippi. He is currently working on a biography of Adelbert Ames.

SAM ELWORTHY is completing a Ph.D. at Rutgers University, New Jersey. His dissertation analyzes the impact of the social sciences on American culture between 1870 and 1920.

TERENCE FINNEGAN is assistant professor of history at William Paterson College, Wayne, New Jersey. He is currently working on a study of lynching in Mississippi and South Carolina.

GRACE ELIZABETH HALE is currently completing a doctorate at Rutgers University, New Jersey on aspects of lynching in the American South.

RHYS ISAAC is professor of history at La Trobe University, Melbourne, Australia. His *Transformation of Virginia, 1740–1790* won the Pulitzer Prize in history for 1983.

CHARLES JOYNER is Burroughs Distinguished Professor of History, Coastal Carolina University, Myrtle Beach, South Carolina, and author of the prize-winning study of a slave community *Down by the Riverside*.

TIMOTHY J. MINCHIN has recently completed a doctorate on postwar southern textile unionism at Cambridge University, England. He currently holds the Mellon Research Fellowship at Cambridge.

JOHN SALMOND is professor of American history at La Trobe University, Melbourne, Australia. His most recent book is *Gastonia 1929: The Story of the Loray Mill Strike*.

SHANE WHITE and **GRAHAM WHITE** both teach history at the University of Sydney, Australia. Shane White is the author of *Somewhat More Independent: The End of Slavery in New York City 1770–1810*, while Graham White's most recent book, co-authored with John Maze, is *Henry A. Wallace: His Search for a New World Order*. They are currently working on a book on African-American expressive culture.

ISBN 0-313-29860-2
90000>
EAN
9 780313 298608
HARDCOVER BAR CODE